To Norman Levine:

I hope we have the opportunity to do something like this together once more.

Love to you and Sandy.

Don Barnes

AF681263

As I See It

Don Barnes

NATIONAL UNDERWRITER

The National Underwriter Co. • 505 Gest Street • Cincinnati, Ohio 45203

First Edition
First Printing

Copyright© 1991 by
THE NATIONAL UNDERWRITER COMPANY
505 Gest Street
Cincinnati, Ohio 45203

All rights reserved.

No part of this book may be reproduced, stored in a retrieval system, or transmitted, in any form or by any means, electronic, mechanical, photocopying, recording or otherwise, without the written permission of the publisher.

Library of Congress Catalog Number 91-62779
ISBN: 0-87218-496-X

Printed in the United States of America

Acknowledgments and Confessions

I have spent my life going to conventions and meetings. Sometimes I even attend the sessions. But most of what I have learned has come in corridor discussions, cocktail parties (I believe "receptions" is the proper word), and elevator discourses. During platform appearances people say what their scripts dictate. In less formal occasions you meet the real man or woman. That is probably why I have been in all the wrong places in hotels, at the same time the Great Leader was unloading his priceless knowledge on a fascinated audience. I could get the Leader's script later, but I could never catch up with the wonderful random remarks my friends made over a hot or cold toddy.

What you will be reading is a collection of columns—all written in the heat of enthusiasm, or anger, or even, sometimes, laughter—that reflect on man's opinion of the life insurance business during one of its most crucial times—1986 into 1991. Some event pushed my ignition switch and off I went. No one censored me; no one said, "This is not *National Underwriter* material."

My editors and I have selected, out of the nearly 300 columns I have written during that period, the ones which still have validity. We eliminated those which have been superseded by later events, as well as a few where my point of view changed radically. I did not want to confuse readers by looking like a writer arguing with his mirror.

These columns differ from most articles in the *National Underwriter* in that they do not presume to report the news. That is the job of the national staff of the newspaper. I have tried to draw a few moral judgments about where we might be going until the millennium ends, but I am not a moralist at heart. I see myself as a rudimentary threshing machine, undertaking to separate the wheat from the chaff in what is thrown at you in the press every day.

I guess I have a strong sense of history. Having been in the life insurance business for 55 years, occasionally I will reminisce about how we got were we are now, for good or ill. You may recall that my favorite quotation is from George Santayana: "Those who forget the past are condemned to repeat it."

I owe an endless debt to those who have advised me, and there are many. I have tried to credit them every time, but I am sure I have slipped. When I go to meetings I engage people in corridor conversations. My telephone bills when I operate from my Key Biscayne headquarters are not paltry sums. I try never to quote anyone capriciously.

Tom Slattery, editor of the *National Underwriter*, is of course my principal editor. Of special importance in compiling this volume are Carole King, senior editor in Hoboken, and Alice Fossett, retired editor of the Advanced Sales Reference Department in Cincinnati. The final draft was overseen by Steve Nieman.

I also need people who will grab me by the seat of the pants and throw me across the chasms I am threatening to fall in. Alan Press of New York, Joe Razza of Washington, and John Donohue of Chicago have been especially useful. Since they are longtime industry watchers, I take what they say very seriously.

In addition, I have a literary agent who exists, as far as I'm concerned, on a daily can of Heineken beer and an occasional lunch. His name is George Grim and he would be the voice of my conscience if I had one. George retired some years ago as one of the most famous newspapermen in Minnesota and he now devotes, as my neighbor, a good deal of time disagreeing with what I write. Every person needs a disagreer (if I may coin a word) but few have had a more amiable and compatible one than George has been to me.

Don Barnes
Key Biscayne, Florida
September, 1991

Table of Contents

Candles Of The Business

Every Business Has Its Dark Side

An Agent's World

The Political Arena

Foreword

The privilege of writing this introduction about Don Barnes and the book you are about to read is a truly significant honor. I am doubly honored because it has been my good fortune to know Donald Frederic Barnes for two or three years more than five full decades.

While young Mr. Barnes was at Bowdoin College, he wrote for the Associated Press, the *Boston Transcript*, and the *New York Herald Tribune*. After graduating, he spent some more time with the *Trib* before becoming a member of the headquarters staff of the National Association of Life Underwriters. Starting as an assistant editor of *Life Association News*, Barnes was quickly promoted to editor. There he came to know, and be known by, a very large portion of the men and women of distinction in American and Canadian life insurance.

Across fifteen years with the NALU, Barnes reached a very high level of duties and repute, including responsibility for veterans affairs. In this post he worked closely with General Omar Bradley, who had become head of the Veterans Administration.

In July of 1948, Barnes moved on to become the head of advertising and promotion for the Institute of Life Insurance. Shortly thereafter, he was named a vice-president, a post he would hold for twenty years.

That move was a great step for Don in his career, and a happy event for the Institute and its successor by merger, The American Council of Life Insurance. But of equal or greater moment, the life insurance business acquired his extraordinary perception, the constant clarity of his prose, and the elegance of his diction.

During these years Barnes was deeply involved in many of the innovations of the life insurance business. He helped create the Life Underwriter Training Council; he worked with John Henry Russell to shape the form of the John Newton Russell Memorial Award; he created the Louis I. Dublin Public Service Award for life underwriter associations; he was an original director of the Million Dollar Round Table Foundation; and he devised and presided over the Life Insurance Public Relations Council for twenty years.

Today, as a man honorably retired after 50-plus years in our business, he has authored this series of observations, historical recollections, personal interpretations, prognostications, and weekly commentary called "As I See It." His column appears weekly in the pages of the *National Underwriter.*

These columns are an unsurpassed composite of serious reporting and commentary, couched in friendly, informal, and often humorous style. They contain recollections of industry leaders throughout the years, as well as quotations and interpretations of those comments. There are criticisms and accolades of today's or tomorrow's leaders or events of significance to the industry.

It is these sources, coupled with Don's wisdom, experience, and writing skill, that have made "As I See It" immensely valuable to the life insurance world. It has been these friendships, strengthened by his discretion and responsibility, which has enabled him to reach virtually any person of position in the life insurance business at almost any place and at almost any time.

Donald Frederic Barnes might be the best qualified person in American insurance to do exactly what he is now doing. So read on, dear fellow reader! Read on and be grateful that Don Barnes had the energy and determination, as well as the talent, to write the essays that are the content of this book. . .and be glad that you and I had the wisdom to acquire it.

Benjamin N. Woodson, CLU
September, 1991

Introduction

Contrary to popular belief, the man who runs the *National Underwriter* is an ancient gent who reigns, not from Hoboken, NJ, but from a small, tropical island in Biscayne Bay. Trust me on this. I know. I work for him.

Don Barnes is a gentle but relentless boss. He counsels and cajoles me, often and insistently, by mail and by telephone, on a dizzying range of editorial concerns. Why were his papers late *again*? Precisely *which* of the composing room gremlins is *permanently* assigned to bedevil *his* copy? When are we going to relax his *ridiculous* deadlines? *Why* am I not going to the NALU annual meeting this year? Would it help if he wrote to NU's president, Clarence Barnes (Cousin Clarence, he calls him), about *any* or *all* of this?

I once thought, naively as it turns out, that such matters were beyond the purview or interest of a simple columnist, especially one subsisting on the modest sum we pay him and which he so richly deserves.

Granted, the man is a nuisance. But you learn over the years to take the bad with the good, and I long ago came to terms with the notion that the very qualities which make Don such an irritating human being in the aggregate are what, in the bargain, make him such a fine columnist. In fact, he embodies what a newspaper "op ed" writer should be:

First, he is opinionated. Even better, he is an opinionated exhibitionist. Better yet, he is quite old—which is to say he draws from a deep well of life insurance history. He's also nosey, a compulsive poker, and prodder. And his insolence knows no bounds: he perversely delights in putting his own "spin" on the news, and he freely agrees or disagrees with any and all comers, even the institutionalized opinion of his own newspaper printed just across "the gutter" on the editorial page. And—oh yes—he is, incidentally, a writer of uncommon grace, economy, civility, and good humor who truly loves the life and health insurance business.

I am proud to say that Don Barnes wrote this book on the "op ed" page of his favorite newspaper, the *National Underwriter*, which has been home to his column, "Don Barnes: As I See It", for the past six years. He asked the landlord for a benediction when it was decided to make a book of his better columns. He has that, and my genuflection as well, for blessing me and us all over many, many years with his lucid, witty, wise, and elegant voice.

I would like to walk you into this book a bit further, but I'm afraid you will have to excuse me for a moment. I'll catch up with you in a while. My 'phone is ringing, and I think I know who it is.

Thomas J. Slattery
Editor, *National Underwriter*
Hoboken, New Jersey
September, 1991

1

As I See It

"What Does This Person Believe?"

No. 36, September 6, 1986, Page 13

Whenever a new columnist pops up in one of the publications I read, I try to get a handle on the kind of stuff he or she is going to feed me over time—if I decide to continue reading that column. As my first—but I hope not my last—service to readers, I'd like to describe where I stand on some matters of general interest.

- Alexander E. Patterson was president of NALU some 46 years ago and later became president of Mutual of New York. He was noted for quoting what he called "Rule Number Four": "Always take your job seriously but never take yourself seriously." Not once did he mention any of his other numbered rules, so it was easy for me to remember this one. I still do, and it has stood me in good stead during fair times and foul. It's going to get involved in what I talk with you about, so remember I said it.

- I have been cranking around in this business for more than 50 years, and never once have I longed for "the good old days." As I look back, it all seems to have been so simple—a cottage industry, almost. Once a titan of the business spent an hour with me at the 19th hole musing about which of his associates and agents—if any—he should allow to call him by his first name. I rather suspect that our current CEOs have something weightier on their minds. If you catch me going on about how sweet it was, write me quickly.

- I do not believe that just because the boards of directors of our great institutional organizations have made a decision on some vast industrywide problem, that decision was necessarily right. They have a very good track record, but infallibility is not in them. They need some gentle guidance and some tender loving care just as we all do.

- No company practice is either completely right or completely wrong. People who condemn a point of view usually weren't there when the determination was made. What you don't know can hurt you if you fail to go to the source before shooting off your mouth.

- I have always wanted to believe that all members of the field force are saints or angels, as their CEOs tell me they are (when they happen to think of it). However, I have known too many of them to swallow this philosophy. What they **are**: some of the best conversationalists, friends, philosophers and drinking companions that a person could want. They are also some of the best businessmen and women in the world. But let's not put them up for canonization.

- Someday I am going to start a Society for the Preservation of Actuaries. They are the most maligned men and women in our business, and possibly in any business I know. They tend to have sneaky senses of humor that creep up on you when you least expect it, and blow your pomposity apart. They are also very brilliant people. I promise never to join the crowd that makes fun of actuaries—unless, of course, they deserve it.

- I have never known an unworthy person to receive the John Newton Russell Award for "having done the most for the life insurance business." My trouble is that I know a hundred other people who are equally worthy of the award but have never received it—and probably never will. That's why, even though I'm happy for the person who receives the accolade, I always leave an award banquet feeling sorry for friends who have framed a small acceptance speech in their minds but have never had the chance to deliver it.

- Will Rogers' proclamation, "I never met a man I didn't like," has always nauseated me slightly. (Ghaddafi? Hitler?) I have always preferred Honest Abe's remark, "I don't like that man. I must get to know him better." Will's phrase connotes a complete lack of discretion: Lincoln's implies that there may just be something lacking in me. I'd prefer to buy that.

These paragraphs should at least give the reader some angles on me. There are others: I'm afraid I don't know them all myself.

"Voltaire, Get Lost"

No. 1, January 5, 1987, Page 13

One of the real pleasures of cranking out this column is that I have acquired more pen pals than I ever knew existed. Let me share with you some of their comments on my first cycle of attempts to entertain and enlighten you:

The erudition of *National Underwriter* readers passeth all understanding. In an item commenting on the National Underwriter Co.'s decision to publish Bob MacDonald's *Control Your Future* I quoted an aphorism that the philosopher Voltaire was "supposed to have said" (my words): "I disapprove of what you say but will defend to the death your right to say it." A large number of you—including Bob MacDonald—reminded me that Voltaire never said any such thing.

Right on! Anyone with access to Bartlett's *Familiar Quotations* can find that out. Trouble is nobody knows who did say it first and it keeps getting attributed to the crusty Frenchman. So I decided to use Voltaire rather than pretending I had made it up myself in a moment of unbridled nobility.

I will never quote Voltaire again without your permission.

* * * *

In the same column I ended by saying, "Note to unbelievers: As I type these words, not a single person at the National Underwriter knows I'm preparing them." Norris Rumsey of King of Prussia, PA, asks, "Can you clarify what you meant by this?"

Yes, Mr. Rumsey. In my sly way (I thought), I was trying to dispel any notion that the *National Underwriter* had hired me to be its house apologist. Since it was my first formal column, I figured it might have popped into someone's mind. I'd probably have done better not to bring the issue up at all.

* * * *

I expected to get disagreement when I questioned the total sanctity of political action committees, and I did. One particularly well-reasoned letter came from an executive of a major trade association who asked for anonymity since he was writing personally. I found myself nodding approvingly until I arrived at this sentence: "I believe PACs are instruments of rank-and-file voters and give them more power than they would have by themselves."

No way. PACs may give the rank-and-file life insurance agent more power over how certain legislators vote on life insurance issues, but they don't give the rank-and-file voter any power over how legislators vote on non-insurance issues. Or, for that matter, any control over whatever cruel, biting TV commercials, made possible through PAC money, his campaign people may dream up in a frenzied fight for votes.

Besides, I had been carefully taught that the word "power" should not be used when discussing PACs.

* * * *

When I mentioned Elizur Wright as the first "muckraker" in the life insurance business, and probably Joe Belth's spiritual predecessor, I struck a responsive chord in the mind of Gene Bussian of Rockford, IL. He characterizes Mr. Wright, and apparently with complete accuracy, as the father of the buy-term-and-invest-the-difference philosophy. Wright was an enthusiastic proponent of the provident Savings Society whose "chief mission," according to the distinguished actuary M. Albert Linton, "was to sell renewable term insurance."

After 20 years the Society got itself into a terrible mortality problem and wholeheartedly clasped level premium life to its bosom. Mr. Bussian dryly suggests that Wright's enthusiasm "certainly seems to be the grandfather of the A.L. Williams-type approach."

Even the mighty always appear to have at least two or three toes of clay.

* * * *

Two true leaders, John O. Todd of Chicago and Buddy Zais of Montpelier, have led me back to the paths of righteousness as far as the Million Dollar Round Table annual meeting program is concerned. They have convinced me that the list of speakers is indeed balanced, and that a certain amount of schmaltz is needed. "Everyone in that audience feels the need to go forth and slay his own particular dragons for another day," John reminds me.

The MDRT's program development committee also makes me eager to go to its Chicago meeting next July. ". . . Our Chicago audience will be more experienced and more sophisticated than previous audiences," according to Arlen I. Prentice, first vice-president. "This allows us to program to an even higher level. So members can expect the '87 meeting to be faster-paced, more informative and even more thorough." A tough task for what is already the best meeting around.

* * * *

Letters have come to me through the National Underwriter's offices in Cincinnati, Chicago and Hoboken. I get them all eventually, and undertake to reply when it seems useful. If you are looking for specific information, feel free to write me where I really hang out: 611 Ocean Drive, Key Biscayne, FL 33149.

"Who's In Charge Here?"

No. 5, February 2, 1987, Page 27
Property & Casualty/Employee Benefits edition

When I was a tad, you didn't have to ask who the boss was in an insurance company. He was the President (with a capital P in all communications and press releases, please). If the title was good enough for F.D.R. and Harry Truman, why invent a new one?

Since that time, the executive suites of the larger insurance companies have become so crowded that you can't tell the players without a program. If you don't have one, you may find yourself talking with a person who has a fine-sounding title but not even a key to the executive washroom.

As a service to readers, I present my own interpretation of what titles mean today, beginning at the top (I think), and proceeding downward in some sort of irregular fashion:

Chairman of the Executive Committee. This is indisputably the Old Boy himself, who has become weary of coming in at 7:30 a.m. as an example to employees. He is finding time to play a little golf or tie his trout flies. But when the chips are down, he usually has all the crunch he needs.

Chairman of the Board. In most cases he is the top dog, or chief executive officer, although in some instances he may bow to the gentleman just described above. Alternatively, he may be the company's chief spokesman and front man, while the president is in the trenches manufacturing silk purses or golden parachutes.

Vice-Chairman (or men) of the Board. This person—and there may be more than one of them—has helped in a major way to build the company but has missed out on becoming chief executive because he was in the wrong age group or too highly specialized. It's a fine title for an invaluable person, but I've never heard of one advancing to become chairman and CEO. (Of course, just as I had written this so confidently, Prudential proved me wrong by elevating Robert Winters from the vice-chairmanship so that he's now chairman and CEO. Pru never feels the need to go by the book.)

President. Well, here you are, little man—or maybe you're not so little. You are usually CEO in companies not afflicted by title-itis. In others you may be being groomed or at the very least watched carefully. If you aren't CEO, be wary of being offered a vice-chairmanship.

Senior Executive Vice-President. President of all vice-presidents, of whatever shape or size. Possibly being groomed, possibly rewarded for outstanding service. A prime candidate for vice-chairman, if not something more gaudy. It's a highly complicated title, but there are those who are comfortable with it.

Executive Vice-President. Super-head of a staff—investment, actuarial, underwriting or marketing, to name a few. Certainly a comer; if the age is right, the possibilities are endless.

Vice-President. Formerly a magnificent title, tending to cast fear among the troops. Today less glamorous, except in companies where titles are given sparingly and cherished highly. Doubtless on the ladder of success, barring a faux pas that might cause him to be waived or traded.

The Troops. Everyone else.

This may remind you, as it does me, of the Star Wars of the Generals during World War II. Great Britain, with its Field Marshals and Admirals of the Fleet, tended to look down its royal nose at Americans who came to top-level meetings with a mere two or three stars. So, in order to get decent seats at the table, we escalated, and generals had to wear longer epaulets so their stars wouldn't bruise the neck. A truce was finally reached at five stars; otherwise, the military would surely have had to use them as necklaces.

While there seems to be no similar situation among America's life insurance companies, the very increase in company officialdom has caused an escalation in titles. After all, you can't manage a staff of computer programmers looking like a second lieutenant.

Unhappily, even the title of CEO is no longer sacrosanct, according to William Safire, who writes about words in the *New York Times*. He tells about Robert Galvin, chairman and CEO of Motorola, who relinquished his CEO-ship. The press naturally thought he was "stepping down" and said so. Said Motorola in a press release:

"This is incorrect. Mr. Galvin will continue to work and **lead** (emphasis theirs) the company just as before. . . He relinquished one of his titles, chief executive officer, so that other eminently deserving long-service associates can carry this richly deserved recognition." Obviously, nothing is sacred any more, at least in Motorola's grammar.

I do hope we have ended our hunger for titles. After all, how would our government be run if Ronald Reagan decided he would like to be a Chairman of the Executive Committee in '88?

"Second Takes"

No. 12, March 23, 1987, Page 21

Some columnists and TV commentators have what I call the "out there affliction." They refer often to "you readers (or viewers) out there." I don't buy that; I consider the people who read my stuff to be just as "in there" as I am, and maybe more so. That's why, when I say something that needs amplification or correction, I propose to share my new thoughts with you.

I agree with Jimmy Breslin, the Great Guru of Astoria, who is reported to have said, "When you do a column, some are singles, some are home runs, and sometimes you strike out. A columnist who takes a lot of pitches, keeps the bat on his shoulder and hopes for a base on balls is not going to be a columnist for long." You may assume that I will continue to take my weekly swings.

Here are some comments from all over on articles I've recently written:

When I got excited about the slender role of women at major life insurance conventions and said, "Unhappily, the figure for female registrants at such meetings is something under five percent," Lynn Merritt, the principal panjandrum of the Life Office Management Association, took issue with me by firing off a few facts. Here are some of them:

"In 1985, a record high of 720 women, insurance professionals from LOMA member companies, comprised 47 percent of the total number conference registrants. Two hundred thirty-five women, experts in their respective fields, currently serve on LOMA's four councils and more than 50 committees... 56 percent of all FLMI designations since 1984 have been earned by women...18 percent of the first class in the relatively new Master Fellow Life Management Institute program were women, and 30 percent of those eligible for the 1987 class are women."

I guess I had better say in great haste that women in the LOMA disciplines are far better represented than their peers in other organizations.

When I wrote about "Loyalty—the Phoniest Word" I quoted Bill Clark, chairman of Massachusetts Mutual. He demurred:

"You quote me exactly, but then you state that is my view of loyalty... 'Loyalty' is a word I don't use. I like it no better than you do. I honestly think that an agent should do what is to the best interest of the client, but to do this properly takes a fair amount of sophistication and it was this lack of sophistication that I was deploring..."

Bill Clark was right and I was wrong. Do not put concepts into the other guy's mouth.

Remember when I wrote about the various titles that senior executives have assumed and how difficult it has been to tell who ranks whom? I received a hilarious letter from the president (and CEO) of a midwestern company that has recently spawned an umbrella holding company. There are titles for the life company and for the senior board. He has a title for each. Some have titles in one but not in the other. He concluded, "All of this is written for the purpose of adding to your obviously vast store of knowledge of titles!"

I suggested to him that in adding holding companies to the mix he had opened a can of worms of awesome dimensions. I don't even want to think about it.

On the same subject, not even the good, gray *New York Times* can figure out the title business. Recently it ran a headline: "Jenrette Is Chosen Equitable Life Head." Not quite. He simply replaced the retiring Bob Froehlke as chairman. Sixteen lines into the article it dropped the other shoe: "John Carter continues as chief executive."

Indeed you can't tell the players without a program.

A few weeks ago I described with some awe how financial planners at their conventions "scurried from session to session," in contrast to life underwriters who, at their meetings, adopted a more leisurely pace.

Maggie Doyle, a member of IAFP, took me apart on this one. "It obviously didn't occur to you that most IAFP members attend conferences in order to get their tickets for continuing education validated. They cover every session they can get to, whether they learn anything or not, because they get brownie points."

But I don't suppose there's any law against their picking up a new idea, is there?

"Planning To Change Your Lifestyle?"

No. 38, September 21, 1987, Page 19

Lately there has been public talk by prominent life insurance field people about changing their lifestyles.

Norman Levine, most recent winner of the John Newton Russell Award "for having done the most for the life insurance business," has told sales congresses that he has a new schedule of working 14-to-15-hour days for seven months and then taking the rest of the year off.

John Savage, one of the most popular speakers around, says, "I never even contact my office for five months."

Ralph G. Engelsman, Jr., a second-generation life insurance person who has a reputation as an innovative thinker, writes that he is taking the last six months of '87 off to write a book, to start to learn a second language, and "to explore ways I can be more effective. . ."

A friend of mine, whose name you probably know, tells me that he is adopting a regimen of "three workdays a week for nine months then three months off." (He asked that I not use his name "until I've proved I can do it.")

These and others—all of whom have been in the sales force for from 20 to 35 years—are adopting new habits that most of us just dream about.

I will stoutly defend their right to make these changes, but I wonder whether or not they should talk them around as much as they do. The reason? They are expressing the fulfillment of a longing that most of us have, but they are perhaps better equipped to make it work than we would be if we arose and shouted, "Right on, man! I'm with you!" Changing lifestyles means more than having the cash in hand to support it. For those who may be contemplating the same course—or something vaguely similar to it—here are some points to ponder on:

1. You can't go home again. Adopting a relaxed way of life should be relatively simple for nose-to-the-grindstone people, but shifting back into high gear if the need should arise isn't easy. Is Norm Levine, after five months of nibbling at the lotus flower, going to be able to leap from his bed with a glad cry, pull on his three-piece suit, and go back to managing his stable of agents without missing a beat? Will John Savage's employees recognize him? This is an important point to consider.

2. Some of us can't even leave home. We don't realize what our dedication to our business is until we try to shuck it. There may be individuals we are bringing along, organizations where our roots are hip-deep, activities that won't wait for us. If we still remember what was on our desk after we took a month off, can we bear the thought of seeing it increased five-fold?

3. Most of our clients are content with our being away for a month. What happens after that? Since this is a service business, I can't see our clients accepting a long term of nonservice while we expand our minds. If we assign someone else to do our jobs, there is some chance that we won't have a client when we return. Not much, maybe, but some.

4. As Engelsman is doing, you must fill up—in advance—the time you propose to take off. Retirement areas are strewn with the bones of ol' boys who looked upon quitting as "a chance to improve my golf, get a little more sleep and inhale a few brews." It won't work. Ask any retiree after the first four months.

Fortune tells us, "Just about every student of the human life cycle has detected in fiftyish men a propensity to insulate themselves." Can that be the subconscious wish of those who are leaning slowly into retirement? Since there is little change—and even desire—for further advance, some people tend to crawl into a corner at the very time when they could be most valuable to their associates.

Winding down from a life's work is a complicated job itself. It demands at least introspection and sometimes counselling. It shouldn't be taken lightly.

"On Actuaries, Meetings, Spokesmen, Etc."

No. 31, August 1, 1988, Page 25

Here are a few summer items that ought to distract you from the heat or whatever else may be bothering you:

What is the least stressful, most highly paid job one can aspire to?

According to the *Jobs Rated Almanac*, it's the job of the actuary, which ranks just above the piano tuner, petroleum engineer and lithographer and pays an average salary of $45,780. The stress categories included 22 job demands, including physical demands, speed required, life of worker at risk, stamina required, meeting in public, and competitiveness. Apparently actuaries were ranked rather low on all these elements.

I rather think actuaries would take a dim view of this assessment, particularly those who have been asked to whip up a new universal-variable policy that would beat everyone else, or who were struggling to maintain a Best's A+ rating.

However, I must sadly report that most industry people seem to think that the assessment of the actuary is just jim-dandy.

* * * *

Meetings, the man said, are what we get involved in more of than anything else. These include staff meetings, board meetings, annual meetings, agency meetings, kaffee-klatsches and you name its. Most of them are only half-useful because the preparation for them is half-baked. How many times have we come out of a meeting mumbling that if it had been properly organized we could have saved half the time?

Finally something has been done about it. The Minnesota Mining and Manufacturing Company, known as 3M, has opened a "3M Meeting Management Institute" aimed at increasing the productivity of America's business meetings. Hallelujah!

Virginia Johnson of 3M, who will act as manager of the new Meeting Management Institute, has assembled an advisory group of major names, and has already published a book called, *How to Run Better Business Meetings*. She divides meetings into several categories: sharing information, solving problems, training, building morale and recognizing achievement. Presumably she and her advisers will have hints about them all.

It is entirely possible that Ms. Johnson and her advisory group have struck the greatest blow against boredom since the invention of the Blab-Off. At the very least, they ought to be able to help you streamline all kinds of meetings. For more information about the institute, write Virginia Johnson at 3M Center, Building 225 3-NE, St. Paul, MN 55144. My notion is that you'll be glad you did.

* * * *

For some time now you have read my growlings about celebrity spokesmen who talk about life and health insurance on TV with a blithe disregard (or maybe we should just call it ignorance) for the full facts involved. I have always maintained that celebrity spokesmen are utterly incompetent to advise a family about its insurance needs.

I now have an ally in Bill Gunter, the Florida insurance commissioner. He has recently fined Continental American Life of Delaware (whose spokesman was Eddie Albert) and Union Fidelity Life of Pennsylvania (whose spokesman was Betty White) $10,000 each for misleading advertising. Mr. Gunter claimed that their ads misrepresented the actual costs and benefits of the life insurance and Medicare policies.

Hearings are pending with National Benefit Life (Dick Van Dyke), National Home Life (Tennessee Ernie Ford) and Colonial Penn (Ed McMahon).

The reasons these commercials are distasteful to me is that people assume they are getting a certain amount of expertise that just isn't there. I don't mind Ricardo Montalban standing by a car and saying he likes the way it looks and rides, because there's no special knowledge involved in that assessment. Not so in the case of celebrities and insurance.

It will be interesting to see if other states follow the Gunter doctrine. If companies are going to give information, let it be complete and accurate—or let it be admitted that the spokesman is just being paid to mouth words.

"Old Folks At Home—Or On A Cruise"

No. 44, October 31, 1988, Page 17

Most Americans seem to be of two minds about retirees in the '80s, none more so than the American Association of Retired Persons. In its bimonthly magazine, *Modern Maturity*, it lavishes upon them advertisements for cruises, airline discounts, mutual funds, luxury hotels and retirement homes in Beverly Hills, to name just a few.

In its monthly news bulletin, a totally separate publication, it illustrates how it is fighting for the rights of senior citizens and is either holding the line on or attempting to increase benefits, COLAs and other perks they have acquired over the years.

Somehow, AARP has become, in the words of *Newsweek*, "the Big Gray Money Machine." First it dropped its minimum age from 55 to 50, and then, working with Prudential and The Hartford, began to offer health, homeowners and auto policies. It hauls in some $99 million to cover the administrative costs it offers.

On the other hand, legislators like Teddy Kennedy and Claude Pepper want us to perceive oldsters as people at the mercy of bureaucrats, doctors, hospitals and insurance companies. AARP agrees with them. But, with the single and rather ominous exception of long-term or catastrophic disability, they seem to be doing very well. Retirees are a prime market for everything, including all types of insurance.

Older people have 50 percent of all discretionary income and 70 percent of all financial assets, according to AARP. But the retiree who has run out of funds and is in no physical shape to get back into the work force is a much sadder figure than the younger indigent, and he or she makes more sympathetic newspaper copy.

Congressmen cater to retirees because they tend to vote in every election and on every issue. When AARP, the Gray Panthers, or other senior groups form a block, it is a formidable one. This can be especially true when legislators convince them that they are being treated unfairly by insurance companies. They are a suspicious group because they have survived in a long life during which all manner of people have tried to take advantage of them—and, quite possibly, they have done a little of the same themselves.

They are acquisitive. I know quite a few people driving top-of-the-line autos who, if their Social Security checks are a couple of days late, start calling their congressmen.

But they are a good market for sales people who are willing to make some substantial alternations in their usual marketing procedures. Here are just a few:

They want extremely simple plans to consider. They have given up trying to cope with life in the fast lane; they don't pretend to be abreast of the latest wrinkles in the financial security market anymore. So the clearer a presentation is, using the old familiar words, the more chance it has of being accepted by the senior.

They want service without end. This is illustrated by the high percentage (85) of them who use direct response (mail order if you will) services in the course of a year. They are reluctant to get in their cars and come downtown to talk with you. They have, remember, done their share of rushing around during their lives. Now they'd dearly like to have you come to them.

They are very proud. They have made it to a life of retirement, although for some it may not be as grandiose as they had anticipated. They have fought the good fight. They will feel a kinship with the salesperson who acknowledges this.

So let us disabuse ourselves of the popular notion that a good many retirees are at a subsistence level and look upon them as active prospects. They are where a lot of the money is.

"I've Told You A Hundred Times. . . "

No. 4, January 23, 1989, Page 13

Give or take an issue (depending on when my sainted editors choose to run it), this should be my hundredth column for the *National Underwriter.* It wouldn't have been more than a trickle in the careers of old pros like Walter Lippman or Red Smith, but for Barnes it's quite a feat. It seems appropriate that I pause and refresh your minds where I'm coming from and where I'm going.

Several readers have written me gravely to say they consider my attitude toward life insurance and financial services to be too frivolous. I don't think they understand my style. A viewer with alarm has got to see some light at the end of the tunnel, just as a pointer with pride has got to be aware of the tunnel. I see no issue, however complex, in the life insurance business today that is not susceptible to solution. Because I am a commentator and not a reporter, I can pursue those solutions (sometimes in the manner of the blind leading the blind) in a lighthearted way. Reporters are wise to use the "just the facts, ma'am" approach. I can mess around with issues in a way that may give my colleagues throughout the business food for thought.

Sometimes I'm chided for not pursuing "gut issues." I have a friend in my home town, one Jay Schaffer, who believes I should spend more time writing about such matters as company financial stability and "the coming global market." Fact is, I'm researching both of them, but to go off half-cocked on either would be a disservice to the *National Underwriter* and its readers. I'll get there eventually. You should see my phone bill for soliciting expert opinions. I constantly undertake to have my stories represent more than just me talking.

One element that makes me different from my fellows on the *National Underwriter* (except the one who writes its editorials) is that I'm seldom on assignment and can write about anything I think will interest you. I can also express my personal opinions. (Those of you with total recall will know that I have already used the perpendicular pronoun "I" 21 times in this column and I'm not through yet. It's not ego speaking, I hope, but just a reminder that one person is talking who may or may not represent the editorial policy of this publication.) Many columnists avoid the perpendicular by hiding behind such circumlocutions as "this reporter" or "a friend of mine," neither of which is totally accurate.

The problem with the life insurance business today is that it has ceased to be a compact, caring institution and has segmentized itself, company vs.

company, company vs. agent, discipline vs. discipline, stock vs. mutual, large vs. small, state vs. state. Both the prospect and the client are caught somewhere in the crush. The very communications capacities—the computer and its new-found cousins—that were supposed to simplify everything have now complicated the marketing process to the point where every insurance shopper believes he can find a person with a computer who can give him the straight deal on what he ought to buy.

Despite the fact that mathematics is the very heartbeat of life insurance, it isn't the function that makes the sale. The foxes of technocracy have taken over the hen house of marketing. Only when the various elements of the business stop fighting with one another and the companies reassemble themselves into cohesive wholes can the long-term goals of the institution be met.

These words may sound like the pipings of a visionary, but how else are we going to work it all out? We see surveys showing that field and home office suspect each other, and that various company elements are struggling for supremacy. If this isn't stopped, chaos can't be far away.

Now that I have stamped myself as a lighthearted thinker, I seem to have become a doom-shouter with the best of them. Not so; I just believe that those in the business need to get together, lighten up, work in concert and cast the burden of contentiousness aside. There is enough within the institution for all, if the participants are willing to let it be so.

I have had the good fortune to talk to you a hundred times. Perhaps I will be able to do so many times more. Share with me your best and brightest thoughts.

"Summer Meanderings"

No. 31, July 31, 1989, Page 27

Ever since people began collecting statistics on life insurance, the sales curve for the months of July and August has resembled a whale's underbelly. Just as conventional wisdom tells us that all psychiatrists take the summer off (presumably leaving their patients to go mad during this period), or that all Frenchmen leave Paris in August (leaving tourists to cook their own meals and run the Metro), it is assumed that nobody buys life insurance when the sun is high and hot.

But I know people who are using this myth to their own high advantage. Consider these facts: more and more well-to-do people in the temperate climates save their vacations for the winter, to escape the Alberta Express (or whatever it is that comes down from Canada in the winter); all manufacturing and service industries must remain more or less fully staffed because the nation doesn't close up like Paris; and senior executives have to be as worried about a hostile takeover before Labor Day as they are before the Fourth of July.

I will quote just one agent, a member of MDRT:

"Warm days give people a relaxed feeling even when they are on the job. They are more approachable. Tax worries aren't on their mind. Family occasions are. I work harder during the summer than any other time, and it pays off. That's why I can spend January and February in the Virgin Islands."

This isn't a scientific survey—just an observation. But it might work for any well-organized agent.

* * * *

The question of whether life insurance companies and their agents should be allowed to state that they are members of a life insurance company guaranty organization is still moot, even though New York companies voted to continue the ban on such a statement. Others would like to be able to use a phrase similar to the banks' "Member, Federal Deposit Insurance Corporation" to reassure their policyholders.

Several people have asked me where the best thinking on this issue is being done. I have two good sources for them, in the form of two interesting papers:

For continuing the ban: Alan M. Neiditch, Vice-President, Metropolitan Life, 1 Madison Avenue, New York, NY 10010.

For eliminating the ban: Deborah I. Roffman, Vice-President, Unity Mutual Life, One Unity Plaza, Syracuse, NY 13215.

There is much to be said on both sides of the matter. In many instances, the policyholder's right to know who stands behind a policy is self-evident, but Mr. Neiditch's explanation of why companies are reluctant to go along with the theory of unasked-for disclosure may change a good many minds. If you have a legitimate interest in the entire situation, I'm sure that Neiditch and Roffman will give you resumes of what they have written.

* * * *

Over the past year I have read with deep interest two consumer booklets published by the Canadian Life and Health Association. One, *This Business of Life*, is an 80-page booklet that describes in simple and unforced language the ins and outs of life insurance. The other, *Retirement: As You'd Like It*, is a 56-page "hands-on" workbook for Canadians planning to retire within 10 years. Both are brilliantly done in language and typography.

But I feel that I have seen the last of a rare breed of publication, designed to educate people about life insurance and reinforce their beliefs in it.

At its annual meeting on May 30, Daniel Damov, chairman of the organization, reported on a survey made of its members. He said these words:

"The major reorientation of the CLHIA that our members wanted to see was a change from our emphasis on advertising and public relations to a very strong focus on government relations, particularly on policymaking. The study defines the role of the CLHIA as an instrument for identifying the major external issues. . .The emphasis is on consensus-building and on the representation of our industry's interest of government."

Well, here we go again. The CLHIA seems to be following unwaveringly in the footsteps of the American Council of Life Insurance, which made the same decision more than a year ago. It appears that the life insurance business, both in the United States and Canada, is the only institution unwilling to charge each of its clients 25 cents a year more in order to explain to them how to use its product to best advantage.

I have often felt that Canadians had a better grasp on life's realities than their friends south of the border, but perhaps we are all cut from the same cloth.

* * * *

Steve Piontek's measured assessment of financial planning organizations in the June 19 [1989, page 39] issue of the *National Underwriter* entitled "Does the IAFP Know Where It Is Going?" was to my mind a masterpiece of logical thinking. An association simply cannot exist if the practitioners who started it are outnumbered by their suppliers—although IAFP disputes this. And the fact that only 5 percent of its members have chosen to take the steps necessary for them to be members of the Registry of Financial Planning Practitioners speaks more loudly than a hundred adjectives.

Alan Press, president of the National Association of Life Underwriters, seems to be on the bottom when he says that the threat of life underwriters from financial planners is very much in the past.

"The New Internationalism"

No. 45, November 6, 1989, Page 37

In life insurance, it used to be the dollar and the dollar alone—or almost alone. Now, in addition to the dollar, it's the yen, the pound sterling, the guilder, the peso, the deutsche mark and the franc. People are buying life insurance in all these currencies, and buying lots of it.

In 1992, when the 12 nations of the European Community unify trade laws and eliminate trade barriers, a $4 trillion market of more than 320 million people will be created. Quite a change from the days when North American companies patted their international brethren on their heads and patiently explained to them the difference between term and ordinary life, and what the agency system was.

Ernie Cragg, president of the Life Insurance Marketing and Research Association, which now calls itself LIMRA International on its letterhead, used his talk at his annual meeting in Toronto last month to open some minds on this rapidly developing market. Where do the North American companies stand in relationship to it? Here is how he sees the future:

"It will be a market to share, not to capture—for regardless of what form a company's presence takes there, the motive should be one of true partnership, just as it should be here when a European or Asian insurer seeks to sell in North America."

I felt that he was trying to tell his audience, in the kindest possible way, that insurance is already facing the same situation that the electronics, automobile, banking, advertising and other industries have been grappling with for a couple of decades: we are no longer anointed to lead the world just because we exist.

Because marketing is probably the single most significant area where what used to be called "good old American know-how" is still pretty far ahead of the rest of the world, 300 companies from all the inhabited continents have become members of LIMRA, in addition to the 300 in the United States and Canada.

Even our marketing methods, which are generally acknowledged to be the most productive, are under challenge from other countries. For instance, Japan has drawn far ahead of North America in its employment of women as agents. Some of the top producers in the world are Japanese women, while most American companies still haven't found the handle to making women a major element in the field force. Women may be moving quite rapidly into the upper executive echelons of home offices, but our training procedures appear to have failed many of those who opt for personal production or agency management.

Like LIMRA, the Million Dollar Round Table is aware of the shift in the global market, and takes great pride in flaunting the flags of its members in many countries at its annual meeting.

On the other side of the coin (and the balance of trade), U.S. companies have been hesitant to establish a presence in other lands, except in those where it has a large military force, and members of the military can buy life insurance just as though they had never left home. They know it will be necessary to staff foreign outposts with local professionals, and while they may be able to develop an agency system, it will be harder to find actuarial and investment people.

Two of Ernie Cragg's colleagues, Tom Kelly and Walt Zultowski, see the future of American companies abroad as a series of consortiums of powerful companies, willing to take a licking for 10 years before profits begin to accrue. Weaker companies need not apply. Only the big companies will be able to surmount the cultural barriers that exist now and will probably continue for many years.

That phrase "cultural barriers" is important here because over time American industry has insisted that others do it "our way" rather than their way. This trait, along with the rapidly increasing technical skills of our world neighbors, is doubtless what has caused the trade deficit.

It will be interesting to see if American life insurance companies have the guts to meet this challenge. It's a tough one, but it can be profitable.

"Predicting The Future Is A Tough Profession"

No. 1, January 1, 1990, Page 27

As soon as mankind grew mature enough to realize there was such a thing as the future, its members started to predict what it would be like. Some, like Nostradamus, veiled their predictions so carefully that no one could criticize them, pro or con. Others—you see them most often in magazines at supermarket checkout counters—are bold enough to predict almost anything. However, they never publish a periodic won-and-lost box score, so they survive somehow.

Recently, at the 100th convention of the National Association of Life Underwriters, I was given the rare opportunity to examine some letters written by association leaders 50 years ago, forecasting what the state of the agent would be as the last decade of the 20th century began. I will not mention their names, because their remarks were no more than innocent noodlings by distinguished people, but I'm glad they all stayed in life insurance and decided not to make their livings as futurists. I don't think it would have paid. However, some of their ideas almost came true because they illustrated the aspirations these men and women had, not grim realities. Here are a few of their guesses:

- Unanimously, they believed that by now a college degree would be a prerequisite for a license to sell life insurance. They were prescient, but they couldn't know the education stirrings that went on within the business in those 50 years: the immense surge of CLU/ChFC, and the invention of the Life Underwriter Training Council, as well as the various other designations available to the student. Many colleges and universities dragged their feet, so the business created its own learning system. Not far off the mark!

- They saw federal supervision as being just around the corner, even though they didn't like it. They couldn't know that the McCarran-Ferguson Act, which would stem the tide of federal intervention for half a century, was also just around the corner. But I'll bet that if these same worthies were given a shot at the same issue today, they'd reply, "Some form of federal supervision isn't far off."

- Three said something like this: "Due to the decentralization of industry, the typical life underwriter will live in a small suburban community, piloting his own plane, enjoying worldwide television broadcasts and accepting as necessities many products about which we don't even dream." Was someone whispering into their ears about computerization?

- They all considerably underestimated the growth of the professional movements in life insurance. They felt that the National Association of Life Underwriters would top out at about 50,000 members. It was then 27,000. As you know, it has reached about 140,000 and is still growing.

- But even this was a minor miss compared to their estimates of the growth of the business: they concluded that in 1990 it would have $50 billion of assets, and volume "in excess of $200 billion." The most recent figures show about $1.1 trillion of assets, and $8 trillion of business in force. Of course, inflation was hardly a threat at the time, and the population explosion unheard of. Growth was as hard to predict then as it is today.

- They zeroed in unerringly on the fact that the population was beginning to grow older, and that the market for those beyond the age of 50 would become a major one. They understood the strides being made in medical and scientific research. One even predicted, "There will be four times as many people over 65 as there are now, and even more over 75. They will still need insurance."

- Belief that the role of the agent is fundamental to the business lay in every prediction. One phrased it felicitously: "Like the life underwriter of 1939, he will derive his strength and enthusiasm from the deep conviction that his profession is one that makes it possible to transform the finest instincts of mankind into service to society."

These were brave and wonderful people, filled with enthusiasm for the future of their craft. Furthermore, they had the courage to predict the future of a world they never made. If someone were to ask me to predict what life insurance around the globe would be like in 2040, I'm afraid I'd answer, "I'm not really very sure about next month."

"Too Broad A Constituency"

No. 6, February 5, 1990, Page 33

For five bucks, anyone over the age of 50 can become a member of the American Association of Retired Persons, and more than 30 million of us have done so. Membership in AARP entitles you to a lavish bimonthly magazine, a 16 page monthly newsletter, and access to insurance of all kinds; group life and health underwritten by the Prudential, group auto insurance through the Hartford. You can also tap into a cut-rate pharmaceutical service, a credit union with its own VISA card, an IRA managed by Scudder, discounts on rental cars, and a host of other goodies. There is no reason I can think of why any American who wants to save a little money here and there shouldn't plunk down his or her fiver, although as time passes I'm beginning to consider the age of 50 rather juvenile to be carrying the appellation "retired."

It follows as the night the day that any organization of 30 million individuals with a common, if somewhat tenuous, bond is going to get into the business of lobbying—and AARP has done so with a vengeance.

Trouble is, AARP has a habit of depicting us oldsters in widely differing ways depending on the issue at hand. When it is fighting before congressional committees for increases in benefits for the elderly, it shows us as rather down-at-the-heels folk with a desperate need for every dollar Congress can vote us.

When it is selling its mutual fund we become better off. When it sells advertising in its magazine *Modern Maturity* it describes it as "...the nation's most widely circulated—surpassing *TV Guide* and *Reader's Digest*." We have indeed achieved the look of affluence—our age is surely golden.

It reaped the whirlwind of its widely varying constituency when it got involved with the Medicare Catastrophic Coverage Act—that sad piece of legislation, passed to a great many hurrahs and then repealed by what seemed to be even louder cheers.

AARP apparently believed that it would be a considerable benefit to most older people, regardless of the fact that it failed to cover nursing home care. As Barbara Coleman of AARP put it, "Hailed on all sides in Washington as a major advance in health care for the elderly, the law collapsed after many older Americans saw themselves as being forced to bear alone a costly burden for benefits they said they didn't need."

The fact of the matter was that the law was trashed by the more comfortably off oldsters, who are great letter writers and highly articulate citizens. Nothing went right, and the legislators who enacted the law felt that they had been bushwhacked by the very people they were trying to please. According to Sen. Jay Rockefeller (D—W.Va.), chairman of the Senate Finance Subcommittee on Medicare and Long-term Care, "I think there will be a backlash, and I think it will be substantial."

What he is obviously hinting at is that senior citizens are going to have to wait a long, long time before legislators take up the cudgels on behalf of bills that the over-50 crowd appears to want. AARP quotes one congressional staffer as saying that "the changing mood in Congress opens up the possibility that lawmakers will do something for children," and another that the setback may "push the question of health insurance for the uninsured more to the forefront."

It would be unfair to blame AARP for the mess, because it is more or less mandated to support bills that will give its constituents a better break than they are getting now. But it failed to realize that its membership had become so broad that it was no longer a cohesive, single-minded force. I'd be willing to bet it will do some very substantial sampling before it takes a position on the next bill that is touted to perform miracles for oldsters.

Conventional wisdom has taught us that retired people constitute the most overwhelming pressure group in the nation. Congress obviously thought so. But now that it has gone through the trauma of the Medicare Catastrophic

Coverage Act it may not be so quick to lick the boots of the oldsters. They have proved that they don't necessarily speak with one voice.

Which leaves the insurance business where it usually is—in the middle.

"Approaching The New Century—Whenever It Begins"

No. 16, April 16, 1990, Page 23

Never have I read so much gibbering in the letter columns of publications as the current argument about when the 21st century will officially begin. Learned, learned stuff, all of it. Unsophisticated people like me believe that when we start dating our documents "2000" rather than "1999" we will have reached the millennium, assuming we last that long.

But people with broader vision insist that the year 2000 properly belongs in the 20th century, and we really shouldn't launch the new millennium until January 1, 2001. One of my dear insurance friends (not an actuary, you may be sure), even posed this question in a letter to me:

"Is it better to have lived at the end of a century, or at the beginning? Do you end wondering how it will end, or how it will begin?" My answer, of course, was, "If possible, both." I would have preferred to use Rhett Butler's final statement to Scarlett O'Hara: "Frankly, my dear, I don't give a damn" but that might appear to beg the question.

The fact is, over the next decade every pundit you have ever heard of will be trying to tell us the shape of the 21st century, and all of them will be wrong—with the possible exception of the one who says that a large meteorite will destroy the earth, and he will have little chance to gloat.

We are very poor soothsayers, and the reason is that we stick carefully with the law of probabilities. Two years ago did you hear anyone predict the tragedy of Tianenmen Square? You get my drift.

Today you can't open a financial magazine without reading about the coming internationalism of insurance. It may happen, if major currencies continue to remain stable. But let there be a bust in one major power, and the other powers may upset what today seems to be a delicate balance. Greed and nationalism are, of course, the two words of significance, and there seem to be no laws that can limit them.

Greed is the trait that upsets me the most because I literally cannot understand it. Why a person, a company, or a country would try to amass more than they could conceivably use defeats me, especially if, in the course of building this fortune, it wrecks the futures of thousands of others. Yet it looks right now as though greed would be the motivating force as we move toward the 21st century.

And here we must not forget the insurance business. While the infighting is probably not so great as it was five years ago, the wounds are far from being healed, and proselyting goes on apace, particularly among companies that are too lazy to build their own field forces. The bottom lines are fragile, and when this situation exists management tends to make moves that would seem stupid in calmer circumstances.

During the '90s we will see the pundits playing their two favorite tunes: more companies will fail, and the field force will be cut by many thousands. It's curious that when we entered the '80s, the same people were saying the same things, and not much happened during the decade. Now the scratchy needle has been put on the record once more, and we are hearing the same tunes. I dislike them both. Some companies may get into severe financial straits, but the business is big and strong enough to see that no policyholder emerges empty-handed.

As for the agency system of selling life insurance, I believe it has gained strength in the last five years, not lost it. Its continuing education plans, plus the resilience of its agents, has been something of a miracle. As one of my correspondents puts it, "The enlightened self-interest of its participants is proving out."

My thoughts, like those of my fellow writers throughout the industry, are subject to instant cancellation. But I did one thing that gave me some confidence: I went back to the published proceedings of two institutional organizations at the beginning of the 20th century and found that they had all underestimated their capacity to grow and prosper. Let that be so today.

"'A Hundred Years From Today'"

No. 24, June 11, 1990, Page 25

More than 55 years ago, when I was in short pants—if any—a great trombonist and singer named Jack Teagarden recorded a slow-drag blues by the composer Victor Young entitled "A Hundred Years from Today." It was, of course, a love song to a young lady imploring her not to let everything sit on the back burner until she was too old to enjoy it.

I dug it out of my archives a couple of days ago when I received a letter from Dave Woods, chairman of the NALU centennial committee, asking me (and, I guess, a great many others) to write a few lines for the bicentennial committee to chuckle over when it opened a time capsule in the year 2090. I'm a sucker, as you well know, but not that big a sucker. For the guidance of those of you who may have received a similar request—and even for those of you who didn't—here is how I tried to sidestep looking more ridiculous than I already do:

May 22, 1990

TO THE BOARD OF TRUSTEES OF THE NATIONAL ASSOCIATION OF LIFE UNDERWRITERS IN THE YEAR OF OUR LORD 2090:

The Centennial Committee of NALU has asked me, along with many others, to send you a prediction of what things will be like in the insurance business when you open their "time capsule" at the celebration of your bicentennial.

While I find this to be a great challenge, I'm afraid I will have to cop out. (If slang has changed over the years, "cop out" means to quail, shirk or refuse to do one's duty. I assume you will still be speaking English.) Here are some of my reasons:

- I will have to consult with my scientific friends to determine whether the warming of the atmosphere will have increased the sea level to the point where most of the east-and west-coast home offices will be under water. This will, of course, include their agencies and perhaps even their agents. This might cause a profound change in the distribution system.

- If we have colonized the moon or some nearby planet there will be significant changes in the actuarial tables. Have you bred a corps of actuaries sufficiently bold to go to the moon or some nearby planet?

- If insurance goes global, will you have designed wallets subtle enough to contain dollars, yen, pounds, marks, rubles and other legal tender? If you have invented a worldwide currency will you have also invented a place like Switzerland where it can be stashed away, laundered (a quaint 20th century phrase), or otherwise hidden? Do not underestimate the importance of this.

- Will agents ever have to leave home, or can they conduct all their business, including prospecting, electronically? If such is the case, do you not envisage the breakup up of the American family, with Dad underfoot all day?

- As you read this, 150 years ago I was involved in asking the same questions of NALU leaders that they are asking me today. And all they were asked to do was to look 50 years in the future. The result was a fiasco, so much so that at the centennial the responses were quietly hidden in a back room. I hope you will have sufficient respect for your forebears to do the same—if it should prove to be necessary. Do not make fun of us. We do the best we can, but if we fail to heed the immutable laws of probability we are looked upon to be crazy people. Quite probably the craziest will be the one you will cherish most on June 18, 2090.

I hope to be with you, of course, but I may be limping a little. After all, the occasion will be three days after my 176th birthday.

Godspeed!

"A Person's Judgment"

No. 26, June 25, 1990, Page 21

Jim Rutherford, executive vice-president of the National Association of Life Underwriters during the harrowing years of World War II, and the one person who set the association on the course of eminence that it has achieved today, had a wonderful phrase he used when a discussion got contentious.

It was, "A person's judgment is no better than the information on which it is based." Bartlett's *Familiar Quotations* attributes it to Arthur Hays Sulzberger of the *New York Times* in a 1948 speech, but heard it from Jim many years before that. He probably borrowed it from Socrates.

Today too many of us are making judgment calls without doing our homework. And sometimes the information we so badly need is tightly held by a small group and is unavailable to us—although it should be published.

Let me give you a specific example. Some weeks ago I wrote a piece in this column hailing the life insurance business for contemplating an all-industry group that would undertake to cut down on the duplication of education and training programs for field management and agents. I said it was getting too expensive, and needed such an examination.

The day after it appeared, I received three phone calls, all with a similar set of questions: Don't you know that we're well along the road to doing what you want? And how much duplication of training and education efforts really exists?

My knee-jerk response was, "Why didn't you tell me? Tell me more." It turns out that the time isn't yet ripe for telling anyone anything, but plans are in the mill. I was left with the feeling that I had egg on my face, but it wasn't my egg. An investigative reporter (which I sometimes fancy I am) goes to the best sources he can find to keep his readers informed, but sometimes the sources are out in the bayous planning marvelous things, and won't talk. There is reason for this, of course. In the case of education and training, many organizations must be brought together so they may explain their philosophies and their input. Loose talk too early in the game may effectively kill a worthy project.

Unhappily, there is mutual suspicion between those who are creating the news and those, like me, who are purveying it. They think I will spill the beans, and I think they are clamming up on me. If they would trust me and my colleagues more—even with off-the-record comments that would never reach the light of print—all of us would probably have less egg on our faces.

The insurance business has become increasingly suspicious of those who report its doings, and exceedingly sensitive to criticism. Some of its leaders appear to feel that there is an inalienable sanctity about what they do. I disagree. When the press is a toady, as it has sometimes been, it has no reason for existence. As an individual writer, I badly need the ability to disagree with you, just as I need the pride to agree with you.

But I must know what I am talking about. If I go off half-cocked, I am an embarrassment to us all. Back to the Rutherford dictum, which places squarely on me the need to get my facts straight before I make judgment calls. But I cannot get them without your help. Nor can any other insurance reporter. The suspicions that many life insurance leaders have about their press seem to stem from a single thought: "They don't agree with us." Ah, but perhaps they would if they understood your motives and your decision making processes more clearly. Sometimes you mumble; sometimes you go into catatonic silence. The Calvin Coolidge style of communications is long dead. Even your own troops are sometimes puzzled about what you tell them.

Damn, I hate these lectures. But if I don't indulge in them now and then, my colleagues and I won't be able to collect the facts, and we will be accused of "bashing." Bashing is the last thing I want to do.

"'Why Women Fear Money'—WHAT?"

No. 27, July 2, 1990, Page 23

An exceedingly brave woman named Esther Berger, a vice-president of Paine Webber in Beverly Hills, went out on a long, long limb in a column published in the March 12 [1990] *Newsweek*. It was headlined "Why Women Fear Money," and it painstakingly nailed down Ms. Berger's beliefs on the subject.

It is entirely possible that she has been burned in effigy by every responsible women's group in this land. Conceivably, the Supreme Court will have to affirm a decision that burning Esther in effigy is a federal offense, before the practice gets out of hand.

Her thesis is that there is "a disturbing discrepancy between women's achievements during the last two decades and their continuing inability to deal with one of the most commonly accepted measures of achievement: money."

She continues, "Many women still cling to the belief that handling money is a man's job, derived from intrinsic knowledge that women simply do not possess. As a result, women resist taking responsibility for their financial well-being, a situation that has severe consequences at every social and economic level."

Ladies and gentlemen of the jury, let us examine her theory. We will do so without reference to names like Helmsley, Trump and Marcos, because they might tend to prejudice you. We will talk simply about the Modern American Woman.

I will go along with Esther to this extent: women tend to be more conservative in their handling of money, and with good reason. Because they see themselves, at some time in the indefinite future, as the conservator of the corpus of old Dad's estate, they tend not to get into wild speculation.

My own late wife, Peg, was vice-president and treasurer of a corporation that handled many millions of dollars yearly. For the business, she was prudent in the investments she recommended, and they did well. But for the Barnes family she was an arch-conservative. Occasionally, I would come home, eyes alight, with a hot tip. Her lip would curl with disbelief. That's probably why I am not passing among you with a tin cup today.

Where Esther Berger fails in her theory, I believe, is that she blames women for thinking that men know it all financially. Maybe that is true of some of today's matrons who were children of the depression. They saw their fathers and husbands desperately dig themselves out of debt and help them toward a life of some comfort, if not wealth. But that was yesterday, trailing over into today.

Can Esther be talking about today's woman, in her forties and fifties? She must know a strange crew in Beverly Hills, which I remember as a strange crew unto itself. Of the ten couples I consider my closest friends, every wife is wise in the ways of financial management, and half of them are at least as astute as their husbands.

Esther Berger might well have written this paragraph in the year 1950, however, she delayed it until 1990:

"Women must confront once and for all the questions of financial entitlement and control. Taking financial responsibility is a necessary and invaluable element of security, prosperity and maturity. What's at stake involves much more than dollars and cents."

If the *Newsweek* article had been written by a man, it would probably not have been published. If it had reached the pages of the magazine, it would have been excoriated as sexist and biased. But because a woman wrote it, the magazine asks us to look upon it as gospel.

Insurance people, particularly in the field force, have been accused of being unrealistic in their attitude toward women as colleagues and prospects. But I fear Ms. Berger has outdone them all.

"The Two Invasions"

No. 45, November 5, 1990, Page 43

Ask yourself these two questions:

1. When the European Community succeeds in lowering barriers to free trade in 1992, will American financial institutions, including insurance companies, undertake to become a part of the act?

2. Have European and Japanese companies already made inroads in buying control of established U.S. life insurance companies? If you have been following the news recently, your answer to the first question is "Probably," and your answer to the second is "Absolutely."

If you were a military strategist, this could remind you of two great armies circling each others' flanks and plunging into enemy territory without having engaged in combat. But I doubt that it will come out that way at all, at least as the 21st century opens.

Each of these land masses has special skills that they have honed over time, and each will try to use them to its own advantage.

The Japanese, for instance, have been studying U.S. life insurance practices with great care since they financially recovered from the debacle of World War II. For many years an austere gentleman named Gen Hirosi seemed to turn up at the most important company and agent meetings in this country, taking copious notes and accompanied by a cloud of assistants and interpreters. I managed to interview him, with considerable help from others, and discovered that he was CEO of one of Japan's biggest and fastest-growing life insurance companies.

What Hirosi and his colleagues set out to do was to take every transferable element of American life insurance and adapt it to Japan. They did it very well; today they have 659 members of the Million Dollar Round Table, more than any country except the U.S. and Canada. And, of course, they added their own spin to the idea. They have found that women are among their most accomplished sales people. Eight of them are in the premium organization, the Top of the Table, and nearly 500 are members of the MDRT.

Japan has tentatively begun to invade the U.S. market, and American companies have started to strike deals with their Japanese counterparts. There seems to be a fair exchange here; as far as the experts at LIMRA can tell us, both sides are profiting. While Japan has the strictest regulations separating insurance and banking of any country on the Pacific Rim, the financial businesses work amiably together.

U.S. companies' relations with their European counterparts will probably be more difficult, for a whole host of reasons. Europeans feel they invented life insurance, and they are probably right. This makes them reluctant to look across the Atlantic for ideas or help. Their distribution system has evolved differently from the American agency system, but it suits them.

Most importantly, throughout Europe banks and insurance companies are blood brothers, working out of the same offices and with the same techniques. When the European Community formalizes in two years, this is bound to continue. As far as I can see, there are no laws contemplated to separate the two. As we all know, American insurance is totally united in keeping banks and insurance as separate as laws can make them. This will make it hard to move into a European market where the distinction does not exist. One of our favorite business expressions these days is "the level playing field," but any incursion into European insurance is not likely to occur if European companies have the leverage of their banks and American ones do not. The playing field will always say, "Tilt."

The same is not true of European organizations that now control what used to be purely domestic companies in the United States. They operate under our laws, but their masters across the sea have their own set of rules. And there are constantly more companies coming our way.

So, unless American companies can set up subsidiaries that can work under European strictures, our prospects for becoming a factor in the European Community of the future will be difficult indeed.

(I am deeply in debt to Betty Tovian of LIMRA for having helped me crystallize my thoughts in this important area.)

"Tracking The Equitable In Its Quest"

No. 3, January 21, 1991, Page 19

The Equitable Life Assurance Society of the United States—to endow it with its full title and to separate it from the various other Equitables in the world—has decided on a demutualization plan. It is by far the largest mutual company to undertake to stock itself. Its decision created shock waves throughout the life insurance business. Shocks and curiosity will continue until its new status is in place and operating.

Not an easy undertaking. It would have been impossible for a New York company to do it until the state legislature passed a law governing demutualization proceedings in 1988. Union Mutual of Maine did it six years ago, but split itself into three corporations, all with UNUM in their names, to facilitate the transition, and to satisfy state insurance departments.

None of the other great mutuals—Prudential, Metropolitan, New York Life, Northwestern Mutual, Mass Mutual, Connecticut Mutual, Mutual Benefit, Mutual of New York, to name just a few—has indicated that it will follow Equitable's lead, but it would be folly to assume they have not put together task forces to monitor what is going on, just in case.

Does this mean the ultimate conversions of what used to be called "the giant Eastern mutuals" into stock companies? I doubt it. Equitable says it wants to "gain greater flexibility in being able to finance growth." The company has made some errors in recent years, and admits it. Those that have maintained their conservatism during a time when this trait was scorned may not have such motivation. But it would be folly for them not to watch through microscopes, telescopes and any other scopes they have how "the Goddess of Protection" — as Equitable calls itself once again—makes out.

A little history is in order here. Prior to the famous Armstrong investigation in 1906, almost all large life insurance companies sold stock as a matter of course. But the excesses that were revealed were so widespread that many decided to mutualize in order to place themselves above suspicion. Equitable completed its mutualization in 1918. Most big companies that chose to do so accomplished the transition in the 1910-20 decade. They had trouble with their faithful stockholders, particularly institutional investors, but they made the idea work. Smaller and younger companies weren't in the least bit interested in the notion, and hung onto the stock concept that created them. But the public enjoyed mutualization, particularly with policyholder dividends, and the new mutuals blossomed.

But if you think mutualizing was a tough task, consider the problems of demutualizing. Public hearings must be held by the state. The company goes under the scrutiny of everyone involved with finance, and will be required to respond to all sorts of criticism, some sage and some totally outrageous. And what about all those participating (dividend earning) policies? Their owners are entitled to vote on the new plan, and every single one of them will ask, "What will I get in place of dividends?"

The answer is that they will receive stock in the demutualized Equitable, or cash, or additional life insurance, depending on the terms and conditions authorized by the Equitable and the states. Talk about a labor of Hercules!

It isn't as easy for a mutual life insurance company to go public as it is for, say, a family-held organization. The logistics are difficult for a layman to imagine, although it is perfectly clear that Equitable senior management and its board had examined every one of them before making their fateful decision. Even now the company cannot answer many questions until its demutualization plan has been developed and approved by just about everyone you can think of.

One could say that Equitable is a scout, pioneering in the wilderness for all those who may choose to follow it. Just one problem: it was a stock company once before, so it is pioneering into the past.

"'Stop Generalizing. . .You Idiot'"

No. 5, February 4, 1991, Page 27

"Research" isn't what I do. Research is a gang of people telephoning some two thousand respondents, asking specific questions of each, and coming away with a two percent margin for error.

When I decide to write on a contentious subject, I call up perhaps ten of my old buddies, all of whom I consider to be well-versed on the issue at hand, and ask for their reactions about what I propose to say. Sometimes their replies are so violent that I scrap the project and go on to something else. And sometimes they lull me into a sense of false security.

One of the mistakes I make, in my desire to cause everything to be perfectly clear to you, is to generalize too much. You have seen two instances of this trait lately in letters that have appeared just below my column. (Can't they put them in a less embarrassing place?)

The first was a letter from Bob Oberst, president-elect of the International Association for Financial Planning. I had said that the craft of financial planning was "in a state of confusion." In a kind way, he replied that it was not. What I had failed to do was to separate the financial planner who has paid his or her dues and has all the proper designations from the person who has simply decided to call himself a financial planner because the name has a good ring to it.

Unhappily, it appears to be impossible to copyright the title. So, until the genuine article is unable to separate himself from the fake, there will be a state of confusion. I hope I have completed the clarification.

More recently, you may have read the letter from Kay Doughty, public counsel for the Office of Consumer Protection for the State of Texas. She took me to task for saying that "consumer advocates deal in great and sweeping generalities" and accused me of doing the same thing myself. She was right, of course. I should have leveled my sights directly on the person I was criticizing—Bob Hunter, president of the National Insurance Consumer Organization—and just one letter he sent out seeking contributions for his cause. I did not like the letter then, and I don't like it now. But I should not have undertaken to tar an entire craft on the basis of one letter by one person.

Consumer advocacy in any field is relatively new. Ralph Nader didn't invent it, but he certainly popularized it. Even before World War II there were a number of people known simply as "critics" of life insurance, most of whom were simply espousing term insurance over whole life. One was Norman Dacey, who at an advanced age still turns up plucking his one-stringed lute. Another was the improbably named team of Gilbert and Sullivan—no relation to *The Mikado*. In more recent times we have had my neighbor, Andy Tobias, who writes books like *The Invisible Bankers*—subtitled "Everything the Insurance Industry Never Wanted You to Know." Many of the new breed grudgingly conceded there are some virtues in insurance.

Ms. Doughty was absolutely right. I generalized too much. If I need protection as a consumer, I may well call on her.

Sometimes a gentle reader throws a left hook at you that comes up right from the floor. One such as Warren James of Pittsburgh. He is a personal producing general agent, and he questioned my reference to the species as "a breed apart who live by a special state of rules." He obviously couldn't understand what rules I had in mind. I had written a sloppy sentence. What I had meant to say was that when a person is partly a producer and partly a general agent, he or she has to abide by the rules of both. That is why Warren and I agreed that they have to be a hardy breed in order not to be a dying breed. It appears that many companies don't like them any more. Too bad!

As you can see, I have communicated by phone with these three people. I try to talk with everyone who is a critic of mine. I might just learn something.

"Will You Join The Lagoon Society?"

No. 6, February 11, 1991, Page 17

Some time ago a friend of mine and I formed The Lagoon Society, an organization of people whose interests were a mile in circumference and six inches deep. In other words, we were dilettantes. We knew Ty Cobb's batting average, how Michelangelo had managed to paint that ceiling of the Sistine Chapel, how many touchdowns Red Grange scored against Michigan, how a deaf person like Beethoven could compose such magnificent symphonies, and where Franklin Roosevelt discovered the phrase "the only thing we have to fear is fear itself." The purpose of the society was to convince its members to dig more deeply into any issues they considered to be of importance, and to cease skipping around the surface of their lagoons like waterbugs.

It has worked well. There are more than 200 members, and each of them has dug into the bottom of his or her lagoon and is starting to make it a lake—

a smaller lake, to be sure, but one that is deeper and more useful than the lagoon used to be. Some have become real experts.

Why do I bring this up in an insurance magazine? Because I want to discuss with you the issue of continuing education, which transforms the lagoon of your first knowledge of life insurance into a lake of facts and understanding.

Recently I received a questionnaire from the New York State Association of Life Underwriters headed "What Do You Think About Mandatory Continuing Education?" I was surprised. To me, mandatory continuing education is like brushing your teeth in the morning. Anyone who doesn't know what advances the insurance business has made in recent months has plaque attached to his or her brain.

So I called Ben Brewster, executive vice-president of the association, and asked him why he would send out a questionnaire with such an obvious answer. His reply surprised me: a certain number of his members, not by any means a majority, didn't want the state government dictating to them what they ought to know. They had no objection to learning more, but they wanted to have what courses they took sanctioned by their various associations, including LUTC and CLU/ChFC, rather than the state.

To my mind, the objectors are simply quibbling. No state, whether it be New York, Florida, California or Montana, is going to ask life insurance agents to assume an impossible burden of education. Their purpose is to make sure that the people they license are qualified to consult wisely with their prospects and clients. For far too many years the state insurance departments were somewhat derelict in their educational duties; now that they are beginning to bring themselves abreast of the situation they shouldn't be knocked down by their own constituents.

Television had made education in insurance easy to come by, if you are alert and willing to spend a little money. Most states have begun to accept sales congresses, conventions and other association meetings—if attendance is certified—as credentials for continuing education. Now TV has been added to the list. The Insurance Television Network in Broomall, PA, (215-356-9500) is producing a series of events [one of them, *ITN News Journal*, in association with this newspaper] that include pay-per view seminars with some of the top professionals in the business. The Financial Satellite Network in Dallas (214-490-1900) is producing four hours a day of financial programming, and is tightly tied to continuing education strictures. Both are affiliated with the best of professional insurance organizations.

My space here is too confined to explain to you how to work, but you have their phone numbers. Education is never totally painless, but bringing highly sophisticated courses into your office or a local meeting place helps a lot.

Today is no day to be a dilettante. The Lagoon Society is a pure mythical fraternity, but the associations you belong to and the networks you subscribe to will make your lake of knowledge a lot deeper. And most states will be helping you, if not prodding you. So get to it.

"Putting The Cartel Before The Facts"

No. 24, June 17, 1991, Page 19

"Cartel" is a word of many meanings, including "a challenge to a duel." But its most frequently used one is "an international syndicate, combine or trust generally formed to regulate prices and output in some field of business."

Recently a group of responsible writers, appearing in esteemed publications, have stated flatly—but with no factual substantiation—that the insurance business in America is a huge cartel, fixing prices, commissions and underwriting practices. They call for the cartel to be destroyed, chiefly by having the federal government step in and supersede the states in regulating all forms of insurance.

This reminds me of the ancient saying, known in almost every language, "to put the cart before the horse." That is, to reverse the right or natural order of things. Any professional researcher trying to make a point has to get his or her facts in line before dragging conclusions behind them.

This is not to say that insurance deserves a whitewashing. It doesn't. There are shady practitioners and greedy people in it. They feed on the fact that consumers are pathetically unaware of its complexities, and are reasonably happy to accept any good, linear explanation of costs and benefits. But those same consumers have recourse. There are hot lines they can call to dispel their confusion. They can comparison shop, which they are accustomed to doing in most big-ticket items. They can go directly to their state insurance commissions if they feel they are being taken advantage of.

Why haven't the writers who talk about cartels done the same thing? Since they are apparently bright enough to get their stuff printed, why can't they devise the dimensions of an insurance policy they may just pretend to want, and ask for quotations on it from several sources? The average agent selling any form of insurance today can tap into computer banks and give writers any quotes they ask for. An inquiring mind can reveal a great many truths—as well as falsehoods.

Pundits seem to have forgotten the competitive nature of American business.

If you offer a product at a given price, your competitors have just two choices: they will try to produce the same product at a lower price, or a better product at a competitive price. If they can't do either, their salespeople will probably come over to you. Of course, a non-competitive company can hang onto them for awhile by boosting their commission scales, but that never lasts long. The proud agent gravitates toward the proud company.

In many cases, insurance people react violently even to mild criticism. They tend to call it "bashing," and they fire off furious letters of complaint either to editors or writers. While such correspondence may give them a certain amount of internal satisfaction, it seldom changes the situation. A well-reasoned letter, buttressed by facts, is likely to have better results.

A concrete example: in May, the *New York Times* dredged up the old "cartel" argument in one of its editorials. Within two weeks, it published three carefully thought out letters in one issue, under a three-column headline reading "There Is No Insurance Industry Cartel to Bust." There was no screaming and yelling; just a parade of facts which the *Times* appeared to feel was unassailable. As far as I and several of my colleagues were concerned, the issue ended right there. If reason didn't prevail, at least the readers of the *Times* were given an opportunity to examine both sides of the story.

If you choose to be a participant in a complex business—and you wouldn't be reading this if you hadn't so chosen—you have got to be prepared for misunderstandings and lack of comprehension, even on the part of people you consider to be experts. Mere anger at what you consider their shortcomings will get you nowhere. The only phrase created by Lyndon Johnson that still sticks in my mind is, "Let us reason together." It makes good sense under almost any situation.

At any rate, if you hear the word "cartel," reason with the person who spoke it.

2

Candles of the Business

"Sidebars From The NALU Convention"

No. 39, September 27, 1986, Page 9

You will read the basic news about the NALU convention, one of the most important meetings in the life insurance business, elsewhere in this gazette, as well as in earlier issues. Here are some comments that certainly didn't escape you if you were there, but may amuse you if you weren't:

By all odds its biggest news happened 1,500 miles away from New Orleans, the site of the meeting: the resignation—or, better yet, let's call it retirement—of Bob Beck as chairman and CEO of the Prudential. It surfaced as a rumor while the clans were gathering for the John Newton Russell Award dinner, the classiest event of the week. Unhappily, as in all such cases where complete information isn't available, the question was bandied about, "Did he fall or was he pushed?"

This seems to be the case in all early retirements, however well programmed they may have been. Pity the gossips the next morning when a straightforward story in the *New York Times* showed that the retirement was planned by Bob Beck, just as it had been by his predecessor, Don MacNaughton. The rumors quickly turned into applause for a stalwart veteran who simply felt he had carried the ball long enough.

The only clear loser was Joe Melone, president of the Pru, who was mentioned by the *Times* as one of the four candidates to succeed Beck, but who didn't make the cut. Joe, as president of the Life Underwriter Training Council, was guest of honor at a cocktail party the following evening. If well-intentioned expressions of sympathy could drown a person, Joe would be down full fathom five.

* * * *

The spirit of this convention of agents seems to be tremendously high—higher than I can remember it for years. Maybe it was the Dixieland music, which seemed to be everywhere. (Pete Fountain certainly proved that Dixieland wasn't dead when he played a triumphant concert in a packjammed ballroom.) Maybe it was the new sense of combativeness in the current breed of highly professionalized agents. Possibly it was because the meeting wasn't as highly politicized as conventions usually are: Alan Press of New York ran unopposed for secretary. This means he is heir presumptive to the presidency of the association three years hence. While there were campaigns for trustee, they tend to be in a slightly lower key. At any rate, a fresh breeze seemed to blow from first to last (which is an event in itself in humid New Orleans).

Most panel sessions tend to be either over-rehearsed or under-thought. But the five men who participated in the forum called "Our Future From the Company Perspective" were the answer to a listener's dream: candid, perceptive, witty and brief. For the record, they were: Jack Bobo, executive head of NALU; Marvin Brower, chairman of State Farm; Skip Pease, senior vice-president of Prudential; John Scully, senior vice-president of John Hancock; and Tom Wheeler, senior v.p. of Mass Mutual. If you can stand some tough talk about your future delivered in a palatable way, you should order a cassette of this session from NALU. And if you think the Hancock isn't seriously interested in getting into banking, listen to John Scully's blunt question.

* * * *

The blue-ribbon panel's choice of Norman Levine, general agent for the Mutual Benefit in San Francisco, as recipient of the John Newton Russell Award ("the person who has done the most for the life insurance business") was inspired. Forthright, outspoken and sometimes contentious fellows aren't usually very good candidates for awards; they are bound to have offended somebody of consequence. But Norman has never pulled a punch in his travels through the chairs of NALU, GAMC, LUTC and sundry other associations. It is refreshing to find a panel that likes a fighter.

* * * *

Tom Wolff, one of the nation's best known life underwriters, delivered a thoroughly upbeat talk on the effect of proposed new tax legislation on life underwriters. While he acknowledges the worries ahead, he also sees plenty of opportunity. He proposed the notion that some forms of life insurance may constitute the last tax shelters. This is comforting, I suppose, but it may be like the woman walking down the streets of Nome during the Gold Rush declaring, "I am the last virtuous woman in Alaska." Somebody is bound to get interested in the concept, and in the case of life insurance it may be members of Congress who are looking for potential tax sources. But since the Wall Street Journal has come pretty close to saying the same thing, I doubt that we have a real secret here.

Perhaps we will do well to heed the words of the old advertising slogan: "If you've got it, flaunt it."

"Belth The Iconoclast"

No. 40, October 4, 1986, Page 11

Supreme Court Justice Brandeis once said to a meeting of businessmen, "All businesses and industries should have their muckrakers. Muckrakers will make them more concerned, more progressive and perhaps even more honest."

The Justice was using the term "muckraker" in the classical sense, which was not in the slightest bit demeaning. Teddy Roosevelt used it to describe a group of journalists and critics who, in the first decade of the 20th century, undertook to expose abuses in business and industry and corruption in politics. Some of the best known were Lincoln Steffens, Ida Tarbell and Upton Sinclair.

The life insurance business has never been blessed—if that's the right word—with many authentic muckrakers.

Elizur Wright, a fiery editor and abolitionist of the 1860s, was undoubtedly the first one. He conceived the legal reserve principle and then went on to shape state supervision as the Massachusetts insurance commissioner.

Charles Evans Hughes conducted the Armstrong investigation which completely recast the life insurance business in 1906-07, but he became afflicted with the desire to become President and ultimately ended up as Chief Justice of the U.S. Supreme Court.

Since then, most people who have posed as insurance critics have been writers in search of a fast buck by ineptly taking apart a business that has more than a hundred million customers. (That magic figure seems to guarantee a wide audience, but such is not always the case.) Most of them have ended up with the limp admonition: "Buy term and invest the difference."

But today we do have on the scene a man who seems to have all the qualifications of a muckraker: (1) he knows his subject inside and out; (2) a considerable number of the members of the establishment dislike him; (3) he does his homework on any subject he tackles; and (4) in many of his approaches to the business he exhibits a lack of tact.

He is Joseph M. Belth, CLU, Ph.D., professor of insurance in the graduate school of business at Indiana University—Joe Belth to most people who care to pronounce his name at all. He runs a monthly newsletter called *The Insurance Forum*, which is the main outlet for his opinions about life insurance and the people in it. He has written *Life Insurance—A Consumer's Handbook*, which is a sprightly, opinionated volume about today's product and those who sell it. Consumers, however, will have to dredge up their knowledge of high school algebra when Joe starts talking about price calculations and rates of return.

To give you some examples of the Belthian mind, here are three of the subjects he has been concentrating on in the recent past:

- The A.L. Williams organization. He has dug more deeply into its pyramid operations than anyone, and has brought to the attention of several state commissioners what he considers to be ALW's unseemly behavior. He is a bulldog on Williams: if legal counsel is necessary for him to fight what he regards as misleading tactics, he brings it to bear.

- The companies reinsuring the business produced by ALW's agents. Some of these companies are at the same time hurting, to one degree or another, from ALW's replacement tactics, and Joe is mildly—but not necessarily politely—inquiring about which side of the fence they think they are on.

- The NAIC's confidential IRIS ratios. The insurance commissioners association has developed an Insurance Regulatory Information System (IRIS) which lists the life/health companies rated B+ or higher that had four or more IRIS ratios outside the range of usual values. According to Belth, "the NAIC considers the ratios valuable in pointing to companies likely to experience financial difficulties," but it refuses to publish them. Belth is trying to get access through appropriate law suits, even though he can come pretty close by working with the A.M. Best Company, on whose calculations the ratios are constructed. I'm betting he will succeed.

Nobody is perfect, and that includes Joe Belth. Sometimes he is blunt to the point of irascibility. Often he seems to go out of his way to make enemies of people who sincerely want to be his friends. But I believe, in Justice Brandeis' words, he is helping to make the life insurance business more concerned, more progressive and even more honest.

Perhaps we should call him Belth, the iconoclast. That fits him, and it keeps him out of the muck.

"At Last, Praiseworthy Advertising"

No. 44, November 1, 1986, Page 9

The word "cognoscenti", in my private dictionary, means a group of people who think they know it all, whether they do or not. The advertising business has more cognoscenti than it can use, and most of them tend to be contemptuous of insurance advertising.

Imagine how the cognoscenti reacted when a life insurance campaign won the Grand Prix at the Cannes International Advertising Awards Film Festival. "While the commercials were the unanimous selection of the judges," according to press reports, "the announcement of their decision at the festival was greeted by an audience of about 5,000 with angry shouts, boos, hisses and even some thrown objects."

It figures. The know-it-alls were unable to comprehend how anyone can advertise triumphantly for an intangible product whose marketing is done principally by sales people. But it happened.

The advertiser: the John Hancock. The campaign: a series of commercials under the heading, "Real life, real answers." Listen to what one prominent Madison Avenue critic had to say about them:

"The characters populating John Hancock's $20 million ad campaign seem so real you'd swear they weren't actors—that their lines bubbled forth from their heads, not from a script. They don't look at the camera; indeed, they look away. They mumble and shrug; their voices overlap; background noises distract.

"The print ads have no headlines, the TV spots no announcer's message. This advertising is shocking not just because it breaks new ground for a financial services campaign but because it breaks new ground for any kind of advertising: This is hard-sell advertising served up in the softest, most palatable way."

You have probably seen one or more in print or on TV.

Takes Awards

I suspect that the executive suite at the John Hancock building was in shock when it realized that the campaign had just about swept the board for advertising awards earlier this year. But Dave D'Alessandro, senior vice-president for corporate communications, was taking the whole matter in stride when I talked with him:

Yes, the field force loved the campaign and thought it had a measurable effectiveness on sales, although sales were up while it was running. Yes, the company plans to continue the program into 1987; this good a campaign should last a long while. Yes, the company was proud of the campaign and highly pleased that even competition seemed impressed that financial services advertising was in the spotlight. And finally, it was a little too early to determine what effect it was having on recruiting.

(For purists among you, the campaign was created by the Boston agency of Hill Holliday Connors Cosmopulos, which did a remarkable job with lean copy and people who looked like anything but actors. However, give D'Alessandro and his colleagues credit for recognizing its virtues and putting the chips behind it.)

Coincidentally, John Hancock was the first insurance company to venture into network TV advertising. Nearly 30 years ago it produced a campaign featuring Paul Clark, its chairman, talking about life insurance from behind his desk. It was a true breakthrough, but it would have a Neanderthal look in today's hot TV commercial market.

Some years ago I recited a formula for life insurance advertising before the Association of National Advertisers: good advertising + a poor sales force = poor sales; poor advertising + a good sales force = good sales; good advertising + a good sales force = superior sales. I contend that this formula still stands up, and is the principal reason why direct response advertising hasn't made greater inroads in insurance sales.

One of the weaknesses of top management in insurance is this: because it cannot see the equation between cause (advertising) and effect (sales) it presumes that advertising is a waste. Only when it turns off the advertising spigot, as the Equitable did a few years ago, does the difference become clear. While I'm not privy to the Equitable's private deliberations, it's significant to me that the company is now very much back in the act with a multimillion dollar program.

I'd better stop this before one of you starts calling me a member of the cognoscenti.

"The Communication Dollar"

No. 47, November 22, 1986, Page 13

When an insurance company's executive committee pulls together the year's budget, part of it is invariably allocated to communicating with people outside the company. To some degree or other, it feels the necessity to tell outsiders about its products, its services, its plans, hopes and fears for the future. It doesn't want to be caught looking like a shapeless monolith, in business just to make a buck for its management and its stockholders, if any.

In recent years the U.S. Congress has been threatening to commit so much nuisance with insurance companies that a higher and higher percentage of the communications dollar has gone toward placating or exhorting senators and representatives.

They must do right by our Nell: they must not tax the inside buildup; they must not let banks flood into the insurance business; they must see to it that the guarantees and privileges of insurance are safeguarded; they must realize that excessive taxation of life and health insurance is a tax on thrift, self- reliance and the ability of citizens to control their own financial future.

That's the way the litany goes, anyhow.

As we have discovered, it costs a lot of money to convince legislators, both federal and state, to do what we think are the appropriate things and to keep them from making inappropriate moves. It is so expensive, in fact, that most companies have had to curtail their communications with their natural publics—their clients, prospects, educators, students, etc., etc.

For years now I have been yapping away—by typewriter and by lip—at the leaders of the American Council of Life Insurance, pleading for a return of the times when the business "spoke with one voice" to educate the public in the virtues of its product and how it can serve the people in a unique way. I have always received a courteous reply: "We're doing the best we can with the money we have to spend."

But suddenly I have acquired an ally so important that I feel I have a fleet of howitzers alongside my popgun. He is Pierre Maurer, vice-chairman of Metropolitan Life. In his remarks as retiring chairman of the Life Insurance Marketing and Research Association entitled *Consumer Perception: The Issue*, he cited these facts, chiefly from LIMRA and ACLI research:

- The public does not really understand our product. About half the public feels uninformed and uneasy when buying life insurance.

- For years, the public has had a very poor opinion of life insurance companies. Only one-third of the people surveyed thought that life insurance companies gave them their money's worth.

- In 1969, 54% of respondents felt that life insurance companies had a very high ethical code. Only 29% agreed in 1984.

- In the most recent survey of our prime market, life insurance companies trailed other institutions in virtually every major category: safety, honesty, trustworthiness, innovativeness, fairness and responsiveness, to name a few.

Pierre Maurer sees these perceptions—which are getting worse—as "an enormous handicap in a deregulated marketplace. And make no mistake about it—deregulation could be right around the corner."

His conclusions:

- "It seems clear that in our communications with the public we are still searching for the key. Obviously we need to improve our communications through simplified language and more effective use of advertising, both TV and the print media."

- "We must find ways to make our companies and our products more consumer-driven. . .The situation is urgent and is becoming more critical every day."

- "Above all, we should look for ways to demystify our products and ourselves. We need some sort of simplifications, some ease of expression, some common communications ground to share with the consumer."

He also had some specific recommendations for internal improvements, but you get the idea.

It is superfluous for me to say that I agree with him wholeheartedly.

But I have been in life insurance communications for half a century, and most inhabitants of executive suites have heard me twang my one-stringed lute to the point of boredom.

But this, gentlemen, is a fresh voice—a spokesman for one of the greatest financial institutions in the world, or at least for one of its most revered associations. Can we all fail to ponder on what he is trying to tell us?

The cost of causing people to listen is admittedly high. Too many people and businesses out there are clamoring for the attention of our prime markets.

(Shakespeare knew that back in 1590: "I can call spirits from the vasty deep." "Yes, but do they come when you call them?") But with wisdom, patience, continuity—and perhaps just a touch of genius—it can be done.

Please, you up there in the executive suites, heed Pierre Maurer's admonition.

"The Straw That Stirs The Drink"

No. 9, March 2, 1987, Page 11

Life insurance people, whatever their position in home office and field, are usually totally busy making a living, distributing their products and services, and dreaming up more inventive ways to perform. When government, state or local, starts cuffing them, probing them or trying to put collars around their necks, they have to down tools and defend themselves. Or do they?

They used to, of course. But over the years they have discovered they had invented a lightning rod which could deflect some of the problems they had to face: the executives of their trade associations.

In the early years, they hired trade association people to take care of the membership rolls, collect dues, and set the stage for their conventions and other meetings. The heavy lifting—the development of position papers, research projects and other technical stuff—was left to the uncompensated officers and boards of directors. As time wore on and the business began to assume a larger position in the economy, there was less time for such volunteer work.

So they began to hire better executives, who knew enough about the problems of the industry to work in harness with senior people in both company and field. Today the staffs of the major trade associations compare favorably with those of the principal companies themselves, and are a major factor in giving the business considerable clout in fields it considers important to its survival.

It's probably not unfair to the other skilled associations that operate in almost every phase of the business to say that the four dominant ones are the American Council of Life Insurance, the Life Insurance Marketing and Research Association, and the Life Office Management Association, which operate chiefly on behalf of the companies, and the National Association of Life Underwriters, the spokesman for 140,000 agents. Let's take a look at them:

ACLI. When you have a president who is a former U.S. Senator and Secretary of what used to be known as Health, Education and Welfare, as Dick Schweiker is, you are starting with power. Add power all down the line in public relations, legislative and actuarial services, and you are a force to deal with in almost every area of the economy. Its only weakness is that its public relations arm has become too much a handmaiden of explaining its legislative positions, and not enough for explaining to the public what life insurance means and does. Its new program on risk classification should help measurably in this field.

LIMRA. Never has life insurance research been as pointed, sophisticated and useful as it is today under the LIMRA banner. President Ernie Cragg has acquired a talented staff and given them their heads. The result is that life insurance people in home office and field know more about their markets than they ever have. LIMRA is also pioneering in research about all areas of financial services, giving companies and agents some interesting points of view about new products and services they may be considering.

LOMA. Under veteran President Lynn Merritt (who seems to have been around since before the Flood), LOMA has been built into an organization that gives courses in all areas of home office management except marketing. Again, sophistication has become the name of the game. Want to know about employee attitudes? Concerned about compensation strategies for investment professionals? Policyholder service killing you? LOMA will help on these things and many more.

NALU. This is a sprawling organization with a membership of about 140,000 field people in 50 state and 1,000 local associations (most of them with dedicated, paid help). Jack Bobo, formerly president of the organization and now its executive v.p., runs a tight ship and an effective one. While he faces the inevitable charge (levied periodically ever since NALU was formed nearly a century ago) of kow-towing to the companies, I don't believe a word of it. Its people cooperate, but they don't toady. Its NALUPAC is probably the most effective grass-roots lobby in the business. Sometimes I feel NALU people don't know their own strength.

I get around to see these association leaders as often as I can, in state and local groups as well as national ones. The business now has a squadron of tough, seasoned professionals on a par with their home office counterparts. They are capable of leading the business down the paths of righteousness. They, and their colleagues in other associations I haven't had time to name, are (in the immortal words of Reggie Jackson) "the straw that stirs the drink."

"Less Is Better—Or Is It?"

No. 29, July 20, 1987, Page 13

The Million Dollar Round Table recently announced, with what appeared to be considerable satisfaction, that it has managed to reduce its membership from more than 21,000 in 1985 to just over 17,000 this year.

In most associations this would be a cause for wailing and keening, but MDRT follows the edict first enunciated in Gilbert and Sullivan's *The Gondoliers*:

"When everybody's somebody, Then no one's anybody."

In other words, you can't call yourself an elite organization when the rabble is at your doors with certified tickets of admission.

I had a little experience with this in 1939, when a great man named Grant Taggart and I sat behind closed doors for several days trying to rewrite the MDRT bylaws. Most of the job was comparatively easy, but when we got to qualification requirements we agonized. Because the organization was so new, no one had properly evaluated the weight that should be given to such products as term and group insurance. Some members were sliding in without earning a decent living.

We stiffened the qualifications measurably, and the executive committee gave our undertaking its blessing. Naturally, howls went up from the membership, but this was just the first in an uncounted number of upgradings of MDRT production requirements. Failing such actions, most of the members of NALU would probably qualify for MDRT today, and exclusivity would have become a thing of the past.

A few years later, I found myself on the other side of the battle lines. When the requirements advanced far beyond the million dollar level, I questioned in print whether the organization hadn't better rethink its name. I even came up with a couple of ideas. I was waited on by a pair of burly ex-presidents named Don Shepherd and Tilly Walker, who told me with great politeness that the name was going to stay the same and that I would do well to go lie down somewhere until my fever for changes had subsided. I did, and have stayed there ever since.

Still, I have an inborn sympathy with the poor guys and gals who determine that they're going to make the Table. They struggle upward, finally near the magic number, and then are told that the executive committee has added another rung to the ladder and they must try just a little harder.

I'm convinced that the motto of the committee is Browning's great line, "A man's reach must exceed his grasp, or what's a heaven for?" The poor applicant has the ignoble alternative of going home and kicking the cat.

Of course, MDRT has now separated itself into the elite, the extra elite, and the you-bet-your-sweet-patootie elite, as represented by the Court of the Table and the Top of the Table. My crystal ball tells me that someday there will be a group called the Real MDRT, consisting of those who have assembled a million in first-year commissions. Then there will be no question about the name or who's the elitest.

Despite all this banter, I have the notion that MDRT is on precisely the right track if it wants to be a meaningful part of the life insurance community. Seventeen thousand out of about 140,000 (members must also belong to NALU) certainly constitutes an elite group. As the MDRT itself has said, "Sales of new products and other factors have meant a considerable growth in insurance earnings, causing our membership to grow by leaps and bounds, jeopardizing the MDRT badge of excellence that is our pride."

The only thing that bothers me, and I suppose it's only because I'm trying to show how compassionate I really am, is that the United States shows a 24.7 percent drop in membership. The qualifications committee put another rung in the ladder, and some people's reach exceeded their grasp.

At least they'll have another shot at it next year. But they will again have to learn to extend their grasp.

"The Devil With White Wings"

No. 40, October 5, 1987, Page 31

A balding man with a white, tight-lipped face stepped onto the platform of the annual meeting of the National Association of Life Underwriters on September 13, 1954. He said, "I hereby withdraw my name as a candidate for the presidency of NALU." He stepped back out of the spotlight and disappeared.

His name was John D. Marsh. He had been president of the General Agents and Managers Conference. He was, for four years a trustee of NALU, and then its secretary and vice-president. And he had been told the previous night that, while he was the sole nominee for the presidency of the organization, the nominating committee had withdrawn its support.

This was the first time such an event had happened in the 65-year history of NALU.

His crime? Along with an actuary named George Johnson, he had invented a product known as the variable annuity.

Fifteen years later he was recipient of the Wilner Award, which the District of Columbia Life Underwriters Association gives to its member who has done the most for the business. To validate his worthiness for the award, the association used the very words NALU had thrown at him those 15 years ago: that he had developed and promoted the idea of the variable annuity and variable life insurance.

On September 10, 1987, John Marsh died, full of happiness that his variable concept had been embraced by the life insurance business, and full of bitterness that NALU had never had the decency to reverse a position that had become intolerable within months after it had been established, and a public disgrace that had never been corrected.

Part of this was due to the fact that C. Carney Smith, his principal opponent in the 1954 struggle, became executive vice-president of NALU, and Carney was a strong, proud man who did not forgive easily.

As you might guess, John and I were friends. I saw his concept as far-reaching and worthy of experimental acceptance by NALU at the very least. But the association, unswervingly committed to the guarantees of life insurance, was unwilling to concede that variable products might be part of the insurance fabric. And, most certainly, that people who thought them up were fit to be president of NALU.

Of course, seldom has anyone been vindicated as thoroughly as John. He became president of the Variable Annuity Life and then, after he sold it to the Aetna, the Equity Annuity Life. He became a millionaire many times over, and a horse breeder of international repute. (I remember traveling with him to Belmont one day when he said, "I won the daily double yesterday." I replied, "Great. What was the payoff?" He looked at me with loathing. "My *horses* won the daily double, you idiot," he replied.)

John was a prideful southerner, a native of Atlanta. At another trip to the track, we picked out a horse that positively couldn't lose. Strangely enough, it didn't, and I came back from the windows pleased at how $2 could blossom. John had a sour look on his face. "Didn't you have the winner?" I asked. "Naah," he replied. "There was another horse I had to bet on." "What was its name?" I asked. He looked at me sheepishly. "Southern Pride," he said. And that about says it.

Another of John's achievements on behalf of the business was his creation of the Personal Affairs Division for the Army Air Force, a badly needed function that gave draftees sound advice about finances and helped insurance people use their skills in the armed forces. At first it was looked upon suspiciously by the brass as a boondoggle, but it survived triumphantly and is now a part of every element of the services. John Marsh never had it easy.

Pride. John Marsh did enough saintly things for the life insurance business to have won the [John Newton] Russell Award in a walk, but he was a tough, uncompromising person—and that is enough to make some leaders treat you as though you had cloven hooves. John Marsh lived by his pride and no one could take it away from him, not NALU nor anyone else. He deserves not to be forgotten.

"Whatever Happened To Public Relations?"

No. 48, November 30, 1987, Page 19

"The bottom line is appallingly clear. People do not understand us; they do not understand our products; and yet they know they need insurance. Can we afford, ten years from now, to let the public have these same perceptions? Can we grow at the rate we have in the past without improving how the public feels? Indeed, our marketing accomplishments in the past seem almost incredible if the attitude surveys are an accurate measure of our public image."—John J. Creedon, president of Metropolitan Life and chairman of the American Council of Life Insurance, at the ACLI annual meeting.

So spoke Mr. Creedon. At the same time, it became apparent to those who were listening carefully that the ACLI advertising program had been put under wraps for the foreseeable future, or at least until there was an important legislative problem to address.

This, then, is how the primary public relations organization of the life insurance business has responded to the urgings of its retiring chairman.

To many people, this is quite understandable. The issues facing life insurance before the Congress seem interminable. McCarran-Ferguson, inside build-up, rebating—those are simply the big three, and there are many more. Any organization that fails to gear up for such frightening possibilities simply isn't with it. Let's just state that for openers.

How, then, do we follow John Creedon's precepts? It's obviously a matter of money, and the life insurance business has got to make up its mind about how important the issue of public attitude is. Lip service simply will not do.

Either the crisis is as serious as John Creedon states it, or it is not. If it is, the business must reach more deeply into its pockets and mount a public relations campaign aimed directly at public understanding. Otherwise, it must stop talking about "public perceptions."

Of course, one of the most delightful things to do is to spend other people's money, at least until the other people catch up with you. That, I suppose, is what I'm advocating now. On the other hand, if Mr. Creedon is right the only way the life insurance business can get out of the situation he outlines is by putting into position some kind of a program that will make people "understand us."

Is it possible to put together the legislative issues and the public relations ones? Conceivably, but it will require some thunderously good copywriting.

The reasons people don't understand life insurance are remarkably simple; the reasons they don't comprehend the inside buildup are unbelievably complex. Putting them together will be the task of a Solomon.

Most laymen don't understand how many advertising and public relations impressions are tossed at them every day. To place an advertisement in a magazine or on TV by no means guarantees its readership. To say that a message "reaches 100 million people" is a lot of nonsense. It reaches only the people who pause and pay attention to the message.

If the life insurance business is going to take John Creedon's ideas seriously, it has got to pay the money to back them up. Please, no more talk without action. And if the funds aren't there to do the job, let the business admit it and fight the good fight as well as it can.

"Are All Those Company Associations Necessary?"

No. 7, February 15, 1988, Page 27

Outlanders often express surprise at the number of institutional associations the life insurance business has, even though at times it professes to be "speaking with one voice." There are five of them run by the chief executives of companies: the American Council of Life Insurance, the Consumer Credit Insurance Association, the Life Insurers Conference, the National Association of Life Companies and the National Insurance Association.

Why five? Whatever happened to the "one voice"? Don't they trip over each other when testifying before Congress? Most people who are heavily involved with any of them know better, but here are some notes for the benefit of those of us who are on the outside looking in:

ACLI is, of course, The Establishment—the major companies that have been organized in one way or another for nearly a century, certainly since the Armstrong investigation coalesced the business in 1906. It handles legislative and regulatory issues on all levels, and "provides the public with information about the purposes of life insurance."

CCLA serves as the official trade organization for insurers that underwrite consumer credit insurance in the areas of life, accident and health, and property insurance.

NALC's membership is made up of small-and medium-sized companies, most of which came into being after World War II. It provides those companies with a forum unavailable elsewhere.

NIA represents companies that principally serve the life insurance needs of black families.

Does each of them perform a vital function that the others can't? Roy Woodall, executive vice-president of NALC, lists three reasons why his organization is separate from the others:

"The first is taxes. The second is taxes. The third is taxes."

Roy came to NALC after a career as a company executive and insurance commissioner for Kentucky. He knows his constituency of 600 life insurance companies like the back of his hand, as they say. Not long ago, I had a delightful lunch with him in Washington during the meeting of ACLI. Roy had just been introduced as a distinguished guest of the meeting, which certainly proves that there is no animosity among the top-line organizations.

"It's just not reasonable to suppose that all life insurance companies have the same tax problems, federal or state," he said. "NALC has been instrumental in getting preferential treatment for small companies ever since the 1959 Life Insurance Tax Act. When Congress started to revamp life company taxation in 1980, the NALC was a key factor in getting special consideration for the smaller companies in the stopgap measures of TEFRA and in the special Small Life Insurance Company Deduction in the 1984 Life Insurance Tax Act. We are continuing to represent our companies vigorously whenever tax matters come up."

Do you get along with the other organizations in most other areas?

"Sure. We're not staffed to do much in the area of public relations or public education, and we're in full support of what ACLI does. As a matter of fact, there are 246 companies that are members of both organizations. Occasionally an issue arises where we have a genuine difference of opinion, such as the guaranty fund regulations. We disagreed on that one, but I don't think that anyone was particularly abrasive. Everybody understands that different companies have different needs."

Roy Woodall and I talked at length about the missions of the various company associations, and came to the general conclusion that there was precious little overlap. The credit insurance people, the home service companies, and those that sell chiefly to black families have special problems that would be boring to others, so it's little wonder that they want to get together and hammer away at them.

No, there aren't too many associations. Just the right number.

"Post Sales Service—A Thorny Problem"

No. 22, May 30, 1988, Page 19

Word comes down from at least three recent research studies that policyholders want more service after they've bought their policies. They don't phrase it that way, of course— "service" is an in-business word. What they say is that they don't fully understand the intricacies of their insurance and over time need more coaching from their agents on how to use it. When they bought they knew the basic facts of what they were getting into, but now, as their situations vary, they want to ask questions.

This situation has, of course, become much more prevalent with the emergence of the interest-sensitive universal and variable life policies. These are not like the policies of our youth, cast in stone and headed unswervingly toward maturity. Clients know they can fiddle with these new policies, but they're not quite sure how to fiddle smartly.

This desire on the part of policyholders clashes strongly with the commission system under which most agents operate. The traditional question most agents ask is, "Why should I be spending time with a 5 percent renewal client when I might be interviewing a 55 percent new prospect?" And that's a hard question to answer.

The idea of a more or less level commission system would provide an instant solution. But then can't you hear the companies asking, "How could we finance agents on level commissions when we lose too many on the 55 percent basis?" Another hard question to answer.

Probably more agents go down the tube by getting charmed with "serviceitis" than for any other single reason. It's a lot more fun to talk with a good old buddy who's a contented customer than it is with a tough, growly prospect who can say "No" in 27 languages.

Is there a solution to the service problem? There had better be, or the replacement experts like A.L. Williams will have eaten up all the business for a number of years—until they too become the victims of second-generation replacement artists.

In this computer age, part of the service problem can be solved by the home office. If we go on the assumption that most policyholder questions fall into well-defined areas, computer science should give an agent reasonably complete answers without consuming a vast amount of time.

Most agents I have known over the years can recite the virtues of good service without missing a beat: repeat business, centers of influence, nest prospecting, persistency, etc. The reason that they don't have much conviction about such recitations is that only occasionally do they get a real payout from considerable time expended. So if companies and field people, working together, can both compress the time and satisfy the client, everyone might be able to go home satisfied.

Yes, you say, but why is the policyholder so essentially dumb about a purchase that, in all reality, isn't all that complicated? Well, one of the clear reasons is that the business has virtually abandoned its effort to keep the public educated about the fundamentals of life insurance. Nearly 50 years ago it created the Institute of Life Insurance for just that purpose. The Institute spent some $10 million annually on advertising and other communications media telling people about what life insurance is and how it works.

It was a great success. Public perception of the business rose markedly. People understood what the business was there for and what the agent was there for. But then in the early '70s the leaders of the business folded the Institute into the American Council of Life Insurance. Today the thrust is educating Congress. Advertising has disappeared, and the considerable work among secondary schools and colleges has all but disappeared.

I'll admit I am a special pleader in this case. I was an officer of the Institute, and I took pride in seeing public understanding rise. I grant the necessity of advising Congress of what the business is doing, but I believe that an informed constituency of citizens is better than any political action committee.

Service will continue to be the job of agents. They must make themselves accessible to their policyholders when the latter have problems or become confused. But with the computer techniques available to them today, the companies must help in the process.

"Does Anybody Here Have An Opinion?"

No. 34, August 22, 1988, Page 13

For a great part of the history of life insurance in America, trade magazine editors have been leaders in molding opinion and giving leadership throughout the business. Most of them were growly, cantankerous men who fitted the label of curmudgeon admirably and bowed to no one.

In 1890 Chauncey Ransom of the *Standard* (Boston) brought a group of agents together at the Parker House in his home city and sparked the creation of the National Association of Life Underwriters. At the same time Champion Hitchcock of the *Insurance Field* (Louisville) was busy organizing state and local associations throughout the midwest.

The Cartwright family, C.M. and his son, Levering, ran the *National Underwriter* from Chicago and cast fear into the hearts of executives who strayed from the straight and narrow course of the business as they saw it. Ed Ackerman edited the *Weekly Underwriter* in New York and was not above diving into the middle of the most contentious issues.

Perhaps the best known was Clarence Axman, who from his perch at the *Eastern Underwriter* in New York was a specialist in "discovering" and profiling men and women who quickly rose to the top of their companies. Clarence seldom made a wrong guess, and annually celebrated his finds at a dinner in December at Sard's Restaurant in New York that was the social event of the year for life insurance people.

And, of course, Halsey Josephson was the firebrand who created *Probe* for the present generation of agents interested in the issues of the day.

No more. As life insurance has grown more complex and the number of trade journals has dwindled, editors have had to stick to their desks in order to cover the fast-moving events affecting the industry. They are too busy assembling facts to allow themselves the luxury of contemplating issues.

There are a few exceptions. Joe Belth, the eminent Indiana University savant, frequently wields a scalpel in his monthly *Insurance Forum*. My colleague, Joe Diamond, unloads his high, hard one on occasion, and it still has plenty of pepper. And *Life Association News* has uncovered in its *Probe* insert a whole new stable of writers who—at least until recently—have seemed willing to take on the giants.

(I say "until recently" because Jack Bobo, executive vice-president of the National Association of Life Underwriters, in his column in the June issue of *LAN*, the publication of which *Probe* has become a part, indicated that he would like to see "both sides" of every issue discussed. I believe that some issue, like A.L. Williams, don't have two responsible sides, and others have three or more. This may make *Probe* a lot more hesitant than it has acquired a reputation for being.)

Of course, it is the unsung writer of letters to the editor who can swing the biggest axe, provided his or her material will stand scrutiny and the test of factual relevance. But the writer of letters to the editor is an uncertain contributor; more letters may be written about a crazy typographical error than an issue of considerable substance to the business. The fact is that opinions are in short supply around the life insurance business today. Some writers are afraid of offending the advertiser, current or potential, forgetting that the most provocative writing attracts the most readers, and readers attract advertisers. Some obviously fear that they know too little about the business to speak with authority about it, which is certainly their own fault; if they can't learn they should be writing for the Cat Food Chronicle. Some feel it is their mission to bring news or descriptions of sales techniques to the reader, not opinion.

A business that doesn't have opinions—informed, exciting opinions—swirling about it isn't as lively or forward-looking as one that does. Opinions aren't always right; how could they be? If they stimulate thought and action, they not only deserve to be voiced, but we need them desperately.

I'd like to see more opinions in the life insurance business. I don't care where they come from or who prints them. I'd like to see trade magazines spouting a few more, but if it simply comes down to expanding the letter columns, I'd be for that, too. My notion is that there are plenty of opinions out there—they simply aren't getting traded the way they used to be in the days of Ransom and Hitchcock and Cartwright and Josephson. Let's trade them.

"What Shall We Call The Baby?"

No. 35, August 29, 1988, Page 13

Life insurance companies have always had a terrible time identifying themselves. Everywhere you look there is a Bankers or an Equitable or a Continental or a Lincoln-something. Among those I recall, only the Metropolitan Life took legal steps to protect its name. Let another life corporation try to use the word Metropolitan and lawyers poured out of 1 Madison Avenue like fire fighters attacking a five-alarmer.

If you think this similarity has been tough on people in the business, think of the consumer.

As companies have spawned subsidiaries or downstream holding companies, the confusion has become compounded because the corporate name, like American General or MONY or Lincoln National, has been attached to an entire gaggle of affiliates.

When Connecticut General and Insurance Co. of North America merged, they threw the initials up in the air and when they came down liked the looks of what they saw ("Daddy, what's a CIGNA?").

Union Mutual of Maine probably had the most vexing problem when it became a stock company. It now calls itself UNUM, which is presumably first cousin to a CIGNA. At least both are unique, even if they don't mean anything.

Insurance companies aren't alone in having troubles identifying themselves by name. Banks are probably worse, trying to devise titles that imply strength,

Americanism and friendly service. Far down the line are law firms, where every partner wants to get his or her name in large type on the door and letterhead. The result often looks like the first eleven stations on a railroad timetable.

Once a company has established a firm reputation, names don't count for much. Metropolitan and Prudential have stood the test of time. Everyone recognizes them. But sometimes companies get itchy about their names or logotypes and decide to try something new just to see who salutes it. Here are a couple of examples:

Bankers Life Co. of Des Moines expanded its customer services measurably. It felt that its name was too confining, so it became the Principal Financial Group, with the Principal Mutual and Principal National Life insurance companies as subsidiaries. While it got out of the Bankers category, which must have been a relief, it is now faced with acquainting the public about the meaning and capacities of Principal. It will take time.

Prudential has had the strength of Gibraltar forever, it seems, and has urged people to get a piece of the rock. Now it has stylized the rock and has virtually stopped talking about a piece of it. The *New York Times* asked editorially, "Didn't Prudential's old rock say 'strength' more clearly than the new, though no doubt careful, arrangement of lines and spaces?" It did to me, and its new Gibraltar seems more like one peak in a large mountain range, particularly on TV.

I don't blame Metropolitan for dropping—temporarily, at least—its old "Light That Never Fails." It now has the delights of Charlie Brown and Snoopy, who connote something quite different, and surely good for Mother Met.

Life insurance leaders, as I discovered long ago, tend to tire quickly of a symbol, a logotype or a phrase. Just when a clever statement begins to catch on, it's dumped. There's a good reason for this: chief executives have studied it in such detail that they are weary of it before it even begins to appear. After it has run for a year—and the public is just starting to associate with it—it's a bore to them. "Let's try something new!" And what would have been a real grabber goes into the ashcan. This is a waste of money. The Rock and the "Light That Never Fails" had decades of success.

If I were in a company executive suite I would do at least three things before changing a name, a logotype or a theme:

- Be certain that my current ideas had run their course.

- Research any new ideas I had until I had convinced myself that they were substantially better than my current ideas.

• Be prepared to stay with my new concepts for a long, long time.

Unless I took these three moves, I'd be afraid I might be throwing away an asset that I had spent a lot of money to build.

"The Gift Of Laughter, And Other Stories"

No. 47, November 21, 1988, Page 25

Life insurance has always been a frightfully serious business, and in these days of flat sales and flatter investment yields it is getting, as Alice might have said, seriouser and seriouser. It certainly sounded that way at the recent annual meeting of the Life Insurance Marketing and Research Association in Washington.

It did, that is, until LIMRA's president, Ernie Cragg, struck a noble blow for humor and its handmaiden, laughter, in his talk. Ernie, who is seldom totally serious, devoted the first half of his address to laughter. Here are some of the things he said:

"What is a sense of humor if it is not also a sense of proportion? Whatever it is that seems to overwhelm us can be reduced to its correct proportions in our successful careers by the injection of laughter. Certainly we can use a sense of proportion.

"When we are open, we are most aware, receptive, creative and in the last analysis, more intelligent. Perhaps we can be most efficient and creative and, indeed, more productive partners. . .

"People like themselves when they laugh. As leaders in a people-oriented business, you absolutely must know that those whom you make like themselves a little better will also like you much better. It can be advantageous when those who like you outnumber those who don't."

Something like this has needed saying for years, but I suspect that many insurance people with great senses of humor haven't done so for fear of seeming trivial. I am not talking about the device of the humorous story— "it seems that this clergyman, this rabbi and this priest were walking along the road one day"—but rather about the injection of wit into what W.S. Gilbert would have called "an otherwise bald and inconclusive statement."

We need more people who will do what Ernie Cragg has done. After all, even the *Readers Digest* has for years been calling laughter "the best medicine."

Jack Bobo, Ernie Cragg's opposite number at the National Association of Life Underwriters, performed a similar service at the association's Dallas convention when he ventured the opinion that financial planning might be anything but "the next step up the evolutionary ladder," at least for insurance agents. In effect, he said that the financial planner, who has been the king of the industry during the '80s, has no clothes.

There has been so much palaver about what a financial planner is, how he is compensated, and how he should be regulated, that we have lost sight of the apparent fact that, among life insurance people, "back to the basics is our own version of back to the future," as Mr. Bobo says.

He concedes that a few full-service financial shops are making the grade, and the fee-based operator will always be with us, but the commissioned life insurance agent has retreated since it became impossible for him to offer the tax savings he used to.

As usual, Jack Bobo's comments are full of logic. If they prove out for the majority of the life insurance business, perhaps we can stop agonizing about the financial planning spinoff.

Alan Press, the proud Brooklyn gentleman who is probably the most renowned basher of the A.L. Williams replacement empire, has succeeded to the presidency of NALU. There were those who felt that his preoccupation with the ALW operation might make him a less effective president than his predecessors. Not to worry. In his maiden speech at the NALU convention he showed concern for just about every interest life underwriters have.

Alan is a pugnacious individual who walks around with a metaphorical baseball bat under his arm but that doesn't mean that he hasn't totally grasped NALU's broad spectrum. The association is in for an exciting year under Alan's direction. Remember, you heard it here first.

"Communications All Over The Place"

No. 48, November 28, 1988, Page 21

A few months ago, when I was worrying about who was going to take effective charge of the life insurance business' communications with the public—

a post now apparently reassumed by the American Council of Life Insurance—I searched for other organizations that might have skills in this area.

My first stop, of course, was the Life Communicators Association. The name was perfect, but the mission of this organization is training in communications skills, chiefly at the company level, not undertaking to do the institutional job itself. LCA is invaluable to the business—it teaches young people to write cogently and to use all the communications tools. But it never was intended to be the public relations arm of life insurance. What its members do contributes effectively to public knowledge. To try to push them beyond this would certainly mess up the landscape. I think I would be surprised if I knew with some certainty how many people's understanding of life insurance is increased by LCA's output every day.

I then traveled to Portland, ME, to attend the fall conference of the Insurance Consumer Affairs Exchange, an organization of which I had heard only vaguely. It turned out to be an all-industry conference, "discussing," as its program said, "the issues affecting our industry and how those issues will impact the products and services we provide to our customers."

It was an eye-opener. Among the speakers were two insurance commissioners (North Carolina and Maine), representatives of three consumer organizations, and a solid group of consumer affairs officers from all types of insurance companies. Every talk hooked sharply into consumer affairs issues, and if this wasn't a discussion of communications at its best, I never heard one.

Like LCA, ICAE has limited goals and is not about to try to be the public relations bellwether for any element of the business. But, again like LCA, it is teaching young people how to relate to consumers, a supremely important function. The talent on its program would easily have felt at home at any insurance convention in America.

Beyond these two specialty groups, almost every trade association in life insurance has its own public relations unit, chiefly talking about its own activities but more often than not discussing in depth the issues of the day. More than most of the others, the American College and the American Society of CLU/ChFC go out of their way to inform the public about the latest issues affecting the policyholder. Some of the smaller associations are served in this area by the larger ones—the ACLI or the National Association of Life Underwriters, to name the principal ones.

Obviously, ACLI needs to remain the centerpiece, the catalyst, of all this, and it seems determined to do so. It has its own public relations council, a tightly-knit group of institutional and company communications people who meet periodically for a discussion in depth of the tough, tough issues confronting the business. This kind of activity helps everyone in insurance, whether they realize it or not.

The real need? Let me quote from two press releases based on speeches made October 17, 1988: In Boston, Thomas H. Schnick, CEO of Commonwealth Life, said to the Institute of Home Office Underwriters, "If there ever was a time when the life insurance industry needed to take an active role in bringing the risk appraisal message to the public, legislators and regulators, and stating it clearly and often, it is now."

In Charleston, SC, Gerald E. Mayo, chairman of Midland Mutual Life, said to the Association of Life Insurance Medical Directors, "By any standard, ours has been a successful business. We manage over $1 trillion in assets, we have not fanned the flames of inflation or speculation, we're good corporate citizens and very few of our beneficiaries are unhappy. The industry has done a good job. It just hasn't done a good job telling people about it. We must do both."

Both press releases arrived on the letterhead of the American Council of Life Insurance. They must be listening to their constituency.

"Should The Life Insurance Business Secede?"

No. 9, February 27, 1989, Page 19

Let's face one fact for which there is ample evidence: the great American public utterly fails to distinguish among the various forms of insurance: life, health, property, casualty, automobile, fire, workmen's compensation, and dozens of other smaller categories that perform a function in the social and economic fabric of the country.

So, when something comes along like Proposition 103 in California, life insurance gets swept into the same basket of rage that people are directing toward automobile, property, and in some cases health insurance. No layman appears to realize that, while auto insurance rates have skyrocketed over the last ten years, life rates are the lowest they have been in the history of the business.

Responsible life insurance leaders are now debating the wisdom of adopting one of three courses of action:

- To work with their property/casualty brethren on a campaign to position the various kinds of insurance in a way that would help people understand how and why costs are what they are.

- To devise a unilateral campaign that would dissociate life insurance from the various other forms of insurance coverage, and to illustrate precisely why this should be so.

- To do neither of the above, and opt to simply maintain the status quo.

There are obviously grave dangers in either of the first two courses. While unity is always a noble thought, the problems of the various types of insurance are so disparate that to try to devise any kind of campaign linking them all as a common and economically viable necessity would require a copywriter better than any I have ever known, and I've known some of the best.

Some types of insurance are subject to random acts of God—or, if not God, then juries. Others, notably life insurance, bow to the actuarial tables and are usually settled without fuss or litigation, except in case of fraud.

Each different kind of insurance must defend its practices in its own way.

To try to defend them all in one campaign that would be completely understandable to policyholders boggles the imagination.

To prepare a unilateral campaign about life insurance alone and how it functions vis-a-vis other types of insurance would be a whale of a lot simpler, but it would have to be prepared with great discretion. It could offend multiline companies like Travelers and Aetna, which have been strong supporters of the institution of life insurance for over a century. And it could alienate property/casualty companies that might view statements singing the praises of the life insurance way of doing business as a slap at their own systems.

But it could be written. Messages about "how life insurance is different" could be framed that wouldn't appear to take a whack at other forms of insurance that don't deal with such predictable elements as human mortality. The American Council of Life Insurance came close to this a couple of years ago when it ran a campaign about risk appraisal, but it was too little and too early.

The third choice open to life insurance people—simply to do nothing and maintain the status quo—seems to be the worst choice of all. Legislators in every state are examining the Prop. 103 success, and it's a good bet that several other states will try it on for size the next time legislatures meet. The fact that it is probably unconstitutional (would a state tell its supermarkets how much they could charge for meat?) isn't currently important. What is important is to extract life insurance from the mess that is being caused by auto insurance rates.

While I have mentioned "campaigns" and "messages" above, I haven't used the word "advertising." Advertising would be the ideal vehicle, of course, but if the companies suffering from a financial crunch were to take another tack—speakers bureaus, press releases, etc.—it wouldn't be a total loss, and might accomplish some kind of a positive result.

Life insurance has got to separate itself from that generic word "insurance" or it will ultimately suffer bad legislative consequences.

"Ten People Who Tell It Like It Is"

No. 11, March 13, 1989, Page 23

When I go to hear a speech about life insurance, I like the person at the lectern to tell me something I don't already know. This is almost impossible in the case of those who talk about how to sell. The last word about selling techniques was probably spouted 50 years ago by the immortal Grant Taggart. The great sales-talkers of today, like John Savage, simply wrap old truisms in new and vibrant language that makes you remember them long after the speaker has left town.

What I want to know when I settle into my little funeral-parlor chair or put my elbows on the lunch table is simple: where is the business I admire going, how will that future affect me, and what can I do to help it along?

There are lots of people who have their fingers on the pulse of the life insurance industry today, but I'm daring to choose three each from the field, the home office, and institutional associations, plus a clean-up hitter who has done duty in all three. If they come to your town, sit in on their talks. If you are in a position to invite them, by all means do. If they show up at a national program you're scheduled to attend, be sure that you don't miss them.

From the field: Norman Levine, Mutual Benefit, San Francisco; Alan Press, Guardian Life, New York; Tom Wolff, independent, Vernon, CT. All three are completely wrapped up in activities that make good agents better. All have gone through the chairs of NALU, and plenty of other chairs as well.

Levine is an emotional motivator who thinks in terms of full financial services as well as life insurance. His devotion to agent education, particularly the continuing variety, is unswerving. Like everyone on this list, he can pin your attention from start to finish, and he has an infallible sense of timing.

Press is current president of NALU, and the major defender of the fair—i.e., cash value life insurance—in the field force. He loves to lambaste A.L. Williams, the nation's prime replacement artist, and has devised video cassettes to this end. But he's not a one-stringed lute. He understands all field issues.

Wolff makes advanced underwriting sound like a great adventure. He is an actor as well as one of the most astute salesmen in the business, and he has the infinite capacity to hold an audience in the palm of his hand. His most memorable asset in the minds of many people I've talked with is his ability to get to the core of complex issues and make them look simple.

From the home offices: Joe Melone, president of Prudential; Denis Mullane, chairman of Connecticut Mutual; Jack Scully, executive vice-president, John Hancock. All three are senior executives of major companies whose pronouncements help determine industry policy. And they all talk with you, not to you.

Melone is an educator who ended up in a major company, but he's no pontificator. He is one of a small group of men who guides the Pru empire through its congeneric activities, he has full command of the complexities of such an operation. To listen to Melone is to see the future unfolding, however deliberately.

Mullane is a West Pointer who rose through his company's field force to become its CEO. Because he has been on both sides of the fence, he sees the issues that sometimes divide the various factions of the business, and he sees them with sympathy. He has a company that is trying to supply all of an agent's needs.

Scully's company is one of the great mavericks of the business, and he is often cast in the role of defending policies that may be under attack by a majority of his competitors. He does so with good humor and a backlog of material to support his position. It's good to understand why Hancock is pursuing its course.

From the institutional associations: Jack Bobo, executive vice-president of NALU; Ernie Cragg, president of LIMRA; Dick Schweiker, president of ACLI. There is no need to heap encomiums on these three gentlemen, all of whom are firmly ensconced at the wheel of major trade associations. Each is a consummate speaker; each has a deep understanding of home office and field policy. To listen to any one of them give a major policy speech is to gain a greater understanding of the statesmanlike way the life insurance business is undertaking to conduct itself. They don't all agree, as one might imagine, but they conduct their disagreements with class. Someday I'd like to see the three of them conduct a seminar.

The clean-up hitter? Why, the gentleman who has been executive vice-president of NALU, CEO of American General Life, and latterly, a life and qualifying member of the Million Dollar Round Table. Woody Woodson, of course. At age 80, he is as vibrant a representative of life insurance as anyone I know.

If you are lucky enough to hear all 10 of them, you will be a wiser person.

"The Best Plan Seems To Be Separatism"

No. 16, April 17, 1989, Page 27

Speaking before the Association for Advanced Life Underwriting in Washington last month, Don Ross, chairman of the New York Life Ins. Co., said this:

"When Californians voted for Proposition 103, they did more than roll back auto insurance rates, allow banks to sell life insurance, and repeal anti-rebate laws. . .Voters told the insurance industry what they think of it. And they don't think much.

"True, the primary target of the voters' wrath was the property/casualty insurance industry. But most people fail to distinguish between segments of the insurance industry. We are all lumped together in the public consciousness. And, it seems, we are also lumped together in the mind of that group that greatly influences the public: the media.

"Recently, when one of my company's executive officers met with the editorial board of *The Los Angeles Times* about the threat AIDS poses to the life insurance industry, he was questioned about auto insurance. Even after he explained that he represented a life insurer, the editors continued to complain about how we were cheating consumers with rapid property/casualty rate increases. . .

"The editorial board of one of the nation's largest and most influential newspapers could not—or would not—make the distinction between the property/casualty and life insurance industries."

Writing in the March [1989] issue of *Council Review*, the house magazine of the American Council of Life Insurance, Dick Schweiker, its president, says:

". . . Proposition 103 passed in large measure because of consumer resentment over high auto insurance prices and what was perceived as the industry's lack of communication about those prices. . .One of the first tasks before us, almost everyone agrees, is to shore up the dismal image of the insurance industry. We knew it was in need of repair prior to Proposition 103, based on research conducted both within and outside the industry. . .Making the insurance industry phoenix rise from the ashes of Proposition 103 will not be easy, but it is something that must be done."

These two leaders, like many of their peers, are annoyed that life insurance is carrying on its shoulders some of the burdens caused by public dissatisfaction with auto insurance rates. Yet, they stop just short of saying that life insurance should point with pride to its own accomplishments of recent years.

I believe the leadership of ACLI should rethink the situation.

Let's visualize a 10-second TV commercial that would use a simple sentence like this: "Most life insurance policies cost you less now than at any time in the 150-year history of the business." Let the ACLI sign it and see to it that it's graphically attractive. It is the most direct of messages, and it has the virtue of simple truth. It may need a little cleaning up, but the point is there.

Yes, it would cost some money, but it would take ACLI's influence well beyond the Washington beltway. Individual companies could use it in a thousand ways, from mailing stuffers to billboards.

No boasts, no pointing fingers at anyone else, no odious comparisons. Just a simple statement that has obviously not been understood by a larger segment of the American people.

Nor is it a panacea. As in the case of any campaign, ACLI and the companies would have to buttress it with written material for the media and the populace in general. But it gets across in 20 words the single most important message the life insurance business owes to the public today.

No, I am not trying to write copy; my copywriting days are long over. What I'm suggesting is a simple method of separating the good things that are happening today in life insurance from the more difficult ones that every other element of the business seems to be undergoing.

"The Toughest Guys On The Block"

No. 17, April 24, 1989, Page 23

Using a superlative like "best" puts a person in heavy going; if he sees something later on that he likes more, he is either at a loss for a word to describe it, or he must admit that his judgment isn't too good.

So I won't use the word "best" to describe the annual meeting (always in March, always in Washington) of the Association for Advanced Life Underwriting. Just let's say that it's tough as nails, highly professional, and as politically oriented as a meeting can be. AALU came into being in 1957 when a tax bill that would measurably affect life insurance sales procedure was in the hopper. A small group of life underwriters gathered in Washington to examine the effect of the bill and to consult with members of Congress on how to turn it to their advantage. In order to assure a high quality of participation, it was required that members of the new organization be holders of the CLU designation and members of the Million Dollar Round Table. It was an immediate success because it operated on a level above that of any other agent organization, and it discussed substantive issues in some depths.

This year nearly a thousand people attended its 32nd annual meeting, held in a palatial hotel almost equidistant from the White House and the Capitol. For four days a Who's Who of government people showed up on the program and discussed what Congress expected to do about life insurance and taxation during the year to come. Included among them were Lloyd Bentsen of Texas, Bob Dole of Kansas, Barbara Kennelly of Connecticut, and Bill Archer of Texas, plus the usual group of Washington know-it-alls such as the McLaughlin Group and Larry Speakes.

While these people were impressive in their lay-it-on-the-line attitude toward insurance people, I was even more struck by the immense depth of the more than 20 workshops dealing with issues on the leading edge of tax and pension legislation today.

AALU is a conference of the National Association of Life Underwriters, and the impressive legal staff of NALU was present in full force, taking part in many sessions and running a couple of their own. (Parenthetically, I was unhappy that the NALU lawyers kicked the press out of their sessions, which no one else did. Some of my unsullied agent friends told me there was no conversation at these times that would have turned our tender ears, and I hope at future meetings they will concede that we can be as mature and prudent as they are.)

But it was the issues the speakers and workshop leaders grappled with that pleased and impressed me most. Here are a few of them: in-depth looks at PC graphics and various computer technologies, S-Corps, the Amway case, planning and strategies in the shadow of tax reform, broad benefit corporate owned life insurance, saving the family business, alternatives in the second-to-die sale, the pension distribution dilemma, group carve-out, Section 89/Cobra/Tamra, non-leveraged COLI and FAS #96, the rationale for selling nonqualified plans with 401(k)s, and many more.

It seems to be true that the companies have virtually ceased to offer advanced training to their agents, and the American College is obliged to offer a broader base of education to seekers after CLU and ChFC designations. This puts AALU and the Million Dollar Round Table squarely in the position of being the only non-commercial groups prepared to give their constituents thorough training in selling large and complex policies. Without making much noise about it, they appear to be doing so admirably.

There has been considerable comment recently about the strong upsurge of educational and training opportunities for agents. They are unfolding in closed-circuit TV seminars, local and state life underwriters association workshops, and increased effort by usual educational bases. It tells me that, if their employers won't give agents the tools to work with, they and their associations will forge those tools themselves. And AALU is in the forefront.

"The Dimensions Of The CEO"

No. 19, May 8, 1989, Page 13

In these days of the complicated, strung-out life insurance company, the chief executive officer must appear to be something resembling the Renaissance man. Because of the profit squeeze his company is undoubtedly undergoing, he must be an investment genius. Because of the need for competitive policies, he must have an actuarial bent. Because of the tax and other legislative issues he faces daily, he must know law. Because of AIDS and the complexities of mortality and morbidity, he must understand underwriting practices.

Because he must market his end product to the consumer, he had better have a deft touch in selling. He would also do well to know the fundamentals of public relations, and to be a motivating speaker.

Now, you and I know that no such individual exists. We also know that the CEO has come up through the ranks in one of the disciplines mentioned above, and surrounds himself with people who understand what he doesn't. That's why the executive suite was invented.

Of course, as some CEOs assume the reins of power, they seem to feel the mantle of omnipotence settling on their shoulders. The splendid actuary begins to feel that he knows how agents should be compensated and inspired; the marketing vice-president who moves up displays a sudden and total understanding of what the company's investment policies should be.

Yes, the instances are rare, but we all have in our minds occasions where CEOs who started out knowing it all ended by blowing it all.

Companies today have two saving graces that more loosely structured ones in the past didn't: a group of senior executives, many of them members of the board of directors, who have considerable influence and are not about to bow to the CEO; and the outside board members, who are no longer merely titular objects, pleasant to have around but of no intrinsic value. Today they are first-team players, and it's possible to name recent instances where they have wisely and forcefully upset a company applecart. I suspect we will see more of this as outside directors realize they are on the premises to direct, not merely to flatter the egos of the home office.

It is perfectly obvious that when a board of directors meet someone has to be in charge. That's why the CEO sits at the head of the table. But in the modern boardroom he has become more of an umpire, enforcing Robert's Rules of Order and keeping the game going, than the captain of the team. Men and women who have served on boards know this; they respect him, but they don't necessarily bow down to him.

There is, of course, the vexing issue of how people get to serve on boards. There can be a tendency toward self-perpetuation, particularly in mutual companies, where nominees are created by those in power and elected by a minuscule vote on the titular owners of the company, the policyholders. Closely held stock companies also tend to perpetuate their bodies, except that the profit motive makes them gravitate to the most brilliant minds they can find.

The days of the monarch, the person who rules the company to suit himself, are just about over. The board won't stand for him and regulatory officials, especially the various state insurance commissioners, despise him. If he assembles a group of puppets to act as his directors, chances are he will be spoken to sternly by some member of the bureaucracy.

Nor is the CEO the "grand old man." He is more the catalyst than the decision-maker. The configuration for the job has changed almost completely in the last 50 years, and is likely to change more by the turn of the century. He (and in an increasing number of cases, she) will no longer be the subject of juvenile adoration by employees and field people, but just another manager who keeps the minds of everyone around him moving.

The business has grown so detailed that no one person can have on his desk "The Buck Stops Here" sign. There are a multitude of buckstoppers, and there will have to be more if life insurance is to run smoothly.

"Sports Events: A Life Insurance PR Tool"

No. 24, June 12, 1989, Page 13

In the early 1960s, when TV sports viewing began to go sky-high, life insurance organizations realized that the people watching these events were the same kind of people who were ideal prospects: upwardly mobile, better-than-average income, enthusiastic. So they began to get into sponsoring major events.

The Travelers was doubtless the granddaddy of them all, taking on major sponsorship of the Masters golf championship 31 years ago. Its president, Doyle DeWitt, an avid golfer, once told me that it was tough sledding to get the funds during the first few years, but today the idea of the Masters not having a red umbrella among its commercials is unthinkable. (This year, the only other major participant was Cadillac, which shows the kind of audience the company expects.)

Shortly after that, my organization, the Institute of Life Insurance, began to participate in TV broadcasts of professional football, golf, and tennis. The results proved to be outstanding: the audiences were good, the agents liked the programming, and so did their clients.

In the quarter-century since that time, dozens of life insurance companies have associated themselves with sports broadcasts, and it is hard to think of a major sports event—the World Series, the Super Bowl, the Final Four in college basketball, to name just a few—where life insurance participation isn't part of the big act.

But in the 1980s, perhaps taking a look at what the other life insurance people were doing, at least two major companies have come to the conclusion that sports sponsorship doesn't have to be all highly expensive commercial time at major events. Rather, it can become total involvement in a sport—involvement that includes financial patronage, close association with the sport itself and the people in it, and participation in-depth by the field force. A company that manages an event can maintain its quality.

To me, the most interesting of these is the Equitable Society's B.A.T. (Baseball Alumni Team) program. Equitable has been involved in managing pension funds for Major League Baseball since 1947. When it discovered that some of the really old-timers had slender pension benefits, it set about to improve them. It now holds Old Timers games in every major league city, pitting nationally known former stars against old-timers principally identified with the 26 cities in which the games are held. It is a knockout locally, with Equitable people everywhere, and with the public generally. Since it is spotlighted in 26 of the nation's best markets, it gets considerable mileage without going to network TV. And it helps a group of great players we saw when we were kids.

Equitable is also involved in a remarkable "Family Tennis Challenge" that starts in 240 cities and ends up in conjunction with the U.S. Tennis Open in New York. All the matches are doubles—every combination of mother, father, son, daughter, husband, wife, and brother, sister. Again, it's not a big TV production, but local interest is always high.

"The Equitable set out to create events which are participation-oriented, rather than attaching our name to an existing event," says Jim Martin, vice-president in charge of these sports operations. "This allows us to tailor the events to reflect our company's goals and beliefs."

Another company that is exceedingly inventive in managing a sports situation is the John Hancock, which is investing heavily in the sport of marathon running. This is logical, since its home office is located in the city where American marathons began, Boston. (However, the company did have to ask the officials to change the finish mark from the Prudential building, where it used to be, to its own backyard. No problem.)

As in the case of old-timers baseball and family tennis, aficionados of the marathon are legion, and Hancock has most of the great performers they admire under contract. Because marathoners can run 26 miles, 385 yards only two or three times a year, the company sees to it that the great ones don't try to overdo themselves.

What these companies seem to be telling us is this: if a life insurance company chooses to identify itself with a sport, any relatively popular sport, it doesn't take millions of TV dollars to create a significant impact for itself and its agents in hundreds of communities. If the Hancock can get mileage out of marathon running (pardon the pun, please), why can't an organization identify itself with a sport like swimming, skiing or skating, volleyball or archery? If I had the choice I'd take rowing, the exciting sport of dedicated, selfless undergraduates who turn out to be business leaders. There's no more exciting sight in sports than a covey of eight-oared crews swooping down on the finish line.

Just an idea.

"What's All This Talk About Leadership?"

No. 38, September 18, 1989, Page 49

The boys and girls at the *National Underwriter*, including the person who writes on the page opposite this one over the initials J.S.D., seem to be worried about the state of leadership in the life insurance business. Would you mind if I threw in my nickel's worth?

Early in my career I got to know two elderly, balding men who looked—and in fact acted—like Certified Public Accountants. Neither was worth a hoot at demonstrating they were leading; they were about as comfortable on a speaking platform as they would have been in a vat of hot lard. But they got things done. Their names were Dwight Eisenhower and Omar Bradley.

It was at about this time that I began to understand what is probably a truism today: you can't recognize a leader by the way he behaves. He doesn't have to be a spellbinding speaker, although that didn't do Mr. Reagan any harm. He may do all his profound thinking in the back room of the executive suite, shielded from the likes of you and me. How are we, the members of the public who may see him at his most unimpressive, going to judge him?

You may say, "Take a look at the balance sheet of the company he presides over." Possibly, but in a weak economy the leader who keeps his firm's nose above water may be doing the job of a giant. In the land of the blind, a one-eyed man is king.

Over the last 20 years the life insurance business has been undergoing the tortures of the damned. The first thing that happened, although everyone seems to have forgotten it now, is that the business prevailed on New York State to relax the stringent investment regulations on life companies it had imposed for a century. Under the new rules, inventive actuaries began to construct new policies unlike any that had ever been dreamed of. Each CEO, together with his board of directors and senior officers, was caught in a fierce dilemma: go with the flow or hold back and hope the whole thing was a nightmare.

Each company made its own decision; some put every new policy into their own portfolios, started real estate and investment subsidiaries, cut down on their full-time agency force and cast sheeps' eyes at brokers of all kinds. Others honed the cost of their traditional ordinary life policies to the bone, and stuck with their agents. There are success stories in both areas. Who is to say where leadership lies?

The idea that the CEO must be out in the foxholes, brandishing his sword and exhorting his troops, is in my mind a bunch of bunk. Good strategy is seldom conceived in foxholes. It is likely to come out of the war room, hidden away from the public at large.

If the CEO is a private person, ineffectual behind a lectern but brilliant in his executive suite, let him have a spokesperson or two—or even three. But let those spokespersons be senior officers, with enough clout to enunciate company policy and enough charisma to make his listeners understand what he represents. Even the president of our country has a man named Marlin Fitzwater who handles the press 90 percent of the time.

Every now and again an Iacocca, a Lorenzo or an A.L. Williams comes along who positions himself squarely in the spotlight and tries to convince the public that he is the brains behind everything that happens in his corporation. What a lot of nonsense! Without a team to support each of them, they would be crying in the desert.

Leadership is nothing more than inspired teamwork. One person must wield the gavel, of course, but it is not to be presumed that he is substantially more brilliant than the people he and his board have put into the positions of decision.

The company with the best leadership is the company that performs the best day in and day out. Let us not try to confer sainthood on a single individual. The company had better survive when he leaves.

"A Noble Centennial"

No. 43, October 23, 1989, Page 11

The National Association of Life Underwriters was astute enough to realize that many American institutions have passed or are fast approaching the 100-year mark. So it did not try to celebrate its centennial in Boston last September with tall ships, fireworks, or other ornate attractions. It was strictly a family affair, and a magnificent one.

It was made memorable to me by these people: Alan Press, the outgoing president; Bob Wernecke, incoming chief and program chairman; Holgar Johnson and Charlie Zimmerman, who had occupied the same positions a half-century ago at the 50th convention; Ernie Cragg, who appeared on the program twice as representative of the companies and as the John Newton Russell Award winner; plus, the remarkable but faceless staff of NALU who kept everything going with the crispness of a digital watch.

The setting was perfect: two interconnected hotels with a comfortable auditorium between them, in Boston's Back Bay area. There were just a couple of places where rain could fall on the delegates, and it did, but no one was drenched.

Press, who presided over just about everything as the reigning president, was well-nigh faultless. He had the right words for each occasion, and his lightness of spirit was totally in tune with the celebration. Wernecke operated behind the scenes, as program chairmen are supposed to, until he was elected, when he delivered a rousing challenge to the future.

Johnson (age 96) and Zimmerman (88) provided some moments that will probably never be repeated at an NALU convention. They refused to allow themselves to be bound by reminiscences of what went on 50 years ago when they were in charge of the convention. They talked about the present and the future, and the delegates responded to their words with a standing ovation the likes of which I have never seen in my all-too-many years of convention-going. Everything was captured on video tape, and I understand that this and other highlights of the meeting will be made available to local associations for their meetings in the near future. Holgar and Charlie demonstrated that NALU has chosen its presidents wisely over the years—a fact confirmed by the 25 other past presidents who were introduced.

Ernie Cragg, president of the Life Insurance Marketing and Research Association, spoke as the principal link between the home offices and the field force, and no one could have expressed the innate warmth and affection between these two sometimes contentious groups any better. But his best moment came when he received the John Newton Russell Award for "the person who has done the most for the life insurance business." While the name of the recipient is a carefully guarded secret, he himself is tipped off a bit in advance, so he can collect his thoughts and say something cogent to his audience. Ernie's remarks in accepting the award were probably the most masterly he has ever uttered. They were carefully balanced to bring both laughter and, yes, tears to his overflow crowd. Future recipients had better get a copy of his manuscript (if, indeed, he had one) as a guide for what they might say. It was a profound moment for the entire life insurance business.

It was a comfortable convention, made so—as most conventions of any kind are—chiefly by the attentiveness of the staff that superintends it without asking for rounds of applause. In all, it was spectacular.

Hey! I almost forgot (and you'd better read it here because you won't see it anywhere else): The National Underwriter threw a reception for the official family of NALU in celebration of the centennial. Jim Bunning, the only U.S. Congressman who ever pitched a perfect major legal baseball game, and I were supposed to be the hosts. But the entire staff of the publication was on board, and I believe they made everyone feel at home. If the NALU people enjoyed it as much as I did, we may have seen the beginnings of a tradition. It, too, was spectacular.

"The Lion In Winter"

No. 46, November 13, 1989, Page 17

"To strengthen and give more muscle to the ear, brain, heart, limbs and FEAT! Atta boy!—Keep up our fight!—ART!—Hard at it!—Don't quit because the ladybirds don't like it!"

Sound like a general agent exhorting the troops? Well, it was a general agent, but his "troops" were composed of the American music-loving public and the musicians who played what he wrote.

His name was Charles E. Ives. He was the partner of Julian S. Myrick, another person of strong character (Julian was president of the National Association of Life Underwriters and the United States Lawn Tennis Association at the same time) in a downtown New York City agency for the Mutual Life of New York.

What a pair they were! Myrick was a soft-spoken North Carolinian with an affinity for the very dry martini and the ability to handle it. Ives was a peppery, bearded Yale graduate who was one of the creators of the estate planning concept in life insurance and who rose to the very top rank of American composers of classical music—although, as I will try to explain to you, he will never be confused with Brahms or even Gershwin.

In 1912, when Ives wrote the book *The Amount to Carry—Measuring the Prospect*, which preceded S.S. Huebner's theory of human life value, he also wrote his famous "Concord" piano sonata, a piece that is still in the portfolios of today's virtuosi. Curiously, he was not so much interested in having his music performed as he was in perfecting it. He was likely to put it in a drawer, then pull it out on impulse and tinker with it.

It wasn't until after his health had begun to fail in the 1920s that he began to shift his main interest from life insurance to music. Myrick took over the principal duties of the agency, and Ives retired in 1930, although for years he continued to drop in at the office to see how business was doing.

Ives knew he was ahead of his time, so he patiently waited for time to catch up with him. As the critic, Virgil Thompson, said, "He seems to have learned quite early that responsible musicians in general viewed his compositions with such disapproval that fighting for position would have merely wasted his time. His open life was that of a businessman, conventional, respected, impregnable to scrutiny. His secret life was that of a Romantic artist—wildly experimental, ambitious, channeled, undisciplined, and unafraid."

Curiously enough, it was in the "Jazz Age"—the 1920s—when his popularity began to build. Part of it stemmed from his impishness. His listeners would be fighting their way through the huge and complicated dissonances of his Piano Sonata No. 1 when they would find themselves listening to a convoluted version of "How Dry I Am," "Oh, Susannah" or a raucously hilarious setting of "Bringing in the Sheaves."

As public demand for his music grew, Charles Ives didn't have to write up a storm. It was already there, written from 1898 to 1924, waiting for modern taste to catch up with it. His "Concord" sonata had its first public performance in 1939, and his Symphony No. 2 was awarded the Pulitzer Prize in 1947. He dedicated his harum-scarum composition, "The Fourth of July," to Julian Myrick, and it is still a popular piece, played by orchestras everywhere at holiday time.

Ives died in 1954, having had the unique satisfaction of achieving major success in two wildly disparate businesses, life insurance selling and symphonic composition. The only person I can think of who was at all like him was Wallace Stevens, the well-liked American poet of the Ives era, who was, in his more profitable hours, vice-president of the Hartford Accident and Indemnity.

One warning: when Julian Myrick was introducing me to the music of Ives he said, "I know you're a Duke Ellington man. Charlie wasn't. I never understood a damned thing he wrote." Ives has a great legacy. But his music isn't for everyone.

"The All-Industry Hotline"

No. 4, January 22, 1990, Page 27

An 800-number hotline to answer the public's questions about any form of insurance came into being on January 2, 1990. This hotline [1-800-942-4242] is probably the most ambitious all-industry effort ever put together, involving as it does the American Council of Life Insurance, the Health Insurance Association of America, and the Insurance Information Institute, with possible contributions by the National Association of Life Underwriters and the Independent Insurance Agents of America.

Working the hotline will be a group of professional insurance people, licensed in the various disciplines of the business. It will start slowly, so the organizations involved can measure the demand, and if it seems to be paying off it will expand as needed.

Monitoring the calls will be a group of people who will decide which of the experts is best equipped to handle the subject matter of each question, which will then be dealt out appropriately.

This is about as tough a project as I can imagine. Let's just visualize the first two questions:

- "I had a fender-bender two weeks ago and I can't get a claims adjuster to look at my car. What do I do now?"
- "Does the life insurance business have a policy on how it proposes to handle AIDS and AIDS-related cases?"

I dreamed up these two questions to illustrate the enormous spectrum of queries that can be expected, from small one-on-one situations to vast statements that may put an entire industry on the line. I doubt that the public will accept inconclusive or temporizing answers in either case. If the organizations make promises about what the hotline can accomplish, they had better be prepared to live up to them or risk scorn on the part of the questioners. Professional insurance-baiters will surely try to embarrass those who man the hotline, and if they succeed they will make great noise about what they perceive to be its failures.

This is not to say that such fears should cause the industry to turn tail and abandon the project. It simply means that it must have a keen sense of what it is getting into and train its respondents to the very teeth. No matter what ground rules it sets when it announces the hotline, some people will ignore them, ask any questions that come to mind, and bray about their disappointment if they aren't totally satisfied.

It is my understanding that each association involved will contribute to the program in direct ratio to questions asked about its own segment of the business. This will have an interesting side effect, if the numbers in each area are announced. We will then learn which elements attract the most questions (the word "complaints" might be substituted here because people don't usually pick up the phone to express satisfaction), and we will find out which of them annoy the public the most.

For years I have expressed the belief that the life insurance business might undertake to separate itself from the other elements of insurance so that it might logically boast of its own virtues, particularly in the area of costs. I have been shouted down by people whose minds I respect, and I don't intend to press the matter again. "Insurance is insurance," I am told, and the money doesn't exist to inform the public of the various problems that its elements must grapple with. So be it, and now we will find out where the public's gripes are.

A hotline, properly manned and promoted, is probably the gutsiest way to accomplish this. All the transactions will be one-on-one; there should be no room for misunderstandings, especially if questions are answered with clarity.

During my years in the business, the various elements of insurance have generally gone their own ways. At last they have discovered a common goal, and are willing to try to reach it together. If the hotline does nothing more than accomplish this, it will have been a success.

"'We Know Your Gross. . .What's Your Net?'"

No. 9, February 26, 1990, Page 17

The Million Dollar Round Table is probably the most badly named organization in the life insurance business. If you sell a million dollars worth of good, honest life insurance, its members won't even talk to you.

Which is as it should be. When MDRT was founded in 1927 selling a million was regarded as a miraculous feat, and properly so. But as both the economy and inflation began to surge forward, it wasn't so big a deal. The Round Table was faced with a dilemma: change its name, or keep its well-known title and start to escalate its qualification standards. It did the latter.

I had long discussions about this decision with Tilly Walker, a remarkable Floridian who was in the inner circles of MDRT for many years. I was all for trying to devise a name that would more accurately describe the feats of its members. He contended that the name had become generic, and to change it would strip it of its individuality. He won, of course, and in retrospect I have never felt better about losing an argument. "The Million Dollar Round Table" says it. Nobody asks, "A million what?" It's simply impressive, that's all.

The result is that today qualifying for MDRT requires proven first-year commissions of $40,000, and if a member wishes to reach the ultimate glory of the Top of the Table he or she must have received commissions of $240,000. Sounds pretty significant, doesn't it? And we're not even including renewals.

But wait a minute. MDRT knows it's talking gross commissions here, and most of its members don't sit on the curb with a pen and an application, assuming that passersby will sign up. Since 1973 it has conducted a Cost of Doing Business survey which brings these fine and fancy figures back to reality.

For instance: the MDRT agent's largest expense in 1988 was wages and salaries for staff ($15,620, or 29 percent of total expenses), followed by office rental ($6,595 or 12 percent of total). When you start factoring these figures into the mix, the big hitter doesn't look quite as affluent as he did a couple of paragraphs ago, does he?

That's by no means all. There's deferred compensation, legal and accounting fees, professional education expenses, depreciation expenses and a batch of other categories adding up to 21 percent. At times there must seem to be as much give as there is take. Yes, a good many of these categories are tax-deductible, but there are too many of them to live with in comfort.

In 1988, agencies and/or companies contributed an average of $14,227 (21 percent) toward the $68,410 in expenses incurred by the agents who responded to the survey. Surprisingly, in the previous triennial survey, agencies and/or companies contributed 18 percent of the expenses. That means agency/company outlay is on the upswing, which is probably the most remarkable figure in the survey.

As most of us have discovered at one point or another in our lives, even a salaried person whose out-of-pocket expenses are presumably taken care of by his employer is likely to come up short at the end of the year. But his is nothing compared with the person who is part individual entrepreneur and part employee. The expenses add up, and there is no way of hiding them.

The problem in the '90s comes down to who is going to pay the expenses an agent inevitably accrues as a cost of doing business. Home offices are insisting on greater productivity on the part of salespeople, which is a pleasant thought. But even increased productivity means a greater expense factor, and an agent can succeed himself into ultimate failure if his reach continues to exceed his grasp.

The MDRT survey is the only industrywide one I know of that undertakes to measure the agent's cost of doing business directly alongside his productivity, and deserves all the study we can give it. It may give us a handle on two problems: why so many companies feel they can't afford average agents, and why so many seemingly successful agents aren't making it.

"The Carpenters Who Construct Policy"

No. 19, May 7, 1990, Page 37

Every business or industry of any consequence has to have a set of institutional policies that govern it. This, like an election, involves the consent of the majority. There will always be mavericks who march to the beat of their own drums, but no institution can exist without a clear sense of its won proprieties—financial, ethical, economic and, of course, legislative.

This development of policy isn't easy, especially in a business like life insurance. There are more than 2,300 companies doing business in the field (some of them only theoretically since they are mere shells) and to develop a common sense of purpose is a fearsome task.

I submit to you that there are six men, all heads of institutional organizations, who are the carpenters constructing the policy of the business today. They are, of course, surrounded by excellent staffs, and they have committees of volunteers who advise and sometimes instruct them, but the buck stops with them. I know they are all good friends, even though circumstances cause them to disagree occasionally.

Their names are Dick Schweiker, president of the American Council of Life Insurance, which has the 600 most important companies in its ranks; Roy Woodall, president of the National Association of Life Companies, which represent the newer and smaller stock companies; Bruce Dalzell, president of the Life Insurers Conference, a large group of home service companies; Lynn Merritt, president of the Life Office Management Association, whose interest lies in the operation of home offices; Ernie Cragg, president of the Life Insurance Marketing and Research Association, which deals with the distribution arm of life insurance; and Jack Bobo, executive vice-president of the National Association of Life Underwriters, representing the sales force.

If it were not for these men and their staffs (and I should add Carl Schramm, president of the Health Association of America, as a very close consultant) life insurance would be a rudderless ship.

We sometimes lose sight of these organizations and their leaders when the wheeling and dealing is going on, but they are the compromisers and bringers-together when the going gets tough. Nowhere is this more evident than in the stock-mutual tax imbroglio, in which brother is pitted against brother. My guess is, if it hasn't already happened by the time this is published, that some kind of compromise will have been hammered out. And the institutional executives will have led the way.

These six men are a disparate group. Schweiker is a former senator and cabinet member. Woodall is a former insurance commissioner. Dalzell is a former executive of LIMRA. Merritt is a former academician. Cragg is a former company president. Bobo is a former agent and president of NALU.

I can't think of a better group of cowboys (note that I have now turned carpenters who are erecting a great edifice into herdsmen who are moving the cattle in the right direction) to get the job done. They have all earned their spurs.

The issues the business faces today are endless. Ask ten people, "Which is the most important?" and you will get ten different answers. Whether it be the possible repeal of McCarran-Ferguson, the tax situation, the restructuring of the field force, investment problems and junk bonds—oh, well, why recite the litany?—each is significant to a major segment of the business.

The only way any one of them is going to be solved is through joint action, and the only people who can coalesce that action are the people I have mentioned above. They must pull their boards and committees together with their staffs and get action going. They are capable of it; they are doing it. The company or individual who believes that going it alone will solve anything is whistling in the dark.

The rate of the business in the immediate future rests on people like Schweiker, Bobo, Woodall, Cragg, Merritt, Dalzell and Schramm. Believe it!

"Crawling Before Walking: A Wise ACLI Plan"

No. 20, May 14, 1990, Page 13

As some of you with long memories may recollect, I have been critical of the American Council of Life Insurance for throttling back on its public relations-communications programs with the public.

Now, with the full cooperation of Rob Bier, managing director of communications for ACLI, I can report that ACLI's pendulum has begun to swing back in the other direction. As is prudent, the association is starting to crawl before it attempts to walk; its new programs are exploratory in nature. Some will undoubtedly come into full flower; others will be reassessed and a determination will be made as to whether they can stand up over the long haul. This is the only way to do it. To rush pell-mell into advertising and public relations, particularly in view of the uptight financial situations of the companies, would be foolhardy.

Here are some of the issues Rob Bier tells me ACLI is active in. Some you may have heard of, others may be new to you—but all are practical and spirited:

- The All-Industry Consumer Helpline (1-800-942-4242). All elements of the business are now locked into this number, the Insurance Information Institute having rolled into the line on May 1. So far the mix has been 50/30/20 percent in the health/P&C/life areas, but this will undoubtedly change over time. Members of the industry have themselves attempted to trip up the staff, and some rating services have been reluctant to hear themselves quoted. But the Helpline will survive all this, and as the public begins to know more about it, there will be more users.

- ACLI's "Principles of Quality Service Initiative." This is a dead-serious attempt to have every life insurance company adopt a series of seven major recommendations, supervised by a senior executive, to promote quality service in the home office and field. Presently about 160 companies have activated the principles. They are as good for the individual agency as they are for the company, and any member of the life insurance community who wants to know about them should write Rob Bier, ACLI, 1001 Pennsylvania Ave., NW, Washington, DC 20004-2599. It's as good a set of principles as you are likely to find, but too long to print in full here.

- A new (or perhaps you could call it continuing) advertising program. This appears in a small group of publications—many of which you may not have heard of—that covers Congress, the press and other influential people within the Washington beltline. It's about as much as ACLI can afford these days, and while you may not see the ads, which deal with the life insurance impact on the American economy, they are well-read in the nation's capital. If enough people like them, the campaign may be expanded.

- "Improving Our Image—It Is Everyone's Job." This is a stern lecture by Dick Schweiker, president of ACLI, which is currently appearing in *Council Review*, its monthly message to its members. In it he attempts, with considerable success, to separate the public's opinion about life insurance from other elements of the industry. He ruefully accepts the general consensus that "insurance is insurance," but he urges the life insurance shoemakers to stick to their lasts.

- Finally, the Council is working on what might be called a white paper on life insurance company financial practices and investments that undertakes to separate the conservatism of the business from the junk bond craze and unhappy mortgages. It is a notable piece and you will see it soon in various media.

Rob Bier reminds me that Holgar Johnson, founder of the Institute of Life Insurance, was fond of saying, "Public relations is 90 percent performance, and 10 percent talking about it." I believed it then and I believe it now. But I have always contended that the 10 percent is the straw that stirs the drink.

It seems that ACLI is stirring the drink. Hurrah!

"Won Any Good Awards Lately?"

No. 31, July 30, 1990, Page 13

American business is excessively award conscious. Sales awards are, of course, as old as the craft of selling, but lately there have been awards announced for everything imaginable—including, I presume, the most highly polished shoes. Certainly, there is always the Person of the Year, or the Month, or the Week, or even the Day, or the Last Hours. Anyone who hasn't received an award must be miserable.

To show how ridiculous the process can get, I have even received a couple myself. No, I'm not knocking them—I cherish the organizations who found something mildly worthy in me. But as I stood at the podium receiving the award with whatever grace I could muster, I stared squarely into the eyes of maybe ten people I thought deserved the tribute more than I did—and I'm not being a mealymouthed self-effacer when I make that statement.

Over time I have become an award buff. It began when my boss brought into my office, back in 1946, a tall, smiling fellow who wanted to establish an award in memory of his father, who had been a distinguished president of the National Association of Life Underwriters. The father was John Newton Russell—the son was John Henry Russell. The three of us (Jim Rutherford was the boss) leapt into the project with enthusiasm, and created what we thought was an ideal award. It was easy enough to select a jury of the most distinguished people in life insurance to name the recipient; our problem was to give them the right words to define who deserved it.

We waffled a bit on that, and came to a Solomon-like decision: it should be a person who had devoted a lifetime to the improvement of the business, **or** someone who had completed an electrifying achievement in the preceding year. As I look down the list of the 48 recipients, I don't think a single one has met the second requirement. Every one of them has been a wheelhorse for the business. The NALU board and the jury accepted these stipulations, and I was assigned to write the citations for the first six recipients. (Jack Russell wanted the first award to be labeled 1942, the year after his father's death.) I was totally enthralled with the job; there were giants in those days, old friend. And I was equally enthralled at the 1947 convention when Sol Huebner, Julian Myrick, Stanley Edwards, Paul Clark, Albert Linton and Holgar Johnson beamed when various dignitaries read the encomiums that came off my typewriter. (In recent years Marv Kobel has done a much more stirring job on the citations, but I'm not about to make invidious comparisons, especially if I'm on the wrong end of them.)

As in the case of most major awards, the Russell tends to fall into patterns, honoring a leader in one element of the business—home office, field, field management and association leadership—in something resembling rotation. If you know an agent worthy of the award, and an agent won it last year, tell him to hold his peace for a couple of years until the jury gets around to his or her category once more. This wasn't the way we envisioned it, but it seems like a fair division of the spoils.

To me it would be more equable if some benevolent donor would develop awards for each of the four categories I have just mentioned—plus, perhaps, a wild-card for an educator or other specialist. In this way, many more remarkably worthy people wouldn't end their lives unrecognized. (I realize that GAMC already has an award for field managers, but this could be folded into the triumphant package.)

The reader will understand my ambivalence here: on the one hand I am chuckling over the proliferation of awards, and on the other I'm suggesting more. No—the awards I want to see are for selfless devotion to the business, not for sales efficiency. Too many great men and women are going unheralded. At the reception following every Russell dinner, I see delight in the eyes of one person and pain in the eyes of others who did just as well.

This could be restructured.

"'Quality Service'—An Innovative Proposal, But. . ."

No. 33, August 13, 1990, Page 17

The American Council of Life Insurance, through its Public Relations Policy Committee, has put together a "Quality Service Initiative" for its member companies, from the CEO down to the newest agent. It is an earnest and far-reaching proposal to turn around public attitude about all areas of life insurance, which surveys show isn't as good as it should be.

As in all such proposals, the initiative lies with the member companies and their employees, not the Council. The advice can be superior—which it is—but unless company people and their agents choose to act on it, it's a paper tiger. I'm somewhat downcast by the fact—recited by ACLI—that when the Council asked 415 companies in January about ideas and approaches for the project, it received only 136 answers to its questionnaire.

In terms of replies to the usual questionnaire, this isn't at all bad—better than 30 percent—but in this instance the Council was inquiring about an issue of overwhelming interest and importance to the business. Where were the other 279 companies? Maybe they are the followers who have no special ideas of their own but will be galvanized by the thoughts of the leaders. Let us hope so.

The seven recommendations contained in the proposal are almost a primer of decent behavior:

1. Adopt a set of principles for quality service and stick with them.

2. Establish expectations of professional conduct for all company employees. These should include standards understood by everyone in the company and be available to its publics.

3. Make sure that everyone connected with the company is familiar with the principles and train them in that familiarity.

4. Make the company's principles widely know to the public, including policyholders.

5. Monitor employee and agent performance in light of company principles of quality service, incorporating results into each employee's performance appraisals.

6. Establish procedures for eliciting consumers' reasonable expectations and for handling consumer complaints.

7. Designate a senior executive to be the quality service officer.

Who could disagree? I talked with six CEOs who are or have been in the inner circles of ACLI. They had all received a 20-page brochure recounting the responses from the membership to ACLI headquarters. They were all favorable to the plan. One said, "I hope they will give us the ammunition to put into action"—and I'm sure they will. Another said, "It sounds a little bit like a Boy Scout Creed, but that's what they're there for: to challenge people, companies and institutions to do better." Another said, "ACLI must make sure that top management is trained and sets an example." That is the ultimate must. The Quality Service Initiative is an empty tub if top management—including the board of directors—isn't aware of it and participating.

I intend to keep tracking it as best I can, even though I'm an old enough hand to realize that the performance of good public relations doesn't easily reduce itself to statistics.

The prime point is that ACLI and its companies have put their fingers on what is wrong in the marketplace. As Dick Schweiker, president of ACLI, has said, "It is a long-term undertaking. The program is intended to help the industry regain consumer trust. It should put us in a much stronger position when dealing with legislators, regulators and consumer activists. And it has bottom-line significance."

"Service" is an easy word to pronounce but a devilish accomplishment to come through on. Let's keep our fingers crossed.

"The 'Social' Activities Of Life Insurers"

No. 35, August 27, 1990, Page 37

"Social" is an adjective that has too many meanings for me. I think of "social register," "social climber," even "social disease." And I have just barely begun.

At least three elements of the life insurance business are now deeply involved in what is called "social investing." What this procedure involves is putting money or considerable personal effort into organizations and activities that might not ordinarily get any money at all, and not worrying about the yield or the profit. Only a certain amount of this kind of investing is possible, of course, because neither the companies nor their agents are eleemosynary groups.

Luckily, I have been deeply involved in all of them over a period of 30 years. I am excessively proud of them, and I'd like to share my pride with you because you may have been involved with one or another.

The first is the Million Dollar Round Table Foundation. I served four years as one of the original directors of this group.

Starting a foundation is a mess. You have great dreams but no money. Fortunately, the board I served on had the solid backing of the membership of MDRT, although it was nowhere as large as it is today. (It had precisely 1,662 at the time.) They supported it massively.

Its first gifts were modest. It granted $5,000 to the American Association of University Teachers of Insurance for a casebook on life insurance. Then it distributed ten $1,000 scholarships to colleges and universities.

Its first major breakthrough was a gift of $1.5 million to help pay for the $4.5 million MDRT Foundation Hall at the American College in Bryn Mawr, PA.

Since then its focus has changed. It is giving smaller grants to a wide variety of local and state organizations, most of which are suggested by its members. It helps promote FamilyTime; it has helped develop a program to reduce unemployment among the Papago Indians in Arizona; it has provided funds for Medic Alert, and Mothers Against Drunk Driving.

Early this year it released a whole spate of small grants to local organizations trying desperately to improve one of the facets of their communities. Naturally, each came at the suggestion of a member of MDRT or the Foundation.

What do these grants have to do with life insurance? On the face of it, not one blessed thing, I am pleased to say. But they have done wondrous things for the reputation of MDRT members and, through them, all life underwriters. They have become certified Concerned Citizens.

As of today, the MDRT Foundation, during its existence, has contributed to 113 organizations, and is closing in on $4 million in grants. If this isn't enlightened self-interest, I have no idea what is.

Now let's flip the coin over and look at an entirely different project—the Center for Corporate Public Involvement of the American Council of Life Insurance. For 23 years it has been headed by Stan Karson of the ACLI staff.

It defines a social investment by a company as "those made specifically for social desirable purposes that would not have been made otherwise under the company's customary lending standards, or those in which social considerations played a substantial part in the investment decision."

It began with a big bang: a pledge of $2 billion to President Lyndon Johnson for investments that would meet these strictures. The pledge was ultimately fulfilled.

Since then the Center for Corporate Public Involvement has acted as a shepherd for company participation, giving advice and suggestions. The financial agonies of the '80s took its toll, of course, but a recent study of the project by the Ford Foundation shows that it is alive and well. Logically, the larger companies are the leaders, but smaller companies, usually operating near their base of operations, have a measurable effect.

No business can survive through selfishness. The fact that the various elements of life insurance have shown a clear willingness to be good corporate citizens reflects well on everyone in the industry.

"Public Service By Life Underwriters"

No. 36, September 3, 1990, Page 27

Last week I talked about the social investments of the Million Dollar Round Table and life insurance companies, through the guidance of the American Council of Life Insurance. This was principally in the form of money—money that might have gone anywhere, but which life insurance people channeled into areas where the need was greatest. The campaigns have been winners.

The National Association of Life Underwriters has taken a slightly different tack, but with equally satisfying results. Some 40-years ago a group of staff members representing NALU and the Institute of Life Insurance (now the American Council of Life Insurance) sat down to consider how each organization could more firmly support the other, even though their constituencies were different. It quickly became apparent that volunteer public service efforts of the nation's agents were having a measurable effect on almost every community in America, but were largely unknown because no one had counted them, measured them and reported to the public on them.

So a task force was formed to formalize the public service activities of agents, under the guidance of Dr. Louis I. Dublin, a retired Metropolitan vice-president who was serving as a consultant for the Institute. It was announced that plaques would be presented to local and state associations that did the best public service jobs, and that they would be celebrated at a luncheon during the NALU convention.

The Dublin Public Service Award project took off like a rocket and has never looked back. The most recent result: during its centennial year—1989-1990—NALU's local and state associations pledged a million hours of public service on the part of their members. The final total added up to 1.6 million hours. If the participants had been paid a minimum wage, it would total more than $6 million. But it was done voluntarily.

Some of the projects involved money, but most of them involved sweat on the part of members. When Hurricane Hugo hit South Carolina, associations and their members contributed "thousands of dollars and tons of food" to the Red Cross disaster relief fund, according to NALU.

But where the public service program really hits home is in local activities, often unique to a single community. If a 20-mile walk will help bring money into a worthy charity, hundreds of life underwriters will pull on their Nikes and take off. If a group of underprivileged kids deserve a big party, who do you suppose is broiling and passing the hamburgers?

Cynics have always said that public service is simply another way to make contacts. After careful study, I have concluded that this is poppycock. Worse than that, it's almost libelous. What kind of contacts is an agent making if he gets up to his ears in the Big Brother movement? Friendship, that's all. Of course, if he can wait 30 years until his Little Brothers become captains of industry, he may find the pearl in the oyster. But how many of us befriend kids with that in mind?

Activities that have to do directly with selling are not eligible for the Dublin award. There is one humane exception: many associations have devised senior citizens health insurance counselling programs which lead older people through the maze of coordinating government and private health insurance benefits to help them prevent duplication of coverage. This is no way to earn a living, but it's the acme of public service.

In these two articles, I have undertaken to show the public spirit of various elements of the life insurance business, home office and field. It is nearly impossible for me to compare this spirit with what other industries exhibit. So I cannot call it unique, or even rare. And I apologize for programs I have omitted, simply because they haven't come to my attention.

What my project has done is simply to make me prouder of the people I have spent my business life with. I wish it were possible for the publics the business serves to understand them more fully.

"The Man Who Changed The Business"

No. 40, October 1, 1990, Page 37

Most of us have our favorite people who made the life insurance business what it is today. People like Elizur Wright, who solidified both the actuarial and the regulative disciplines; Haley Fiske, who made the Metropolitan into a giant by turning his company's attentions toward the immigrants who flooded the country in the late 19th century; and, of course, Dr. Solomon S. Huebner, who gave life insurance dignity and persuasiveness in the realms of education.

My own nominee was not a hero in any sense of the word—except among the social crowd—but he set in motion the machinery that created the Armstrong investigation in New York State which, in turn, laid the heavy hand of regulation on insurance and spawned the mutual life insurance companies.

His name: James Hazen Hyde, called "Caleb" by his friends. He was the son of Henry Baldwin Hyde, who founded the Equitable Life Assurance Society, and his father's heir apparent. He loved to give parties—in reality, vast costume balls attended by visiting royalty and anyone who was anybody in New York. He left the management of the Equitable principally in the hands of a highly competent staff. But he spent its money—"policyholders' money," as the *New York World* thundered—as though it was his very own.

Then he gave one ball too many, on January 31, 1905. It was held at Sherry's, New York's most elegant restaurant, which had been transformed into the Palace of Versailles for the occasion. The New York press was lying in wait for him. It described the party, the costumes (including that of the Countess de Rougement, nee Edith Clapp), and the entertainment in tender loving detail, including the triumphant entrance of Mr. Hyde on a stallion.

I will spare you recitations of the costumes and entertainment, but the French Kings who lived in the original Versailles should have had it so good. The uproar was instant and overwhelming. The Armstrong Commission was already gearing up, and it invited him to testify on April 1, 1905 (on the "Day of All Fools," as the *World* tactfully described it).

"He drove jauntily down in his private hansom cab, a bunch of violets at the side of the horse's head, another bunch nodding from the coachman's hat, and a third breathing incense from the buttonhole of the young man himself," according to the *World*.

The investigation was conducted by Charles Evans Hughes, later Chief Justice of the U.S. Supreme Court and only a whisker from the Presidency. Mr. Hyde emerged from the hearing a broken man, stripped of his Equitable title and his directorates. He went into voluntary exile in France.

It would be totally unfair to say that Mr. Hyde caused the Armstrong investigation. Insurance was not sufficiently regulated, and the writing of stronger rules for its guidance was certainly inevitable. But James Hazen Hyde was the catalyst; he was the lightning rod. The public needed something to focus on before it could become sufficiently indignant, and the ball at Sherry's was perfect for the occasion. That's why I say he changed the life insurance business more than any other single individual.

* * * *

More than half a century after the Armstrong investigation had concluded, I was sitting in the bar of the Gideon Putnam Hotel in Saratoga Springs, NY, when I ran into an old acquaintance, Monty Wooley, the actor who originated the title role in *The Man Who Came to Dinner.* When I told him I was attending a meeting of the New York State Life Managers Association he said, "There's someone who lives here you absolutely must meet."

He took me into the dining room and introduced me to a frail, old man who was just finishing lunch with his companion. "This is James Hazen Hyde," he said. He told Mr. Hyde that I was in the life insurance business. He looked at me with something approaching a twinkle and said, "I never was. My father was." It turned out that he had returned to the U.S. at the outset of World War II, and had lived a reclusive life ever since. His glory days were over at the age of 28. But he certainly left his mark.

"Two Nice Guys Finish First"

No. 47, November 19, 1990, Page 11

"Nice guys finish last," was the slogan of Leo Durocher, the scrappy manager of the Giants and Dodgers, who spent his life living up to his slogan.

Not always. Two of the best guys I know, Joe Melone and Ron Barbaro, just finished first in one of the most amazing life insurance company personnel changes I have encountered.

As the news columns have reported, Joe is moving from president of the Prudential of America to president of the Equitable Society. Ron has switched from president of the Prudential's Canadian operations to Joe Melone's old job at Newark headquarters.

They are both remarkable people. Joe started out, after graduating from the Wharton School with a Ph.D., as a teacher at the University of Pennsylvania. He became affiliated with the American College as research director of the McCahan Foundation, and in 1968 made the unlikely leap to the Pru, where he started as director of planning and analysis for the staff-insurance area. He moved up the line quickly, and in 1981 became executive vice-president for marketing. He was named president in 1984. He is 59-years old.

Melone is a remarkable speaker and moderator. He has none of the stuffiness that we are accustomed to assigning to the Ph.D. When he gets on a platform and I am anywhere in the territory, I am there in the front row. His thoughtful remarks are always laced with humor and pleasantness. He makes the difficult totally understandable.

Ron Barbaro is also 59. He is an agent, born and bred. He was president of the Million Dollar Round Table in '85 and one of its wittiest. He is also a native Canadian, and one of the most dedicated public servants in Toronto. For instance, he has been volunteer head of the Toronto Zoo for many years, and was even able to borrow two baby giant pandas from Beijing for his fellow Canadians. (This meant a couple of trips to China, which he cheerfully undertook.) He is head of the United Fund to Toronto, and you may be sure it will be a success.

I was surprised that he accepted the presidency of the Pru in Canada, and even more so that he was willing to transfer to Newark when the call came. To me, he has always seemed to be as unfettered as you can get. After he and his wife had worked as volunteers in an AIDS hostel, he dreamed up the idea of living insurance benefits for the terminally ill, payments that would help reduce financial strain. At first the notion was regarded with skepticism, but it has since been embraced by many life insurance companies, most importantly, the Pru.

Why, you may ask, would these two unique men who are sitting in the catbird seat choose to uproot themselves at 59 and undertake new challenges? I think I know them both well enough to hazard a guess—based on conversations with their present and future colleagues.

Prudential has a long history of alternating its CEOs between those who have field backgrounds and those who have been involved in actuarial and investment leadership. Bob Beck was regarded as a field person when he retired as CEO in '87. Surprisingly enough, so was Joe Melone, the Ph.D. and teacher from the Wharton School. So the board named Bob Winters, a past president of the American Academy of Actuaries and vice-chairman of the Pru, as chairman and CEO. Since Winters is just months younger than the other two, the lack of elbow room was obvious.

So when Dick Jenrette, who was occupying the dual titles of chairman and president of Equitable, invited Joe Melone to cross the Hudson River, it seemed like a good idea. Jenrette is a ripe 61, and purely an investment person. Melone will complement his skills.

Why did Ron Barbaro decide to abandon his position as a very big frog in a medium-size puddle and move to the eye of the hurricane? He answered that question in one sentence quoted by the *New York Times*: "I'm a corporate person and the chairman and the board feel that I can help the enterprise, so I will be there." He couldn't say it any plainer than that.

My congratulations to Melone, Barbaro, the Prudential and the Equitable. It's a natural, and couldn't happen to better citizens or nicer people.

"The Real Estate Mess—And Life Insurance"

No. 48, November 26, 1990, Page 11

Anyone who can read understands that the real estate market is, to put it mildly, unsteady. *Newsweek* calls it "the big bust." The *New York Times* headlines, on page one, "Life Insurers Also Weakened By Downturn in Real Estate."

Much of the alarm on the part of the media was triggered when Travelers Corporation acknowledged severe losses on its real estate investments and cut its stock dividends. Another part is the common knowledge that all life insurance companies invest heavily in various forms of real estate, and therefore, by definition, must be losing the same kind of money that causes other investors to weep openly, usually in the press, about their hard times.

Not so fast. Life insurance doesn't operate in the same way as do banks, savings and loans and other lending institutions. They are gaited for the long haul. Here are some facts, compiled by the American Council of Life Insurance, that should clarify where life insurance companies stand.

- Of the $1.3 trillion of assets held by U.S. life companies, 19.2% are invested in mortgages; 3.2% are invested in real estate; delinquent loans represent about one-half of 1% of the business' assets.

- Unlike banks, insurance companies typically do not engage in speculative, high-risk construction lending. They usually make mortgage loans on properties already 75 to 85% leased. They also customarily lend only up to 75% of the appraised value of a given property.

- Foreclosure doesn't necessarily mean a loss to the lending insurance company. Properties held until the market turns around can be profit-making. At the very least, the management or sale of such properties diminishes the impact that bad loans have on the business.

- As the real estate market weakens, some companies have announced that they are increasing their reserves to guard against potential losses. This is pure prudence, since there is no requirement that life companies put up reserves for losses on their mortgage portfolios. They rarely experience the level of loss for which they reserve.

The alarms that the press is sending out come from the contortions of all financial organizations during the '80s, when deregulation enabled banks and savings and loans to be free to pay depositors any rate they chose, the competition for the consumer dollar grew hotter, and some life insurance companies joined the race toward the highest interest rates. That competition has now abated; S&Ls are in a catastrophic state, banks are trying hard to avoid the same fate, and insurance people have furled their sails.

But the press always seems to be a couple of laps behind today's facts, chiefly because the companies clam up when the going gets tough.

That's why it is encouraging to see ACLI issuing bulletins to correspondents in every medium throughout the country. They aren't press releases, but rather "backgrounders" that will enable writers to have a firmer base of facts on insurance subjects—at least the facts as the major organization in life insurance sees them. I have paraphrased one of them at length above, and I hope more will be forthcoming on issues of the day.

Despite the fact that we criticize them for not doing so, it is almost impossible for writers and broadcasters to have a total grasp on what went on yesterday in the financial community. Things are moving too fast.

The time when life insurance qualified for only a line or two on the financial pages is long past. It has become a massive business, and even reporters tend to draw a long breath when they start talking in terms of trillions of dollars. Someone once tried to explain to me precisely what a trillion meant, but I threw up my hands after they had left the solar system and were flying free in the cosmos.

Nonetheless, it is the job of the insurance community to explain what it is doing to keep stable and profitable. ACLI deserves a large share of the credit for doing so. Individual companies would do well to follow its lead.

"The Realities Of Life Insurance Advertising"

No. 49, December 3, 1990, Page 25

Twenty-five years ago all the life insurance companies in America spent about $50 million on media advertising. Today they spend roughly eight times that amount. (Accurate statistics on life insurance are hard to come by, since independent organizations that measure advertising expenditures usually lump all insurance together in a single category.)

Part of this rise can be attributed to the inflation in advertising costs. But the main reason is that major companies have found it important to advertise and, quite likely, profitable although profitability isn't a factor that can be nailed down.

"Why?" asks the Naive One. "Why—since the great bulk of your product is sold through face-to-face contact?"

Well, more than a century ago John Wanamaker, the great retail merchant and profound thinker, said, "Half my advertising is useless, but I don't know which half." I have no doubt that latter-day Wanamakers, including life insurance CEOs, would gladly echo that statement, but they prefer to look at the half that is useful, and keep them and their agents in the public mind.

Advertising agencies themselves—and you may take this from one who knows—have a hard time pinning down a unique theme for a life insurance campaign. And some of their most ingenious ones aren't acceptable to the companies. Often they are out in the wild blue yonder.

Here, among a myriad of reasons, are some of the most important that impel life insurance companies to advertise in the various media:

- To keep the public familiar with their names, so when an agent contacts a prospect the answer won't be, "What did you say the name of your company was?" There is no worse handicap than having to explain who you represent before you begin delivering a sales dialogue.

- To keep a company's agents and prospective agents aware of the fact that their home office is solidly behind their sales efforts. That's simply the other side of the coin.

- To explain the company's philosophy for existence. This isn't an easy job, but it does separate the sheep from the goats, and if it is well-done it attracts the thoughtful prospect.

- To explain a policy or a practice that a company is particularly proud of. This could be a new concept (of which there were probably too many in the '80s) or a business attitude that the field force is equipped to back up.

- Finally, in this truncated list, to reinforce the belief of current policyholders that they have come to the right place, and will not easily be suckered in to replacement or lapse.

There are several companies that are engaged in "direct response" advertising—some of it highly creative. But most major companies use advertising as a support for their salespeople. Among the campaigns that have impressed me most lately are the John Hancock's seminal series in print and on TV which is often referred to as "slice-of-life." It puts the buyer and the seller right across the same desk, and has doubtless been responsible for the thinking behind many other programs. Or the Aetna's "straight talk" commercials that talk frankly about such taboos as AIDS and alcohol.

The one nearest to my heart is the New York Life print series which characterizes the company as "large, conservative and dull. Reassuring in times like these, isn't it?" The ability to see and take advantage of public perception about a business is rare, and it seems to me that New York Life has done it with a series of adjectives that would have been foolish in a time when there was less public doubt about the stability of life insurance companies. I am waiting to see public reaction to it.

Many other companies are involved in lively, innovative messages about the good things that are happening in life insurance. To me, it is the only way to go.

While advertising is a difficult tool for insurance people to handle, it is a necessary one. Let's hope it continues to improve.

"'Unity'—Small Word, Big Problem"

No. 50, December 10, 1990, Page 11

The retiring chairman of the American Council of Life Insurance believes that unity among life insurance companies is the greatest challenge the business will face in the coming years. Good thought.

John E. Fisher, who is also CEO of Nationwide Life, made this statement and expanded on it in his address to the ACLI annual meeting last month in Houston. He called up the matter of factionalism, particularly between stock and mutual companies, and blamed it for the fact that life insurance companies will pay a total of $8 billion additional in taxes over the next five years, a 50 percent increase.

While he conceded that expert lobbying kept the tax increase from being twice that size, he continued, "When you consider the much smaller tax increase we might have gotten had we gone to Capitol Hill as a united industry, then it doesn't look so good. The formula adopted represents a double hit on acquisition costs added to the reserve disallowance of the 1984 tax bill, and the percent of premiums enacted is subject to easy future increases."

He is obviously right, but unity isn't that easy to come by. Even the original 13 colonies of the fledgling United States of America had a rough time achieving it. The fact that they ultimately did makes any kind of unity seem possible.

The one problem they didn't have to deal with was the stock-mutual situation. For some cockeyed reason, the debate brings to mind Rex Harrison's plaint in the immortal musical comedy, *My Fair Lady*: "Why can't a woman be more like a man?" The audience laughed itself silly, but Rex never even came close to solving the problem.

Why can't a mutual be more like a stock? They are different breeds, that's why. Stock companies have stockholders, to whom they are beholden; mutual companies have dividend-receiving policyholders, who blithely assume their dividends will go up or always stay equal, but will never go down. But Congress is determined that each will be taxed equitably. That's tough.

John Fisher's recipe for unity is "having a strong, adaptable, innovative and resilient trade association. Only a united industry could have a trade association that fit that description."

Oh, but it's not that easy; the business has small companies that operate in a handful of states, and big ones that are not only national but international. Each has its own beliefs about how it should be supervised and taxed. Small companies are comfortable with state supervision; they know their commissioners well and are highly sensitive to their points of view.

The big companies are spread thin. While it would be imprudent for them to say so, many of them would be happy to get along with federal supervision. As a CEO of a relatively minor company once said to me, "In the territory where I operate, I'm bigger than the Metropolitan. I don't lose any opportunity to tell my commissioners that."

Points of view like these make the job of a trade association head, like Dick Schweiker of the American Council of Life Insurance, and his colleagues more onerous. It's easy for John Fisher to say, "The pressures to give in to factionalism will only increase with time as the industry experiences rapid and dramatic change." But the business is full of not only apples and oranges, but also bananas, pears and an occasional prune. With more than 600 companies in their act, how do you acquire unity?

The only answer seems to lie in one word: compromise. To hold rigidly to a concept, and never waver from it, will cause Mr. Fisher's worst fears to come true. The leaders of the business will have to give a little as they take a little. They failed to do this as they debated the 1990 budget bill with Congress. That's why $8 billion will be siphoned from their assets over the next five years. Compromise might have kept it from happening.

A confession: it is supremely easy for a columnist to mastermind everything, and then to draw the counterpane over his head and resume napping. I choose not to do that, so I will keep on searching for answers.

"NALU: Conciliatory Or Obstreperous?"

No. 52, December 24, 1990, Page 17

One of the sessions I enjoy most of all during the insurance year is the Tom Grant Breakfast, sponsored by the BMA Life of Kansas City, and currently a feature of the annual meeting of the American Council of Life Insurance. It gives the top executives of the business a chance—maybe their only chance at a single meeting—to hear the newly-elected president of the National Association of Life Underwriters discuss what's on NALU's mind. It was instituted 53 years ago by the elder Tom Grant, continued by his son, Bill, his grandson, Tom II—all chief executives of BMA—and now by the new management of the company. May the idea continue to flourish!

This year the president of NALU, John Neighbors, undoubtedly surprised his listeners with a "modest proposal." It was one that might lead to a resolution of the federal income tax situation confronting the stock and mutual life companies: that a neutral, nine-member panel be formed to adjudicate the differences between the two breeds of companies, each to choose four representatives "with no company affiliation," plus one jointly agreed-upon representative.

The agreement, he said, should be binding, and the business could go to Congress with a united front that might expect an affirmative nod from those who shape tax bills. Details of the plan have appeared in the *National Underwriter.*

NALU has historically stood on the sidelines in stock-mutual disputes, principally because its members are almost equally divided between the two. For it to suggest a plan for mediation seemed, at its best, a highly conciliatory move; at its worst, an obstreperous intervention by salespeople into company and institutional policy. Which?

So I went directly to the two people most deeply concerned with agent and company policy: Jack Bobo, executive vice-president of NALU, and Dick Schweiker, president of ACLI.

Jack Bobo first: he said he had been proposing such mediation since 1984, and read me chapter and verse to prove his point. This was certainly not a case of John Neighbors and his board taking off on a course of its own. It was a decision thought through carefully by staff and elected officers. The Tom Grant Breakfast seemed like the ideal place to express it, and so it was done.

There was almost immediate confusion, all of the gossip variety, about how companies would accept the proposal. So I got Dick Schweiker on the phone.

Schweiker: his staff and his board accept the proposal in precisely the spirit it was offered, and the most deeply involved will discuss it in-depth and act on it. There are obviously some issues to be ironed out: for instance, how binding can an agreement be with all of his 600 companies? Finding nine representatives "with no company affiliation" who are sufficiently immersed in the problem to know its convolutions may be a tough chore, but doable.

In other words, there is amity and understanding between the two groups. My notion that the companies might believe NALU was moving into territories where it had no business was "simply not so."

My relief after having talked with these two open-handed, open-minded men at some length must have been as obvious to them as it was to me. Smaller people might have seen the widening of a rift between home office and field people, a rift that has been overplayed during the last few years. (Was there ever a time when they were soulmates?) But here we have seen—and, I hope, will continue to see—a mutual supportiveness that may be the key point in solving the federal income tax situation, or at least ameliorating it.

I believe the agent has an obvious stake in the issue of what companies must pay in taxes. Increased taxes mean increased costs; increased costs affect the agent's ability to sell and his or her earning power. Life underwriters cannot sit idly by and allow this to happen without contributing their very best thought to the issue.

Consequently, I think NALU leadership is on the right track, and should be supported and commended for its actions.

"Patriarchs—And What They Can Teach You"

No. 2, January 14, 1991, Page 17

The first of the year is a good time to celebrate the patriarchs of our business—and to understand how to emulate them (because they are invariably successful).

What is a patriarch? Here are some of his virtues: he is older than most of us; he has been everywhere and seen it all; he has learned from everywhere he has been and everything he has seen; and he has the ability to transmit this knowledge to his younger colleagues. Here are my nominees for the all-patriarch team of life insurance. (I fully agree that I have missed some of the best, but this column will be open for another—and not necessarily second—team in a future issue, if you will drop me a line and give me some nominees.)

Patriarch Emeritus: Holgar J. Johnson, past Penn Mutual general agent, past NALU president, past president of the Institute of Life Insurance. Age 96. While I suppose most patriarchs are emeritus, Holgar deserves both labels. He has guided the communications of life insurance for more than 50 years.

He carved out a public relations creed that the business still lives by. It works just as well in a time of tremendous upheaval—that is to say, today—as it did in the more tranquil times when he devised it.

Patriarchal President: Charles J. Zimmerman, past general agent and then CEO of Connecticut Mutual, past president of NALU and LIMRA. Age 88. Charlie has been equally a leader in home office and field. In 1940-41 he was a force in turning aside a federal investigation of life insurance and its agents. As head of LIMRA, he reshaped marketing research. When he went to Con-Mu he was a strong link in the chain of solid executives. And he still makes as much sense as he ever did, which is as great a compliment as I can pay. I never knew a person who didn't like Charlie.

Patriarchal Vice-President: Woody Woodson (known to the outer world as Benjamin N.), past executive of NALU and LIMRA, past senior executive of a number of companies, ending up as CEO of American General Life, educator, voluminous writer and, since retirement, an active life member of MDRT. Age 82.

Now that he has chosen to grow a snow-white (only his hairdresser knows for sure) beard, he looks more patriarchal than anybody. But he is still in the middle of everything. He writes a column that, I am sorry to say, is better read than any other in the life insurance business. (You know why I'm sorry, I hope.) Long may he wave.

Patriarchal Agent Vice-President: John O. Todd, a qualifying member and former president of the Million Dollar Round Table for 50 (count 'em, 50) years, an innovator, a leader and a solid citizen. Age 85. First John Todd made his mark as an agent. While he was magnificently successful at this, he decided to bring together a group of super-agents who would sell on a nationwide basis. Others were doing the same thing, but John's prestige made him one of the very best. This, at a time when most super-agents were retiring on their renewals, their pensions, and their occasional jumbo cases. He is a patriarch of agents.

Patriarchal Actuarial Vice-President: Jack Moorhead, inventive company actuary, consultant, past president of the American Academy of Actuaries and the Society of Actuaries, writer of one of the great biographies of the actuarial profession *Our Yesterdays*. Age 80. Jack is the prototype actuary—confident, easy to talk with, full of understanding and humor. (If you didn't think actuaries had a sense of humor, guess again.) To understand the actuarial profession, you have to know someone like Jack Moorhead.

Why do I talk about patriarchs? Because everyone has to have goals. The best way to reach them is to have someone to emulate, and then study them. I submit to you that these five, each 80+, have performed in exemplary fashion over a great many years. As the Good Book says, "Go thou and do likewise."

"Changing Of The Guard—Be Ready For It"

No. 23, June 10, 1991, Page 19

Jack E. Bobo, executive vice-president, National Association of Life Underwriters, born June 24, 1924; age at nearest birthday, 67.

Richard S. Schweiker, president, American Council of Life Insurance, born June 1, 1926; age at nearest birthday, 65.

Ernest E. Cragg, president, Life Insurance Marketing and Research Association, born August 12, 1927; age at nearest birthday, 64.

While the old mandatory retirement at 65 rule has just about disappeared, many executives at the age of three-score years and five feel that they have made their contributions, paid their dues and deserve surcease from the rat race. Others, whose long-term plans for their organizations still haven't quite reached fruition, would like to hang on for a time until they do. Their directors are usually cognizant of this fact, and will support it—but only to a degree.

Bobo, Schweiker and Cragg are three of the most important men in the life insurance business, not because of the profits they generate but because of the influence they wield. Among them, their constituencies include just about everyone of importance in both home office and field. They are persuasive men, full of ideas and skilled in implementing them. They appear to be healthy, happy and in total possession of all their marbles. Their knowledge of the people in the business is unsurpassed.

As far as I know, not one of them has acquired any significant number of enemies, which is almost a miracle, because their business lives are full of compromises, bringing warring factions together, soothing ruffled feathers and helping lions and lambs to get along with a fair amount of amiability.

Now what, old boys?

To begin with, I have been told the obvious: all the three associations have search groups at work. If not formal committees, at least they represent responsible individuals who look to the future. This is a necessity; as far as I know, none of the groups has an heir apparent sitting on the steps to the throne. Powerful though they may be, they don't have the resources to hide away a Bobo, Schweiker or a Cragg until it comes time to reveal him. Of course, veteran association-watchers think they see certain favorites in the wings, but it would be futile and even somewhat disrupting to speculate here on whom they might be.

The one possibility that gives me pause is that these three estimable gentlemen might step down within a matter of months of one another. They, and their opposite numbers in other institutional groups (all of whom are somewhat younger), have evolved a tightly knit little association of their own. Each understands the aspirations and problems of the others without having to launch long explanations of what they are up to.

Having three new leaders at the same time certainly wouldn't set this small group back to square one, because the search committees are not going to bring in neophytes, but there would be a certain amount of backing and filing for a time.

My hope would be that the three associations would ask Bobo, Schweiker and Cragg to serve as advisers emeritus for a year, not to peer over the shoulders of their successors, but simply to make sure that the integration of the three groups remained as sound and fruitful as it is now.

Many people in the business, properly preoccupied with their own duties, don't understand what a powerful influence all institutional organizations have on the entire business, home office and field. They bring together leaders who might not otherwise have more than a nodding acquaintance with each other. Without invading any antitrust laws they search for a commonality of judgment and expertise that helps the life insurance community function effectively.

They will be hard to replace; their organizations have done a similar job before, but not at the same time. Only if it is done with great care will the business survive their loss without missing a beat. Bobo and Schweiker and Cragg—what a lively lilt the three names have when pronounced together. Let's be sure we don't lose them all at one fell swoop.

3

Every Business Has Its Dark Side

"Voltaire Had The Right Idea"

No. 38, September 20, 1986, Page 11

When some of my straight-arrow cronies heard that I was going to write for the *National Underwriter*, their response came back like a trombone bray: "Not that magazine?" Why? "They published Bob MacDonald's book!"

This was followed by mutterings like, "They would probably have published Hitler," or ". . .the Marquis de Sade." I reminded them that this was highly unlikely, since MacMillan and Company, a distinguished American institution, held the rights to *Mein Kampf*, and Grove Press, another venerable New York publisher, owned the copyrights to the American translations of the Marquis' quaint writings.

But that was simply flirting with the issue, not getting to the heart of the matter, and I knew it. I would like to tell them, with you looking over my shoulder, why I disagree with them. Non-violently.

I have never met the author of *Control Your Future*, which must mean that I've been hanging out with the wrong crowd, since he seems to have appeared almost everywhere during the past three years. I reviewed his book for another publication, after having read it twice, cover-to-cover. It was not a rave review. I have scant respect for a person who, having given up selling ordinary life as a means to earn a living, bad-mouths it to everyone who will listen. If he has a better product, let him prove its superiority and sell it.

Even more seriously, I worry about an individual who throws pejorative adjectives at people who are in logical disagreement with him and who casts doubts on their competence, if not their honesty. He seems determined to become the John McEnroe of insurance, but he has neither the serve nor the backhand to make his surly attitude stick.

But this is all a matter of opinion—my opinion. I don't think it should bar Bob MacDonald from being published by a distinguished house.

There are those who say his book is evil and destructive to the life insurance business, and should be kept from the nervous eyes of those agents who might be influenced by it. This reminds me of the testimony contributed to the Attorney General's Commission on Pornography by the Rev. Donald Wildmon of Tupelo, MS. The Reverend has a very broad definition of pornography, and would doubtless ban from our homes every publication up to and including the *National Geographic*—at least those issues which printed photos of bare-breasted Balinese maidens. I suggest that my good friends who are berating National Underwriter for having published Bob MacDonald's book are teetering very close to the precipice of censorship.

Unhappily, the insurance business, which has grown to be one of the greatest money businesses in the world, still thinks of itself as a cottage industry, a closely-knit bunch of buddies who are tolerant of each other's peccadillos but who close ranks when an outsider takes a swipe at them. They are even less tolerant when a member of the club becomes a renegade. They have forgotten—or in some instances never learned—that as they talk in terms of trillions and hundreds of billions of dollars they have become fair game both for those who are critical of what they do and those who would like a piece of the action by vending their own brands of snake oil.

The French author Voltaire, who had an opinion on almost everything, is supposed to have said, "I disapprove of what you say, but I will defend to the death your right to say it." Voltaire was not a publisher, and if he had been it is possible he would not have risked his francs to publish the Gallic equivalent of Bob MacDonald. But in reality I believe he would have done so, and with considerable relish. He would probably have said, "Now you know what MacDonald stands for. If you like his ideas you can applaud them. If you don't like them you can steer clear of him. Until he committed himself to paper, you had a vague idea of what his beliefs were. He has now revealed himself to you."

In its 90 years of existence, *National Underwriter* has printed countless statements that it didn't agree with, because it felt its readers had a right to know them. I presume it has done the same thing with Bob MacDonald's writings, and I commend its editors for publishing what he has to say.

Note to unbelievers: As I type these words, not a single person at the *National Underwriter* knows I'm preparing them.

"A Power Breakfast"

No. 15, April 13, 1987, Page 27

You know about the power breakfast, don't you? Warm juice, cold coffee, soggy toast and some conversation that undertakes to get to the heart of things. I'm usually not very good at such events, because the warmth of the coffee tends to have more attraction for me than the heart of the dialogue, and if I have any power at all it usually doesn't get revved up until after 9 a.m.

Anyhow, the other day I had a power breakfast with Bob MacDonald, on that day president and CEO of ITT Life, author of a book about life insurance marketing called *Control Your Future*, and generally regarded as one of the principal hair shirts draped over the shoulders of the life insurance business. I had read and reviewed his book—not very favorably—but I figured there was no substitute for meeting the man himself.

I didn't know it at the time—and he was not about to tell a practicing journalist who doesn't think very much of off-the-record conversations—but this was his next-to-last day as head of ITT Life. He was on his way to Hartford to submit his resignation to his parent company and announce his plans to form an agent-owned insurance company.

Which was why, I suppose, that the breakfast crackled with a lot of talk about the agent and his position in the life insurance business. Bob professes to see him, as he said many times in the pages of his book, as the key factor in the distribution of life insurance, the catalyst that makes the rest of the company succeed or fail. He will now get full opportunity to put his money, as the crass saying goes, where his mouth is, and the life insurance community will be watching him with considerable interest.

When you maintain a high profile, as Bob MacDonald does—especially by making talks before life underwriters associations at every opportunity—you are going to attract critics, and he has. Some have even gone so far as to try to get associations to break speaking dates they have set up. This I consider to be an insult to association people; if they aren't big enough boys and girls to evaluate their peers, perhaps they should be in a business where brains are not a priority item.

In the same area, I wondered aloud why he seemed offended, as he mentioned more than once in his book, that NALU had denied him membership, since home office people can be no more than associate members anyhow. The answer is that turning him away appears to confer on him a lack of respectability that he doesn't believe he has earned. Perhaps with an agent-owned company he will be able to turn that point of view around.

Bob MacDonald and I talked at length about his downgrading of the ordinary life policy by taking it completely out of the ITT ratebook. I contended that the stabilization of interest rates and the introduction of interest-sensitive o.l. policies had made this a tenuous stance, but he stuck to his guns that better products are available. It will be interesting to see how he handles this thorny issue with an agent-owned company, where a product portfolio that will appeal strongly to the independent agent might well include some form of ordinary life.

Addendum: Quite naturally, as soon as MacDonald's resignation and announcement of his new position hit the press, the question arose: was the change his choice, or that of the Hartford Group, his senior company? I don't know, and in situations like this one never does. But the fact that he was accompanied in the move by his senior vice-president and comptroller, and his vice-president and chief actuary gives me a rather clear point of view. I leave yours to you.

Now, shall we return to the cold coffee and the warm conversation?

"What Does A Director Direct?"

No. 16, April 20, 1987, Page 25

Directors of corporations are a rather shadowy group of people. They inhabit a board room when in residence at the home office, and they are ceremoniously seated in overstuffed chairs, each of which may have a small bronze plaque with the director's name affixed to it. The board room is usually a company's holy of holies; no frivolous pastimes or third-echelon meetings are allowed to sully its grandeur.

Directors come in two sizes: inside directors, who are invariably the company's senior officers, and outside directors, who are either top executives of other companies or recently retired captains of industry.

What are directors supposed to do? Fortune quotes Harold Geneen, former chairman of ITT, with this somewhat rash definition:

"The board's responsibility is to sit in judgment on the management, especially on the performance of the chief executive, and to reward, punish, or replace the management as the board sees fit. That is what is supposed to happen. That is what may appear to happen. But it doesn't."

In insurance, the theoretical job of the director of a stock company is to represent the interests of the shareholders. In a mutual company, he or she looks after the policyholders' affairs.

Does this really happen? Geneen doubts it. Many others—some of whom are directors themselves—doubt it. This is especially true in the case of mutual companies. Every single policyholder has a vote, and the thought of collecting the millions of proxies necessary to overturn the slate is almost laughable. It is more likely in the case of a stock company, but even in this instance entrenched management is usually in close touch with shareholders who own a voting majority of the stock.

Am I trying to imply that most insurance companies are weakened because they aren't paying enough attention to the caliber of people they nominate for their boards? Not at all; most of them are smart enough to realize that a prestigious board helps their investment flow, their procurement of the kind of personnel they need, and their standing in the business community. But when you see a company that is going downhill, chances are it has weak outside board members who have neither the clout nor the desire to question management.

And let's not go on the blithe assumption that day-to-day management doesn't need questioning periodically. In the wildly changing insurance market of the past decade, some voice of authority has to be at hand to ask, "Are you staying abreast of things? Are you making claims that will stand the test of time? Are you trying to find out what your market thinks of you?" And so on, ad infinitum.

I have a friend who, for some time, has been an outside director of a medium-size, A+ insurance company. When we talked about his attitude toward the job he said, "I feel cloistered. I have to make my decisions on just two elements: the senior officers of the company, and the mountains of paper they send me to look over. Sometime I'd like to go to the home office on an off day and talk with some of the people I never get to see. I tried to visit an agency once but I told the home office in advance about my idea. They were so stiff when I arrived that I felt I was in a waxworks."

There's no doubt in my mind that bringing outside directors into closer contact with company employees, home office and field, is a breath of fresh air. Some companies do it now. More should. Reason: directors are beginning to understand very clearly that if they are associated with a company that is impaired or goes down the tube, they will take part of the rap. The more they know about the inside workings of a company, the more likely they are to have confidence in what it's doing and how it's performing.

The day of the director as puppet is over. They have to carry their weight with the company just as other executives do. And when they do, the company is better for it.

"Celebrities As Insurance Spokespersons"

No. 30, July 27, 1987, Page 13

Under certain circumstances, celebrities can be superior spokespersons on TV for the services of life insurance. A group of which I was a member got involved in such a project once, and the ratings surpassed our expectations.

We were involved in a series of sports broadcasts, including the old American Football League. We retained four "immortals" to speak for us: Otto Graham of the Cleveland Browns, Kyle Rote of the New York Giants, Eddie LeBaron of the Dallas Cowboys, and Bob Feller, hall-of-fame pitcher with the Cleveland Indians.

These men were anything but mere script-readers. Feller was an insurance general agent. LeBaron was a tax attorney who knew more about life insurance than most of us. Graham, a faculty member at the Coast Guard Academy, worked on his script with fellow professors. Rote brought his policies to our offices and spent a day with us making sure that his actual financial plans added up to what he proposed to say.

Smart celebrities will do this. They don't see themselves as parrots; they have to believe. At one point we were negotiating with Chet Huntley, who had just retired from the *Huntley-Brinkley Report*, about the possibility of becoming a principal spokesman for the life insurance business. He told us he would consider it only if he could take pertinent CLU courses before he spoke a word. Unhappily, he died before any final agreement could be made.

Of course, knowledge about insurance isn't the only quality needed. Feller, a farm boy from Van Meter, Iowa, pronounced "insurance" with the emphasis on the first syllable. It was like breaking a mule's back to get him to change. And Rote, who showed a picture of his family on-camera while he described his life insurance program, had the effrontery to get divorced shortly after the commercial began to air. Scratch one!

The point is that we searched studiously for well-known athletes with a logical and demonstrable belief in the product.

Today, I'm not so sure that some of the celebrities who speak for life insurance on TV—people like Lorne Greene, Dick Van Dyke, Tennessee Ernie Ford, Ed McMahon and Gavin McLeod, to name the principal ones—are of the same stripe.

To begin with, all of them talk about life insurance for senior citizens, which they aren't. Beyond that, they all say, "You cannot be turned down for any cause"—with no reference to the tiny type, "Benefits limited in the first two years." They indicate that policies will be sent on approval, but nowhere do they discuss what you get for what you pay—which, in the case of elders, can be very sparse. It seems unlikely that any of these TV heroes has ever heard of a mortality table.

Some insurance commissioners seem to be as frayed by these selling tactics as I am. The state of Washington has obtained a cease-and-desist order against some of the advertisers. And the National Association of Insurance Commissioners has appointed a task force to look into special problems caused by advertising to the elderly. Presumably, this will include the soothing statements made by Dick and Lorne and the rest about "protecting your loved ones."

The notion of being able to get life insurance in any amount is comforting to older people who could no more pass a physical examination than they could hit a home run. I will pass for the moment on the motives of the companies that are selling these policies. I'd think that the very bookkeeping problems involved in them, together with the threat of law suits, would drive the carriers crazy. Presumably the NAIC will take a sharp look at the whole mess.

If there should ever be a scapegoat in this advertising matter, I suppose it should be the companies that write the scripts and hire the stars. But I can't help feeling that a certain responsibility lies with the actors themselves. Are they willing to lend themselves to any kind of a pitch for a buck? Do they ever have the feeling that what they have just read off an idiot-card may come back to haunt them?

But then, who ever said that actors have any sense?

"Have We Lost Our Ethical Senses?"

No. 51, December 21, 1987, Page 15

Every pundit worthy of his or her hire has written at least one long, long column about the decline of American business ethics during the past couple of years. *Time* devoted a cover and 14 pages to the subject. The business magazines, sharply tuned into Wall Street, have risen in wrath and indignation about the matter. (*Fortune* has lately taken to calling it "buSINess.")

Even this reporter, who is not above faking an inside straight in stud poker, wrote a most solemn piece about ethics in one of the *National Underwriter*'s sister publications, the *Florida Underwriter* [Vol. 13, No. 11, November, 1986, page 30], quoting such literary mavens as Norman Podhoretz and Arthur Schlesinger, Jr. It reported a somewhat bleak outlook.

Since that article I have been clipping every article I could find in the press about ethical pratfalls, trying to find some common denominator that would explain them to me and, possibly, to those who read this column. I have arrived at a few hypotheses that I think are worth sharing with you:

- The bullish surge of the stock market upgraded the size of swindles from the thousands of dollars to millions and even billions. Ivan Boesky and his fellow insiders have been involved in scams that would make even a wealthy person gasp.

Wall Street has always had its insider deals, but the recent ones have been front page news in every newspaper in America. It's not so much the increased number of under-the-counter deals that are astounding as it is their size.

The recent tobogganing of the market has made such ventures much less succulent, and the fates suffered by some of the more venturesome speculators will doubtless make believers out of a lot of people whose ethics had been up for grabs.

- The press tends to get on a roll when a single problem repeats itself. Take the experiences of two of the country's most experienced airlines: Delta had two near-misses in two days. After these incidents, no Delta plane could as much as blow a tire without attracting nationwide coverage. Northwest Airlines was involved in a tragic accident. Since then the press has faithfully reported every tiny incident that has happened to its planes, even though no one seems to have been endangered. This is known as "bulldog coverage," and it can tarnish the reputation of a company or an entire business in a short time. Ethical slips have been getting the ultimate in bulldog coverage.

- A large segment of the press tends to look sourly on the "baby boom" generation that reached its majority in the '60s and now occupies a big portion of the country's management jobs. Some writers suspected them as youths in the days of Haight-Ashbury and Woodstock, and suspect them still. They are called the "me" generation. As *Fortune* said, "They want power, and if they can't get power they want at least the trappings of power." I'm not sure that I'm quite ready to lump together the bright people of an entire generation under such a generality.

- Press coverage of hard news, particularly news that might disturb readers, has changed dramatically over the past quarter-century. When John F. Kennedy was president, every reporter in Washington knew he had a roving eye. At off-the-record dinners he practically admitted as much. But reporters routinely protected him. Today, when a public figure breaches ethical standards—Gary Hart, for instance—it's front page news. There is no more protection for Washington or Wall Street, banks or insurance companies, Jim Bakker or Princess Di. Newspapers and magazines have become all seeing, all knowing and all-telling.

At this point, the economy is slowing down from several years in the fast lane, but temptations still exist everywhere. We have no accurate instrument to measure whether the situation is worse now than it was 17 or 27 years ago. Yes, insurance has had its Baldwin-United. The investment business has had E.F. Hutton and its checking accounts. Washington has had its defense contractors selling us $500 toilet seats. But are all of us obliged to take the gaff for these unholy few?

I contend that we should not. There are always worms in our apples, but only recently have we developed the microscopes to spot them. If we become disheartened, the worms will proliferate. Instead of wringing our hands, what we ought to be doing is developing a better worm medicine.

"Are You Sure You Want The President?"

No. 52, December 28, 1987, Page 13

Any organization I know would react with sheer delight to the opportunity of having the President of the United States speak before one of its meetings. I'm sure the American Council of Life Insurance did when President Reagan accepted—at the last minute, as presidents will—its invitation to speak before the opening session of its annual meeting on November 17.

But when the tumult and the shouting had died, I found myself nodding in agreement with those in the audience who were questioning whether the Great Man's appearance was really worth the disruption it caused in the meeting.

Of course, in these days of TV, Americans don't get the chance to see their President in person very much, and it's fun to be there even if he simply recites the alphabet. But the appearance of the chief executive in these days of terrorists is a complicated and highly formalized procedure, with security measures taking precedence over everything else. After all, six years before he had been shot outside a hotel just down the street from the one where the meeting took place.

After the opening ceremonies of the meeting, the ballroom was cleared and all members of the audience were sent back to their rooms from 10:00 a.m. to 11:00 a.m. while members of the Secret Service swept the room, accompanied by bomb-sniffing dogs. Enough TV equipment was put in place to run a modest-sized network. At 11:00 a.m. the audience returned, walking single-file through mental [sic] detectors. Every White House correspondent you ever heard of was on hand because the press secretary had hinted that it might be a major speech and that no advance manuscript was available.

Unhappily, it was no such thing. President Reagan spoke amiably for about half an hour, reviewing his disagreements with the Congress, predicting a bright future for America (if the Congress would mind its p's and q's, of course) and telling a few jokes that every alert citizen had heard him tell before. Sam Donaldson seemed to be asleep.

When he had finished, the audience was rooted to its seats in the ballroom until the presidential party was off and away—a major undertaking in itself, since it seemed that half the White House must have been in attendance.

If the President had done either of two things his appearance would have been a ten-strike for ACLI: if he had made a major speech it would certainly have occupied considerable time on the networks that night, but he chose not to do so. Or, he might have talked about his attitudes towards the financial community, which certainly would have attracted attention, but he limited his thoughts on this subject to a couple of inoffensive sentences. Either approach would have spotlighted the meeting but, as it was, the media practically ignored it.

However, I don't need to be reminded that one is wise not to try to tell a president what to say.

On many occasions I have noticed that a talk by an individual who is squarely in the public eye can be a disappointment, even though the thrill of being in an audience listening to such a personality can be worth the price of admission alone. Often these worthy people aren't quite sure about the composition of their audiences, and they can wander pretty far afield.

ACLI was considerably more on target with other Washingtonians who contributed substantially to the success of the meeting and were clearly aware of the interests of the executives sitting before them. I was most impressed by Sen. Daniel Patrick Moynihan (D, NY), who spoke knowledgeably about health care for the elderly. Pat Moynihan is an eccentric speaker, whose explosive rhetoric fairly bounces off the walls, but his points of view come through loud and clear.

President Reagan was great for panoply, and for the importance he conferred on the meeting. But for thoughts to take home on matters of substance, I prefer those who are working directly with the issues.

"The Future Of Direct Response Advertising"

No. 6, February 8, 1988, Page 13

There is a large body of Americans—how big has never been measured—who have an aversion to salespeople bordering on fear. They collect catalogues of every possible description as though they were bubble gum cards; they spend long hours before the Shoppers' Sprees on their cable set and buy something every day; and they search for their insurance via TV commercials and direct-mail solicitations from companies they may never have heard about. They adore supermarkets because no one asks them to buy anything and they can whisk through the checkout line without being recognized. Most of their clothing, whether it fits or not, comes from such direct-mail giants as John Blair and Haband's. They can go for an entire year without being forced to make a buying decision in the presence of a salesperson.

In these days, when most people are carrying around a little paranoia inside them, sales-phobia is probably just as normal as fear of heights or dislike of the number 13. But how did they get that way? Were they bitten by A.L. Williams as children? Did they put all their dough in Baldwin-United?

Chances are neither is true. They probably fear salespeople because they might get talked into something they need. As direct responders they can choose exactly what they want and no one is going to argue them into anything else.

In other words, they are dumb. They believe they know more than any of their contemporaries, and they aren't about to be put off by anyone who is an expert. The direct-responder simply distrusts his fellow man. He takes more credence in advertising, which has presumably been written by a good salesperson, than he does in the salesperson himself—and he hasn't the wisdom to see the anomaly. He can't ask any questions when he buys in his direct-response mode except, possibly, when he is given an 800 number to call. When he calls it, who does he think he's talking to? God?

There is obviously nothing wrong about informing consumers about a product through advertising. Some—detergents, diamonds or drills, for example—are so essentially simple that person-to-person selling is necessary only to verify the warranties made by the seller. Most advertising—autos, home furnishings and liquor, to name just three major categories—is designed merely to bring the consumer into the salesroom or store. But insurance—particularly life and health insurance—is different because it needs to be tailored to the prospect in exactly the same way a dinner jacket or an evening gown is tailored.

Tucked away somewhere in most direct-response advertising is the phrase "No agent will call," as though the absence of sound advice were an added inducement to buy. Well, if the customer knows precisely what product he wants and has done his own price comparisons, direct-response is probably his bag. But how many people can say that they are absolutely sure that what they are buying will fit into their master financial plans at the appropriate cost to them? I don't know many, and I think my friends are typical of middle class America. (For those of you who don't fit that description, my apologies.)

Direct-response people, particularly insurers, like to hint that the absence of a salesperson invariably results in a lower price. Cost comparisons made by independent organizations don't necessarily agree with this concept. Other expenses, like advertising and verification of insurability, tend to take up the slack. If the price were indeed lower, direct writers would fill the media full of statistics proving it. Have you seen any lately?

There is undoubtedly a market for direct-response advertising and direct writers. I described the members of it in the opening paragraphs of this piece. Some consider themselves intellectuals, while others are just plain know-it-alls. Because they exist, they are entitled to the kind of service they want. As far as I'm concerned, the direct-response people can have them.

"Anybody Want A Mental Detector?"

No. 16, April 18, 1988, Page 21

Most writers for periodicals lie awake nights wondering whether anyone reads their stuff. Authors of books don't have this worry; either the royalty checks come in or they don't. Only when a massive blooper occurs does a columnist like me find out if he has any readers.

In the last issue of the *National Underwriter* for 1987 I described some of the travails an organization goes through when it invites the President of the United States to address it. In this case it was the American Council of Life Insurance, an organization of august CEOs. One sentence read, "At 11:00 a.m. the audience returned, walking single-file through mental detectors."

Yes, it said "mental detectors." In the manuscript I had very carefully written "metal detectors," and I can prove it. But the gremlins that infest printing operations dropped in an added "n" just for fun.

Well, this innocent error brought out the comedian in some fifty *National Underwriter* subscribers. Even before the issue had reached me I had received 'phone calls from Pat Taylor of the New York City Life Underwriters wondering if I was trying to tell them something about the President. Then the letters began to pour in. Some typical examples:

- From Jack Burbidge, vice-president of IDS Life: "We assume nothing significant was found."

- From Lillian Landry, superintendent of disability income product marketing for Mass Mutual (with what I think was just a touch of sarcasm): "Don Barnes has been around for quite a while. He tells it like it is and doesn't hold back."

- From Gordon Rose, manager of annual giving for the American College: "If you were accurate in your reporting, Don, it would have taken the rest of your article to explain how so many got through! Maybe it is an idea whose time has come—maybe we could save millions of dollars on CLU exams and just run people through mental detectors and certify them. A whole new era!"

And even the executive editor of this sainted publication, who might have been expected to show a little compassion, felt constrained to comment on the blooper in an editorial, blaming it on "our columnist." As a naive old writer, I always thought the buck stopped with the top man. Live and learn.

Anyhow, the whole episode made me realize that there are some fine, upstanding insurance people who proofread my pieces elegantly. Sleeping at night is a lot easier.

It's probably true that most people don't understand how a line of type goes from my typewriter to your copy, and how many people handle it. It usually proceeds from me—on an island off deepest Florida—to Hoboken, then to Chicago, then to Cincinnati and finally to you. It is treated with tender loving care, but as Executive Editor Diamond said so succinctly, "Despite what you may think, the *National Underwriter* isn't always perfect."

Another example: in a more recent article I was describing the functions of the five major institutional organizations run by chief executives, in an examination of whether they were all necessary ["Are All Those Company Associations Necessary?", No. 7, February 15, 1987]. That same gremlin popped up again and dropped out of the article my one-line description of Life Insurers Conference: "LIC is composed of companies engaged to a large extent in the sale of home service life insurance." It was important to the story, so I cite the omission here, with appropriate apologies to the Conference members.

Yes, they reminded me of the dropped paragraph.

So if you come upon any more bloopers in my columns, remember two things: I have been making them all my life, so be charitable; and even more importantly, it probably wasn't my fault anyway. Do write and tell me about it.

"ACLI's 'Catastrophic Error' Reviewed"

No. 28, July 11, 1988, Page 17

When the American Council of Life Insurance fired or early retired 21 members of its public relations staff on June 1, it undertook to follow journalistic custom by not making a large noise about it. But the bloodbath was too big to escape public notice, and the *National Underwriter* caught up with the story.

As an officer of the public relations arm of the life insurance business for 25 years before my retirement, I reacted predictably with a special column in the June 13 issue of the *National Underwriter* ["ACLI's 'Catastrophic Error'", No. 24, June 13, 1988]. I had gone to considerable effort to get all of the facts, but since the very "spokesmen" one tries to reach in such a situation either had gotten the axe or seen their closest associates get it, there was an obvious reluctance to talk. So I went with the facts I had, although all of us at the *National Underwriter* agreed that no purpose would be served in naming those who had been dismissed.

It was a column full of fire and brimstone, and I'm glad I wrote it. It expressed clearly my belief that the life and health insurance business needs a public information function today more than any time in its history, and I buttressed my opinion with a copious quote from John Creedon, CEO of the Metropolitan Life.

The phone calls and mail I have received since the column appeared have been almost totally supportive. One criticism I have received is, "Why did you lay it all at the feet of Dick Schweiker, the Council's president and CEO?" He not only sits where the buck stops, but he has a broader view of the missions of the Council than any individual volunteer director. I reasoned that if he felt the board was doing ACLI a disservice, his arguments would have impressive weight.

However, there were a couple of things I did not know, and no one told me:

- ACLI changed its "mission"—by that I assume it means its articles of incorporation—in March to downgrade its role in public relations. It never bothered to tell the public of this. A board that changes its organization's purpose and doesn't say so certainly doesn't have much to do with public relations. This action obviously spiked Dick Schweiker's guns at the June 1 meeting.

- The Health Insurance Association of America, which had operated its public relations for years on a joint basis with ACLI, decided to pull itself and its people out of the arrangement. While the *National Underwriter* reported this, no one mentioned the fact that 11 of the 21 reductions in force consisted of people who worked full-or part-time on HIAA projects.

HIAA and its president, Carl Schramm, had good reason for the pullout: health insurance problems were getting bigger and they didn't involve life insurance issues. Better for the organization to go its own way than for it to be a major contributor to snatching life insurance chestnuts out of the fire. This action by an ally left Dick Schweiker with a fistful of useless cards, however he might choose to play them.

So I will withdraw my allegation that the decapitation of the industry's public relations function should be blamed on him, and I apologize to him for having said so in a loud voice. I hope he will give us guidance in time about what organization should handle the massive consumer relations problems of life insurance.

This leaves the board of directors of ACLI. Consumer relations has never been a serious concern of most chief executive officers. They hire people for that, and it is always nearly impossible to measure what those people do. Lobbyists can push a bill though or get it beaten—a concrete achievement.

Communicators have never acquired sufficient substance within the companies; This is a litany of the CEO. How far will deterioration of public attitudes have to go before management will pay attention? Despite its best efforts, the field force can't do it all.

If you don't understand what I mean, you must be a member of the ACLI board who voted for demolition of the central source of information.

"Another Shot At The Coach"

No. 30, July 25, 1988, Page 27

Last year, the National Association of Life Underwriters took the unprecedented step of producing a video cassette about one of its most hated enemies, A.L. ("Coach") Williams, whose replacement antics have upset the life insurance business mightily. Called *Rhetoric vs. Reality*, the 45-minute film was designed to expose to the field force Williams' tactics and methods of doing business.

Apparently the cassette was a success, because at the recent meeting of the Million Dollar Round Table NALU unveiled a 15-minute cassette *What've You Got To Lose?*, this time explaining The Coach and his minions to the consumer.

While both films were produced by John Phillips, an NALU staffer of considerable talent, the spark behind them was provided by Alan Press, NALU's current president-elect and, along with Professor Joe Belth, the industry's most notorious Williams-basher.

However, in *What've You Got To Lose?* Alan has relegated himself to a supporting role, relinquishing the lead to Jim Hunt, former commissioner of insurance and banking for Vermont and now executive vice-president of the National Insurance Consumers Organization. A Fellow of the Society of Actuaries, he has impeccable credentials for talking about the uses and abuses of life insurance. While NICO has sometimes been a hair shirt to the life insurance community, on the matter of the Williams organization and its attitude toward term insurance it stands foursquare with the National Association of Life Underwriters.

In a quiet voice Hunt recommends annual renewable term as opposed to the A.L. Williams' notion of 20-year term "and invest the difference." Hunt is strongly antireplacement, and he advises viewers to "stay away from A.L. Williams." Other types of life insurance are not a significant factor in the discussion.

NALU buttresses Jim Hunt's statements with quotes from *Business Week, Consumer Reports* and the financial writer, Andrew Tobias, all of which take a highly dubious view of the Williams sales approach. The film also shows The Coach himself in action, calling all agents except his own "dad-gum scum."

(Williams has the disconcerting habit of inserting the word "Right?!" three or four times in every sentence of a speech to his agents. I couldn't figure out whether he is asking a question or asking for applause.)

The film also undertakes to illustrate that Williams' policies (issued principally through Massachusetts Indemnity and Life) are not as "low cost" as he says. In the cassette I saw, the comparison was made with the Guardian Life, which happens to be Alan Press's company and is probably a good generic example. However, I understand that any individual company willing to pay the price can have this segment of the film altered to drop Guardian and include its own precise comparisons. This is an obvious necessity, since many agents would hesitate to have only Guardian figures seen in contrast to MILICO's.

The visuals in the film are more than adequate: people are shown taking chances on everything from three-card monte to vending machines that already have "out of order" signs on them, and other examples of stupid risk-taking that are equated, by implication, with The Coach's claims. There is even the obligatory shot of an agent at a kitchen table, explaining his program to two adults and two fascinated children, which actually may have happened at sometime or another in the history of the agency system.

The superior thing NALU has done has been to take several people and publications having considerable prestige, wrap them into a package, throw them broadside at the consumer and ask, "Who do you believe?"

It is a technique that has to be used carefully and sparingly. Any audiovisual device that is used to hurl bombs at a specific target had better be accurate and shatterproof. Fortunately, NALU has a legal department that is well-versed in dealing with precisely this kind of issue, and I will go with General Counsel Jim Douds and his staff all the way.

The best way to find out more is to call NALU at 1-800-247-4074. It may just save you hours of wheelspinning with clients and prospects about The Coach.

"Strength When It Was Needed"

No. 43, October 24, 1988, Page 27

It takes an exceedingly strong association executive and his board of directors to reverse a course of action that may have been embarked on with too much haste.

That is why my profound congratulations go out to Richard S. Schweiker, president of the American Council of Life Insurance, and his board for reconsidering their position to partially abandon ACLI's role as spokesman for the insurance business. My faithful readers (who numbered 17 at the last body count) may recall that since June I have been criticizing ACLI for taking a step that was obviously motivated by a tight budget and the fact that it is well-nigh impossible to measure the precise effectiveness of public relations and public education. I was by no means alone—many people who have the full respect of the business felt the same way, and said so. I just opened my mouth the widest.

The board's willingness to reconstitute its public affairs policy committee and to give it at least three missions that will enable the business to compile an accurate assessment of where it stands in the public marketplace is certainly broad-gauged. When it has in hand the results that will accrue from the actions it has authorized, it will have a clear idea of just how far into the public communications field it can afford to go.

It will start with two in-depth analyses: one to determine how much of the negative image of the life insurance business is caused by the rub-off of poor public perception of the property-casualty business; the other to search for possible causes of poor public perception emanating from aspects of performance by the life insurance business itself. This will evolve into a strategy and plan of action to improve the understanding of the life insurance business among its target publics.

No one could ask for more. Whatever research is done will undoubtedly be keyed to the surveys conducted by Daniel Yankelovich 20 years ago, and this should give the business leadership a clear view of the swings in public acceptance over a period of time.

The ultimate judgment, of course, will be how much ACLI can afford to spend to correct the deficiencies revealed by its analyses.

Few people clearly comprehend the amount it costs to correct misapprehensions about a company, an industry, or a product. Possibly the most interesting case in our generation was that of Tylenol, a product of Johnson and Johnson. When the corporation found that weird people were lacing Tylenol capsules with cyanide, it had two choices: kill Tylenol and start a completely different product, or make such changes that would assure a safe capsule and continue to use the name. It did the latter, because it had a huge investment in the name. It cost J & J something like $200 million to keep the product afloat, but it managed to do so.

Life insurance companies don't have that kind of money. But they can go after target audiences at a fraction of that sum and make a strong impact on the people most important to them. The phrase "thought leader" has fallen into disrepute because it has some unfortunate connotations, but there certainly is a measurable group of people in America whose opinions are listened to and respected. If ACLI can reach them, they have a chance to correct some of the misconception that may be revealed by research.

The fact that the Congress of the United States has become an ideological battleground has caused many businesses and industries to revise their budgets and pour more funds into mechanisms like political action committees. But the voter back home still has incalculable power, and to ignore such people is to court disaster—both for the legislator and for all of the industries keenly interested in specific legislation.

No one should expect miracles out of what ACLI is proposing to do. The key fact is that the organization is going to take action in the field of public information. We can only wish it the best of luck—together with the skill it always has had.

"Not A Very Happy New Year"

No. 50, December 12, 1988, Page 17

Two phrases echoed like thunder at every institutional meeting I attended in the fall of 1988, whether it was a meeting of agents or home office people:

- "Produce more!"
- "Cut costs!"

The exclamation points were most assuredly placed there by the speakers, not by me.

Even the sleepiest company, even the rawest recruit, knows that the life insurance business has arrived at the point where the mindless repetition of giving the public what executives and agents think it ought to want has become outmoded and extremely dangerous.

The first warnings of all this came in 1980 when interest rate sensitive products, like universal life and variable life, began to catch the public fancy. The companies responded wholeheartedly, and as long as interest rates stayed high they gave their customers products that went far beyond their wildest dreams ten years before that time.

But when interest rates retreated, many companies didn't. With computers able to quote the going rates of almost every company, they squeezed every nickel to stay at the top of the heap. Agents, with considerable assistance from their home offices, used illustrations and projections that were tinged with madness.

All this recitation would be kid stuff, of course, if both company and field hadn't found themselves riding a tiger that they can't get off. Now some are teetering on the brink of insolvency, and they are responding by firing at the home office level and turning over to their agency forces services that they no longer choose to perform.

That makes today the winter of our discontent. What can the home offices and their agents do to restore some semblance of normality to the situation?

- Of course, the cries for greater productivity and cost-cutting are the most obvious. Boards of directors must be more alert, particularly outside board members who tend to take a more pragmatic view of company operations. This is particularly true of mutual companies, which have no stockholder surge to back up critical board actions.

- Interest rate projections, dividend scales and home office underwriting must undergo a cynical review. Alert companies are already far along the road in these three areas, but some are still allowing the tail to wag the dog until they face a cataclysm.

- Use of computer capabilities will have to be increased measurably, both in home office and field. The miracle of computerization has been only partially exploited by companies, particularly in their relationships with their agents. While they may have to curtail personal service to the field force, opening up computer communications may offset this somewhat.

- Companies must determine what they and their agents can do best and not try to be all things to all people. Many have moved into areas, like group health insurance, that have not proved profitable in the end. Big egos hate to admit failure, but smart egos look to the bottom line.

- Beating on agents by companies is a practice that has to stop. "Produce more!" is a great slogan, but unless it's accompanied with a distribution of tools to make this happen it's not a realistic rallying cry. Yes, some companies have put together exorbitant commission scales in order to attract business, and they may have to cut back. Companies with full-time field forces ("those precious few") need to share their problems down to the last detail with their agents.

- Whole life insurance is still the money tree for most mature companies. Efforts to create subsidiary money bushes don't seem to have prevailed. Jack Bobo, executive head of NALU, may have sounded the clarion call at his recent convention when he said, "Back to basics (is) our own version of back to the future."

Getting off the tiger may seem to be a risky job, but it may be preferable to riding into oblivion. Happy New Year!

"Is There Public Relations In Our Future?"

No. 8, February 20, 1989, Page 13

A little history for those of you who tuned in late:

Last June 1 the American Council of Life Insurance, which had been the central source of information for the life insurance business for 50 years, said it was reducing its public relations function, and fired or retired 21 staffers. Business reaction to this step was immediate, including a couple of rather agonized columns from me. I contended that the leaders of the business were dumping an important investment in public trust they and their predecessors had made over time, and that they were short-sighted to do so.

In September I had a long and cheerful talk with Dick Schweiker, president of ACLI, in which he told me that the organization was completely reexamining its position to partially dismantle its public relations and public education activities. I reported this to *National Underwriter* readers in the October 3 issue.

In the November elections, California voters shocked the nation by passing, by a bare majority, Proposition 103, which gave the state enormous powers to set insurance premiums and regulated the business in a variety of new ways. While lobbyists poured millions of dollars into the state in an effort to show the ridiculous nature of the proposition, the voters' discomfort with property and casualty rates—particularly in auto insurance premiums—carried the day. The life insurance business was swept along with the tide.

This showed a good many life insurance people that you can't educate the public on an ad hoc basis; that is, you can't wait until the fire of ignorance burns brightly and then put it out quickly with a few buckets of water of understanding. But I didn't feel that an "I told you so" preachment about the virtues of constant and continuing public education was appropriate at that time, so I held my tongue and turned off my typewriter. But now it's five months since ACLI's announcement that it was reexamining its public relations position. What's happening? I asked Rob Bier, managing director of communications for the Council, how things are coming along. Here are some of the actions he cited to me:

- The public relations policy committee has been reconstituted and is meeting. It is composed of 13 senior officers, mostly CEOs, and is headed by Clair E. Strommen, chairman of Lutheran Brotherhood. It has appointed some subcommittees that are working closely with staff to implement a board-approved plan of action to improve the perception of the life insurance business among key audiences.

- The ACLI board has received an analysis of existing research data culled from various sources. This review presented evidence that public belief in the fairness of life insurance pricing goes down as property/casualty prices go up. Other research is ongoing, most of it being done by the Council's research staff.

- Grey Advertising, ACLI's longtime agency, is back on the job and in on the action, but no advertising plans have been announced.

- There have been no staff increases anywhere at ACLI since the June firings or Schweiker's October 3 announcement about the "reconstitution" of the public relations function.

Most of these are optimistic moves, designed to define the problems first and then set about solving them. If they seem a mite tentative, it is probably because the board and the staff are busy reinventing the wheel of public education and information. Most of the staff from the old Institute of Life Insurance are now long gone, and the situation is vastly different now from what it was on the day ILI became a unit of ACLI.

There is little doubt that the Proposition 103 debacle jolted even the most insensitive insurance executive into an awareness of the need for continuing public education. Yes, it's costly, but nowhere near as costly as putting down the threat of little Prop. 103s in every state in the union, a definite possibility if the California measure survives the legal attacks that are now being made on it.

I will continue to sit on the doorstep of ACLI and report every action it deems newsworthy. Rob Bier has promised me full access to the facts.

"Is There Life Outside The Beltway?"

No. 21, May 22, 1989, Page 13

The Beltway is a series of roads circling Washington, D.C., built for motorists who choose not to be mugged or murdered by penetrating the city itself. Inside the Beltway is, in the minds of Washingtonians (most of whom live outside it), Where It's At, at least during working hours. If you're anywhere else in this broad land, you're just camping out.

The new advertising campaign of the American Council of Life Insurance, announced in the *National Underwriter* for April 24, as well as other trade publications, is strictly an inside-the-Beltway production. It appears in 12 magazines and two newspapers, most of which you never heard of. All but two of these have most of their circulation inside the Beltway, a fact made possible by the regional editions of the major newsweeklies.

(While Washingtonians will be able to see the ACLI message in *Time, Newsweek* and *U.S. News & World Report*, if you live in New York, Chicago, or Los Angeles that space will be taken over by other advertisers.)

It is a thoughtful campaign about "The Great State of Security"—life insurance—"that isn't anywhere. . .it's everywhere." It describes the impact of life insurance on the nation and its citizens, and it is, frankly, designed "to help Congress better understand the unique contribution life insurance makes to our society." Its total cost, which also includes 100 sixty-second radio commercials, all in the Washington area, is just under $400,000.

It's encouraging that the great institution of life insurance is once again speaking out on behalf of itself and its policyholders. It's not quite so encouraging that the same institution can afford to spend only about one-tenth of the amount it put into its annual media campaigns in the mid-1960s.

But only a person who has been living in a cave for the past 25 years will fail to understand that times have changed violently: the margins for media spending are simply not there anymore. The companies have cut their rates and gone into interest-sensitive products to the degree that makes you wonder where they found the money for this simplistic, one-advertisement, two-insertion message.

One could see this coming more than a year ago when ACLI altered its mission statement to drastically upgrade its legislative contacts and downgrade its communications with the public. As a former colleague of mine who attended the last annual meeting of ACLI said to me after he returned home, "I felt as if I had attended a meeting of lobbyists."

His feeling was probably right. The relationships between the life insurance business and Congress have never been so tense and intense. Many members of Congress look upon life insurance as a potential money source, and the business, like a great football team, must have superb offensive and defensive units to keep from getting beaten to a pulp. That costs money.

Sometimes when I have advocated opening fuller lines of communications with the public, I have felt that I was asking the coach to spend more money on the cheerleaders. But then I regain my balance when I think clearly about who elects these congressmen.

Happily, ACLI has developed a "communications program kit" that will enable its member companies to redouble their relationships with the publics that it can't afford to reach itself. This is a chancy thing, since it depends wholly on the enthusiasms of the various companies, but it is a far cry from doing nothing.

Life insurance has become the only business I know that doesn't have a high-powered central source of information explaining its actions to the public. In the competitive frenzy of the past decade, it has reduced its margins to the point where it is just too poor to afford one. Planning has been in the hands of those who say, "Be competitive." Those who have pleaded, "Be understood," seem to have been sent to the minor leagues.

Note: if these remarks sound like the musings of a person who spent his life trying to help people understand the many intricacies of life insurance, you are absolutely right.

"What Exactly Is A Board Of Directors?"

No. 12, March 19, 1990, Page 19

I am reliably informed that every self-respecting corporation in the world must have its board of directors. Sometimes they have fancy names like The Supreme Soviet, but they are really directors.

They come in two flavors: one, called "inside directors," inhabits the home office and commands the troops. The others, called "outside directors," have made their marks in some other business and condescend to advise the inside directors on what they appear to be doing right or wrong. That is the theory. The fact is that the inside directors nominate the outside directors, who are always people they respect, not to say revere. On rare occasions stockholders (or, in the case of mutual insurance companies, policyholders) rise in their petulance or wrath and manage to elect directors of their own. If the ancient gods had heard of directorships, one of the twelve labors of Hercules would certainly have been to get an opposition slate elected to the board of the Olympus Life. Cleaning up the Augean Stables would have been a comparative breeze.

Peter Drucker, who probably knows as much about American business as any writer, calls the typical corporate board "an impotent ceremonial and legal fiction." There is much to support his point of view.

Executives of many life insurance companies are now lashing themselves about the mistakes in judgment that they made during the '80s. Isn't cronyism one of the possible answers? "I'll serve on your board if you'll serve on mine." How deeply do the committees that nominate board members probe into the actual expertise the nominee may bring to the board's deliberations? Or is he or she simply a good old boy or girl who has kept a chain of retail stores or a communications company in the black for a reasonable number of years?

Quite naturally, management isn't likely to suggest nominees who will go after their hides. There's the rub. When Ralph Nader becomes a director of General Motors I may have to beat a retreat, but I don't see the possibility on the drawing board.

Some legislatures have tried to devise regulations that would discourage cronyism, but that's an almost impossible chore. When a person with impeccable credentials is asked to join the board of an organization with an unblemished reputation for honesty, who can throw the first stone? And so it goes.

My notion is that management should seriously consider bringing on its board one or more persons who, if we were in Great Britain, would be called

Her Majesty's Loyal Opposition. Not a person who is against everything or throws tantrums on cue, but a questioner who knows something about insurance and finance and isn't averse to standing up to the man at the head of the table. It's a risky business, but it might cause some boards to question the omnipotence of inside management. An interested policyholder who is knowledgeable about finance, for instance? Or (and you may put your hands over your eyes if you can't stand strong language) an agent?

Only once in recent years have I seen a director stand up against the hierarchy, and he won. We needn't go into the details, but it proved to me that a person who has his facts in a row will get the attention of the board, if not always its concurrence.

When I think of Drucker's characterization of a board as a "fiction," I have to ask myself, "What's the alternative?" Shall we allow the fox to build a condominium in the chicken coop, or shall we allow government to appoint people who will breathe heavily over our shoulders? No, I believe the only answer is to spread the gospel that the board of directors need not be a rubber stamp but rather a force for improving the company. The courts have begun to tell them so. Some states have told them so, and more are likely to.

The American Bar Association, in its Corporate Director's Guidebook, says "A board's responsibility is to represent the interests of the shareholders as a group. . . in directing the affairs of the corporation within the law."

This obviously doesn't include toadying to the inside directors or being a mindless "aye" sayer.

"'Proliferation' Can Be An Ugly Word"

No. 13, March 26, 1990, Page 13

"Proliferation" was devised as a kind and gentle word. It means simply to grow or produce by multiplication of parts, as in budding or cell division. Presumably that also includes pregnancy, which should make us all more or less happy that it was invented.

But organizational proliferation isn't as kindly, and its effects can be wide-ranging and often ugly. We seem to be going through a spate of it in insurance these days, and I have some reservations about the whole thing.

Let me give you just two of the most recent examples:

- The people who sell life insurance and those who sell health insurance just can't get together, despite the perfectly obvious fact that most of them sell both. Having failed in its attempts to reach some accommodation with the National Association of Health Underwriters, the National Association of Life Underwriters has announced the formation of some form of health insurance conference (similar to its general agents and managers and advanced life underwriters organizations) with its own board of trustees and administrative staff.

- At almost the same time, NAHU revealed its Registered Employee Benefit Consultant (REBEC) professional designation program, which expands its Registered Health Underwriter (RHU) designation program. This appears to ignore the fact that the American College, a sound and accredited educational organization for insurance people, is in existence.

There has got to be some form of almost sublime stubbornness in these kinds of actions, and I'm at a loss to see what its source is. NALU, with 140,000 members, could eat NAHU, with some 10,000, for lunch. But now we will have two organizations plus another professional designation to deal with. Plus parallel executive staffs.

Presumably, no one would object to this kind of proliferation if it was all free. But it's not. The very executive staff I just mentioned, plus their housing, will be in the six figure range. And somebody (including you, your fellow field people and the home offices that take an interest in such projects) is going to have to foot the bill. I have heard it said that people who are sufficiently enthusiastic about the issues, and feel that they have the solutions in hand, will gladly pay the tab. Nonsense! In the long run will two organizations who have the same goals avoid speaking with one another? Will two groups who offer similar, carefully considered designations, go their own ways? You answer the questions—I hope I don't have to.

If the above illustrations seem to be taking a tough shot at the people who sell health insurance, they weren't meant to be. They are by no means alone because there is proliferation everywhere today, and a lot of it is costly and counterproductive. For example: I am a total enthusiast for PACE, the continuing education program of the American College. But I'm not so happy about the endless circus of closed-circuit television seminars that the CLU and GAMC people are offering to earn PACE and other credits. They are expensive to the viewer, and there is no way to have interchange between the speakers, who are presumably located somewhere in Heaven, and the earthlings who are listening to them. As one past president of MDRT said to me, "The closer I can get to one-on-one, the better I like it."

Education used to be available without reaching out to the superstars, who appear on the TV shows—presumably at some expense to the sponsors—to attract a crowd. I have been at state sales congresses that would blow some of the TV epics apart.

It is, as everything in life insurance is today, a matter of money. Neither agents nor their companies can afford more proliferation. What is called for is an all-industry committee to determine what's needed in institutional areas, and then to enforce its dictums. If this isn't done, let the two of us start our own association, possibly with a building in Washington.

"NALU—The Giant Stops Being Gentle"

No. 15, April 9, 1990, Page 11

If there is one flaw in the remarkable centennial history of the National Association of Life Underwriters, entitled *Voices from the Field* and reviewed in this column on September 11, 1989, it is that NALU is depicted as always having been a strong force in the inner councils of the life insurance business.

In its early days, the major companies paid little attention to it because it hadn't earned its wings and there were fears that it might become an abrasive new element to deal with.

Slowly, the major companies began to pay it tribute, but in the manner of a kindly uncle patting a small nephew on the head. While it was a vital force in improving the caliber of agents, its clout in helping put forward major issues was sporadic and sometimes ineffectual.

Just before the beginning of World War II it did begin to acquire real muscles and flex them. Since then it has grown stronger every year, and today it is an 800-pound gorilla that everyone listens to very, very carefully. But it has been a benign gorilla, working amicably and carefully with its fellow gorillas from the other major institutional organizations, as well as the companies. It has practically never raised its voice; it is a patient beast.

In my mind—and I have been watching carefully all this time—two major moves have caused this growth. The first, and by all odds the most important, has been the development of an immensely talented headquarters staff that grows more potent every year. No dues-paying member of NALU should discount this because the officers and trustees, who are volunteers, have their own fish to fry, and should be allowed to limit themselves to policymaking decisions, not day-to-day work. The staff, whose members seem to work around the clock, lays the groundwork and drafts policy. And it seems to be good policy.

The second has been the establishment of the Life Underwriters Political Action Committee, which has injected NALU into the very heart of governmental decisions. Whether or not you like the idea of PACs, as long as they have a part in our political scheme they should be used to the utmost, and NALU is doing just that. It is the most powerful PAC in life insurance, and that grants NALU a chair in every inner circle.

Over time NALU created the CLU movement and the Million Dollar Round Table, both of which grew powerful enough in their own right to become independent, although they still maintain strong ties with the Mother Church. NALU still has under its wing the General Agents and Managers Conference and the Association for Advanced Life Underwriting, both of which benefit from being housed with NALU, and bring it considerable clout. To say nothing of the Life Underwriter Training Council, which will also leave the nest and go out on its own, but which will probably never totally sever its umbilical cord with NALU.

Now NALU has lost patience with one of its sister organizations, and proposes to invade its turf. As has been reported here, the other group is the National Association of Health Underwriters. I see nothing wrong with this invasion, if only for one reason: NAHU has something less than 10,000 members, most of whom sell life insurance; NALU has 140,000 members, most of whom have health insurance programs in their portfolios.

With the immense concern about health care—short-term, long-term, catastrophic or what have you—it is time to roll out the big guns, and that seems to be what is happening throughout the business.

This is no time to protect turf; let's forget that nonsense until some rational plans for health care come down the pike. Everyone knows it will be a difficult job to somehow meld the private and the public sectors, but it has to be done. Let NALU develop its conference on health insurance and employee benefits; let NAHU be as supportive as it wishes; let the Health Insurance Association of America and the American Council of Life Insurance get their artillery on the line.

Let's just not quibble.

"'Look, Everybody's Out Of Step But Johnny'"

No. 25, June 18, 1990, Page 17

OK, people. I guess I'm Johnny.

I have just finished my fourth rereading of a seven-page article in the April 23 *Newsweek*, written by Steven Waldman, with a long sidebar by the redoubtable Jane Bryant Quinn. It is entitled "The Insurance Mess."

In Waldman's five pages of acerbic criticism, barely a paragraph refers to life insurance. Quinn's sidebar devotes two columns to the life insurance industry, mostly dealing with two of her favorite crusades: the usefulness of term insurance for most families, and the manipulative use of "illustrations" by salespeople.

The entire remainder of the piece focuses on auto insurance, property and casualty insurance of various kinds, and health insurance. Part of it details the helplessness that property and casualty people and health insurers feel about the cards that have been dealt them, including ridiculous claims and uninformed legislators. A few paragraphs try to illustrate the "greed" of insurers. It attempts to be balanced in its discussions, but the title word—"Mess"—permeates the article.

Very well—here's "out-of-step Johnny."

For some time now I have been bringing up the possibility of the life insurance business undertaking to illustrate its singularity: the fact that it is less expensive and offers more options today than any time in its history, that its professional salespeople are better trained and more up-to-date in their thinking than they have ever been, and that the business is rock-solid—even if it takes state guaranty organizations to keep it so in the face of get-rich-quick artists.

Every time I express this point of view, my conservative friends slap either my wrist or a more tender part of my anatomy. They say to me, "Insurance has become a generic word. You can't separate wind storm or auto insurance from life insurance. The public simply won't understand what you're getting at."

If an effort had been made to prove that my contention is worthless, and it proved to be so, I would retreat to my little grass shack and start whacking away at more obvious evils. But I suggest that in recent years no such attempt has been made. Companies that advertise low costs today are doing so at the expense of other life companies, not with a broad look at the economy in general.

The last thing I would recommend is an invidious comparison with other forms of insurance. If a person stands tall, he has a right to say so. He need not say, "Everyone else is short." He might accidentally find someone who is taller than he is.

I'm totally unhappy with advertising that casts aspersions, but today it is all the rage. Company A says, "A cures your burps twice as fast as B." Company B says, "B cures your burps just as fast as A, and has no side effects. So there!" To my thinking, messages like these leave the public confused, unsure of what it ought to buy, and desperately seeking a product C that simply sells itself for what it is. That's all I ask.

One of the sections in *Newsweek*'s long article is entitled, "Why Rates Go Up." It goes on for nearly a page and there isn't a single sentence in it about life insurance. Yet one of its illustrations shows a pig, its mouth full of money, labeled "INSURANCE COMPANIES," under the caption "Never Has Enough!"

We could, I suppose, blame our forebears for the generic approach. When insurance became popular in the 1840s, many companies undertook to cover all kinds of risks. Separating the various species never occurred to them. And even today, of course, multiple-line companies are everywhere, and easily annoyed.

I still believe that the life insurance companies, without denigrating other types of insurance in the slightest bit, should give it a spin. They have much to be proud about. To be swept up in the whirlwind of California' Prop. 103 should never have happened. But it will occur again and again in other states unless life insurance shows its trumps.

Is there anything wrong with declaring you are part of a business that is better than it ever has been?

"Will We Be Condemned To Repeat It"

No. 8, February 25, 1991, Page 15

George Santayana's dictum, "Those who cannot remember the past are condemned to repeat it" always lies in the forefront of my mind, particularly when I think of the insurance business over the last 15 years. How many mistakes were made, and how many remembered?

As every schoolchild knows, the entire insurance business got caught on the horns of an enormous dilemma during those years: whether to maintain its innate conservatism or to plunge forward into untrodden ways. As long as the stock market was bullish and interest rates were rising beyond belief, the temptation on the part of all kinds of insurance companies to expand, experiment, and move into new areas was well-nigh irresistible.

In general, the more venturesome companies found that it didn't work. When interest rates returned to normality, the promises they made became unkeepable, and the projections they saw turned out to be unrealistic. When real estate became more of a glut than an opportunity, retrenchment became the order of the day, and many major companies are still fighting their way out of the morass.

Why am I bringing up these sordid facts that everyone in the business recognizes all too clearly? For one simple reason: in the year 1991, the media—particularly magazines and newspapers—have begun to see what has happened, and many are trying to paint insurance as a failing business, unable to recoup the losses it suffered, and is still suffering.

For instance, the *New York Times*, admittedly the grande dame of American journalism, on February 7 ran a front page, two-column headline: "Insurance Giants No Longer Ask To Be All Things to All People; Many Are Abandoning Entire Areas of Coverage." The article that followed seemed bent on destroying whatever confidence policyholders and stockholders might have in their insurance. Here are excerpts from the first two paragraphs:

- "The change could substantially affect rates for many kinds of insurance, the prices of insurance stocks, and the economy of the Northeast, where the largest insurance companies are based.

- "Stung by losses or shrinking profits in many of their businesses, the insurers are sharply cutting back on or abandoning entire areas of insurance, selling unrelated businesses, closing offices and laying off workers."

This kind of nonsense is like yelling "Fire!" in a crowded theater. Granted, misguided expansion has required prudent retreat. Granted, many employees who were hired during the boom years will be victims of the bust. Granted, the shoemaker has decided to stick to his last. Granted, reality has reluctantly returned to the insurance business.

But does this mean that any consequential number of policyholders or stockholders—or, for that matter, major companies themselves—are going to become victims of the times? I think not. The forces of conservatism are in full cry, and in a relatively brief time balance will be regained and the doom-shouters will be in disarray. Too many writers are confusing retrenchment with insolvency.

As the *Times* itself points out, insurance company failures fell to 35 in 1990 after reaching a 1980's peak of 44 in 1989. When one considers the many thousands of insurers and their hundreds of billions in assets, this is minuscule.

It is the nature of the press to become Chicken Little and to cry that the sky is falling. This is conventionally known as "alertness," and sometimes it pays off. When it does, there is considerable self-congratulation. When it doesn't, well, there will be another publication in your hands in a few minutes. "Yesterday's newspaper" is a phrase of contempt in the business, unless it contained something spectacular.

I have a gut feeling that the insurance business isn't going to be condemned to repeat the past. There are too many wise minds in it, and too much understanding of the hazards.

4

An Agent's World

"What Does The Agent Want To Hear?"

No. 41, October 11, 1986, Page 13

Frank Friedler, retiring president of the Million Dollar Round Table, had recently been engaged in a gentlemanly discussion with a few of us regarding the nature of the speakers at the MDRT annual meeting (widely acclaimed as one of the best institutional meetings anywhere). It seems that some of us churlish fellows have been complaining that the platforms have been loaded with too many football coaches, track stars, huggers (Dr. Leo Buscaglia, of course), and assorted performers who have a message of faith and confidence but are not quite certain of the nature of the audience they are addressing.

Frank said this during the course of his presidential address in Orlando in June (I was there, and I caught his thunderbolts):

"I have read in recent years criticism of our meeting as spending 50 percent of our main platform time on 'whole person' values, rather than on the meat of our business, sales ideas. I disagree with this criticism 100 percent. I come to the Round Table each year to become recharged and rededicated—to become not just a better sales professional, but a better person . . . it is difficult to believe that when 6,000 of us joined hands last year to sing 'We Are the World' we didn't receive a special gift. Selling life insurance is not child's play. We deserve four special days, where we are nurtured and loved. I tell you that it is the MDRT's concern about me as a person that has brought me back year after year."

Anyone who doesn't concede at least a major portion of Frank's point hasn't been attending many MDRT meetings lately. Two years ago at the Radio City Music Hall, a track star ran a tape of himself breaking the 3:50 barrier in the indoor mile run. As he neared the finish, the entire audience rose to its feet and cheered him on. What if he had failed—and on videotape, too?

Enthusiastic Audience

Any audience with that kind of enthusiasm gets what it deserves, and deserves what it gets. Don't knock it.

Frank Friedler could have made an equally important point in his talk, one that would have knocked all my prunefaced arguments into a cocked hat, but he forbore to do so.

During its afternoon breakout sessions, the MDRT offers about 40 seminars, mostly dealing with sales and educational ideas. Members had an opportunity to attend at least two of these during any one of three afternoons. My estimate—although I couldn't be everywhere—was that at least half the members didn't attend any.

Non-existent Questions

For example, what could have been a lively session dealing with the current issues facing the business and featuring its top leaders (Jack Bobo of NALU and Dick Schweiker of ACLI, to name just two) more or less fell on its face. The reason: there were only 61 people present. The penetrating questions from the floor about where the business is going were almost non-existent.

In other words, when MDRT offers its members the kind of meaty fare that my cronies and I have been crying for, a reasonable number of members find themselves otherwise engaged.

So old pruneface here is going to get off the backs of the MDRT program committee and let it go its own way. I have a gnawing fear that it might just have done so anyhow.

Maybe under current technological advances, program chairmen everywhere will have to change their ideas about what will attract field people to any meeting—local, state or national. The audio cassette—and, to some degree, the video cassette—has enabled the agent to get hold of most of the brilliant sales ideas going the rounds. Conceivably, the only plan that will get him out of the cuppa-soup-and-cassette lunch will include two factors: a speaker who challenges his ideas and beliefs about the business, and an opportunity to talk back to said speaker after he or she has finished. I might even be willing to face the rubber chicken myself in order to be involved in such a session.

Yes, I'm afraid I'm going to have to bow to Frank Friedler and his colleagues for having achieved the right mix of coaches, advanced underwriters, huggers, estate planners, and shrinks. It definitely ain't broke, so why try to fix it?

"Big Query, Small Reply"

No. 52, December 29, 1986, Page 29

The following is a transcript of a portion of a forum at the CLU/ChFC annual meeting last fall in San Antonio. The participants were: Joe Melone, president of Prudential, who was the moderator, and the executive heads of three major agent associations, NALU (Jack Bobo), MDRT (Rod Geer), and ASCLU/ChFC (John Driskill).

MELONE: I read with interest and jotted down Don Barnes' comment in *Probe* a few issues back. Let me quote it here:

"If NALU, IAFP, the American College and the College for Financial Planning could quit their bickering and form a 'Center for Continuing Education in Financial Services' they could damned well decide who is a financial planner and who isn't, and come down hard on those who fail to measure up to their standards." Now, we don't have all parties that Don referenced there on the panel, but we've got pretty good industry representation. What do you think of the main thrust of Don's observation?

DRISKILL: I like that idea of creating a Center for Continuing Education. I think we've done that. It's called Bryn Mawr, Pa. (Laughter and applause.) Thank you, Don.

MELONE: Now we're jockeying for position as to who's going to be the boss—that's what we're coming down to, I think.

GEER: I think Don's comment gives validity to the old adage, "To err is human. To get paid for it is divine." (Laughter.) I'm not aware of the bickering he refers to. I think it's a figment. By and large, the College in Denver and IAFP enjoy a very excellent relationship with the life insurance industry. Their leadership attends the Round Table meetings; we attend theirs. Our executive committees have met jointly. I know that John Driskill and his leadership have met with the folks at the Denver College and have worked very harmoniously with them in developing ideas and concepts for the future. I think what he refers to as "bickering" is merely honest differences, and that's inevitable. Good music is composed of both harmony and discord and I think that has to be equally true of our industry differences from time to time.

MELONE: Jack, do you have anything to add?

BOBO: I have nothing to add. I agree with Rod. I don't even know what he's talking about, about "bickering." (Laughter.)

* * * *

I consider those to be a relatively vapid group of answers to a proposal that Joe Melone must have taken seriously or he wouldn't have brought it to the panel's attention. No answer was truly responsive to the idea that a center for continuing education in financial services, embraced and funded by all the major financial services organizations, should be considered on the highest levels.

Any person who has studied the situation knows that the laws are in place to punish those who commit fraud or any other serious malfeasance on their clients, whether they call themselves financial planners or not.

But there is no law anywhere that prevents a person from calling himself a financial planner and then going out to give his prospects half-baked advice on how they should handle financial matters. IAFP seems to be groping for such regulations. The life insurance business appears content to say, "Acquire your ChFC designation and you will be anointed."

I concluded my article—which was a long one—with this sentence:

"Only by making modest proposals like this—however flawed they may be—can we direct our thoughts to making the educational processes within the financial services business a single entity."

I did not expect my proposal—which received some small acclaim from responsible people in life insurance—to be brought before a panel at the CLU/ChFC forum. But, once there, I certainly failed to anticipate that it would be greeted by titters and giggles on the part of three men who are certainly among the most influential in the business, and rightly so. Let John Driskill volunteer to head Bryn Mawr. Let Rod Geer worry that I get paid to err. And let Jack Bobo feel that all is comfy between NALU and IAFP. The issue of who may fob himself off as a professional financial planner to an unsuspecting and untutored public simply won't go away.

When the New York attorney general's office filed a multimillion dollar lawsuit against First Meridian Planning Corp. in November, that office said that it had found new ammunition to use in its campaign for legislation aimed at regulating financial planners. If the financial services community won't act to clean up its own act, it may be leaving the job to the courts and the legislators. In my book, that's a solution of last resort.

"The Woman In Life Insurance"

No. 2, January 12, 1987, Page 17

For years it's been mildly pointed out, by LIMRA in its research studies and by individuals from various platforms, that life insurance people had never properly caught the hang of hiring women and promoting them to leadership positions, either in the home office or field. It's a rare insurance woman who ever gets a place on one of the industry's prestigious convention programs and, no matter how competent in her discipline she may be, she seems to be given the aura of Sir Samuel Johnson's female preacher: "Like a dog standing on its hind legs, you are not so surprised to see it done well as you are to see it done at all."

But in November, at the annual meeting of the American Council of Life Insurance, the business was grabbed by its lapels and given an old-fashioned lecture about its treatment of women. The lecturer was Victor Fuchs, Stanford University professor of economics and director of research for health economics at the National Bureau for Economic Research.

He began by noting that in 1984, only 2 percent of women employed by insurance companies made more than $25,000 a year, compared with 42 percent of male employees. By comparison to that 20:1 ratio, he noted that the ratio for retailing is 7:1 and it ranges down to 4:1 for real estate.

"Is there a particular reason for this profile, or are you missing talent and opportunity?" he asked. "Aren't you going to need to rethink jobs, how to set up jobs, and the kinds of benefits you offer?"

Certain Attractions

Insurance jobs hold particular attractions for women, he said: most do not rely on physical strength, many are in residential areas, and many lend themselves to part-time work and flexible hours.

I consider his point of view unassailable. There are precious few female "fast-track kids" in any area of insurance, although they abound in every other financial services business. One young woman I know who is a life insurance expert with a brokerage house, but not on commission, said to me, "I'll earn a hundred thousand just doing the job they demand of me. If I achieve more, I'll get more."

The fastest track in selling is the Top of the Table, where commission income of $210,000 is required for qualification. Of the 875 current qualifiers,

10 are women—and two of those are from Japan. American women, then, represent less than one percent of the big hitters. And so it goes, down the line.

It isn't easy to make such clear distinctions in home office positions, where there aren't such obvious benchmarks as production clubs. One guideline might be, how many women attend the major institutional conventions of home office people—ACLI, LIMRA, LIC, LOMA, NALC? If you go to one or more of those, you must have acquired some standing. Unhappily, the figure for female registrants at such meetings is something under five percent.

As a longtime enthusiast for women's rights, I have tried to figure out why life insurance is so hopeless in its recruitment and promotion of the best and brightest women. I have come up with two notions; you may take them apart if you wish:

Men who have risen to top management posts, both in home office and field, have never taught themselves to be comfortable with women associates. There are no courses to guide them. Their experience with women has been limited to mothers, sisters, wives and secretaries—and many of them will admit the fact off the record. If some enterprising and prestigious organization were to offer them such a course, I'll bet the response would be surprising—especially if they could attend in false beards and fright wigs.

While women throughout the country are petitioning such male strongholds as the Jaycees, Kiwanis, Lions, etc. for admission and equality, life insurance women tend to huddle off in self-segregated groups. The Women Life Underwriters Conference of NALU is a prime example. It holds its own meetings at NALU conventions; in local communities it has created its own chapters. It seems to be saying, "We are not like you. We are different. We have our own problems to solve."

The natural reaction of the male, hearing these words, is to reply, "If that's how you see yourselves, go right ahead." I can think of no way for women to keep out of the mainstream of life insurance more effectively than to create their own rivulet.

This isn't true of all insurance women, of course. A majority of female members of NALU are not members of WLUC. Recently, I spoke at a life underwriters association where both the president and the president-elect were women. Neither was a member of WLUC. Why? "We're perfectly comfortable with the association as our base," one told me. (Both, incidentally, are members of MDRT.)

Still, the main problem continues to be the ineptitude of male managers in bringing women along to become their peers. When they do this, the face of life insurance will change for the better.

"The Phoniest Word"

No. 7, February 16, 1987, Page 15

In the waning years of the 20th century, one of the phoniest words in the English language is "loyalty." The reason it has become phony is that it is used almost exclusively by people who expect to receive loyalty; those who freely give it use the word hardly at all.

We hear phrases like "my loyal wife," "my loyal servant," and even "my loyal dog." Not to mention, of course, "our loyal agents." Never have I heard anyone refer to "our loyal CEO," even though I have known several men in that category who would surely qualify.

I would go so far as to say that indiscriminate use of the word "loyalty" is serving only to exacerbate agent-company relations in the year 1987. Larry Albright, who writes perceptively for *Life Insurance Selling*, equates the word with "becoming less independent," and sees it as "a threat to the innovative, consumer-oriented progress the business has made in the late 1970s and 1980s."

He asks, "Would universal life have revolutionized the life insurance business if agents had remained 'loyal' to their primary (career agency) companies? How long would agents have had to wait for their primary companies to come up with universal life?"

His point is well-taken, even though sliding interest rates have tarnished the original glamor of the universal life policy. And it is the very soaring and swooping of interest rates that causes many CEOs to say to their agents something like, "Hang tight. Hang tough. What goes around comes around. Stay with us."

Bill Clark, president of the Massachusetts Mutual, expresses his philosophy this way:

"The successful, sophisticated agent knows that today's projection will be tomorrow's fairy tale. He clearly understands that volatile interest rates can cause today's good deal to be tomorrow's disaster."

What he is saying, in sum, is that the agent who is chasing the best buy for his client by examining the wares of several companies may have to do a lot of replacing over the years. And, he says, "If replacement is called for with every change of interest rates, the result is no more credible than churning an investment portfolio, and we all know who is the winner in that game."

All right. I conclude that Bill Clark's vision of loyalty on the part of an agent is for him to stay with a reputable company on the theory that in the long run everything will come out favorably for the client. But it collides forcibly with Larry Albright's contention that only pressure by the sales force causes a company to innovate. Experience has shown that there is considerable substance in such a belief.

Sy Raboy, president of Connecticut Mutual, prefers the word "commitment" to the toplofty "loyalty." Says he, "Companies make significant investments in the business success of career agents by recruiting, financing, training and otherwise supporting agents, with life, health and professional liability insurance as well as pension plans and the employer's portion of the Social Security tax. To be a career agent and accept fringe benefits and other company offerings seems to be in conflict with the spirit, and usually the practice, of shopping each situation."

And so the lines are drawn. For an agent to accept all the goodies described by Sy Raboy and then take his or her business elsewhere would seem like the act of an ingrate—except that it happens every day in every American business. It comes with the territory. Somewhere along the line there has to be an agreed-upon end to commitment, or every career agent would find himself indentured to the company that recruited him. Further, let it be remembered that the company has profited to some extent by the business the agent has submitted to it before he decided to stray from the nest. Commitment, too, is mutual.

To me, "loyalty" is a word that should be stricken from the manuscripts of speeches or articles by company officials exhorting members of their field forces, and vice versa. "Commitment" may surely be used, although we may expect it to be followed by a bout of arm wrestling over which side has committed what to the other.

Here are two certain truths:

- Neither the agent nor the company selling a top product at a fair commission rate has to worry about loyalty or commitment.
- If any element of American business had to concern itself about loyalty to keep its head above water, it would drown.

"The Agent As Pawn"

No. 8, February 23, 1987, Page 25

No one can deny that it is the duty of life insurance top management to keep its company viable, competitive, aggressive and profitable. How senior executives go about doing this is up to them, their board of directors, the various insurance commissions and the public that either buys or doesn't buy.

Over time, most of them accepted the conventional wisdom that trained salespeople formed the perfect bridge for transmitting the product to the consumer. So they hired and trained and compensated as many such people as they could afford.

But on some occasion not recorded in the history books, a bright executive said to himself, "Why do I bother to do all the training? Why don't I wait until someone else trains them and just hire them away? Think of the money I'll save!"

And another said, "Why don't I get cozy with the banks? Look at the prospect lists they have! Our agents won't have to spend time doing the onerous, unprofitable prospecting job. And if we supply them with prospects, we won't have to pay them as much."

Still another said, "Why don't I install a high-powered advanced underwriting specialist in a brokerage house, let the stockbrokers bring their clients into the office for professional advice, and split the commissions? We'll need just one agent to handle a whole stable of brokers."

There are enough other "Why-don't-I's" in the minds of companies or already on the drawing boards today to fill this page. And the person who is the pawn in them all is the agent, the person who led in building the insurance business to whatever eminence it has today. Nobody asks the agent anything. On the chessboard of marketing today, the agent doesn't have many moves.

Take the Mayflower Group, called by the *National Underwriter* "a diverse group of financial service giants, including some insurance companies, (which) have signed a statement of principles urging a complete restructuring of financial services laws and a more open, competitive financial services market."

No one can be so naive as to fail to realize that smashing the barriers in the broad field of financial services means developing new distribution systems and marketing strategies. Where the agent will fit into such new horizons provides chancy speculation at best.

Or, from the other side of the coin, take the recent proposal by E. Gerald Corrigan, president of the Federal Reserve Bank of New York, to revamp the financial system by eliminating many distinctions between banks, securities firms, and insurance companies, and allow common ownership of these companies. "Banks are special," Mr. Corrigan said. So special that they should be allowed to invade new marketing areas now denied them by federal and state laws, I presume.

In all such jockeying for position—and with most insurance companies sitting attentively on the sidelines, all eyes and ears for what actions they should take next—who speaks for the individual agent? Hardly anyone, because he and his institutional organization are only a small drop in this bucket of change.

My notion is that the agent has got to be more alert to what is going on in his marketplace than ever before. If he feels that his company isn't dealing off the top of the deck, he must take action. Insurance marketing has become a contact sport, and if he doesn't want to end up with his nose in the mud, he must seek a friendly environment.

Please look back at the first paragraph of this article. I wasn't able to mention the agent in it because I'm sure that most top managements don't feel he belongs there. Breathes there the executive with soul so unimaginative that he doesn't go to sleep asking, "What can I do to lower those acquisition costs?" He may not have found the answer, but it's a safe bet he will keep trying.

The era of the untouchable agent is over. Whatever new era he creates will depend, I believe, on three factors: his ability to adapt, his sense of consummate professionalism, and his willingness to keep learning.

"Paying The Agent"

No. 17, April 27, 1987, Page 31

You can't get into any panel discussion about life insurance marketing these days without diving headlong into the matter of how the agent for the future is going to be compensated. Even companies with almost identical backgrounds can have widely differing notions about what it should cost to move the product from the home office computer into the home of the insured.

There are three possibilities most frequently bandied about, as they were at the recent meeting of NALU's General Agents and Managers Conference:

- The traditional, high first-year plus nominal renewal commission system, usually on the order of 50 percent and nine fives, followed by a permanent 2 percent fee for the life of the policy.

- A level commission for the life of the policy.

- A fee for all services provided by the agent, negotiated by the agent and the client.

Nobody likes the traditional system very much, but it has stumbled along for these many years and a number of the brightest minds in the business seem to believe they're stuck with it. It gives the recruits a smidgen of take-home pay, although they invariably have to be helped out for a few years by additional financing. It is a bonanza for the quick-buck failures who can sell their sisters and their cousins and their aunts and then return to pumping gas. The front-end load makes lapsations costly for the company. And, of course, it makes rebating a delectable possibility.

Most veteran agents I have talked to (and let's define them as ones who are nearing a decade in selling) wouldn't mind the level commission system at all now that renewals have begun to flow into their incomes. But they pause to wonder whether they would have lasted ten years if they hadn't had good front money in the early days. To authentic successes, it doesn't matter how they are compensated as long as they get their share of the pie.

Fee-based compensation is never likely to enter the life insurance business as long as it limits itself to insurance products. But if it branches out into other forms of investment and hires a corps of elite financial planners who are prepared to give sage advice on all a family's financial aspirations, there will probably be those who charge fees. But they had better produce in a very, very smart fashion, because no one is going to pay a fee to a loser.

Some actuaries who are dreamers visualize an agent's contract that moves over a period of years from a high front-end load to level commissions. But even they are willing to admit that agent retention will have to improve. Only a company with very deep pockets would be able to handle a double standard like this one until it became stabilized.

Not that there is much agreement on future commission systems. At a recent industry meeting, Pierre Maurer, vice-chairman of the Metropolitan, speculated that if rebating became a thorn in the side of the life insurance business, his company might try some variations on the level commission route. The very next day Joe Melone, president of the Prudential, addressing the same issue, said, "No way!" If the two authentic giants of the business, who hire the best minds they can find, end up 180 degrees apart, you have to wonder where the truth lies—and, indeed, if there is any at all.

I see the problem as one that minds far keener than mine are still grappling with: the life insurance business is still not retaining a sufficient number of the people it hires. LIMRA burns the midnight oil unendingly to figure out why. Every agency manager will tell you it's the prime reason he loses sleep. But until the companies can stop wasting money on failures, any conceivable compensation system has built-in hazards.

"Maybe 'Commitment' Is The Word"

No. 18, May 4, 1987, Page 27

When I wrote a column several weeks ago condemning the indiscriminate use of the word "loyalty" ["The Phoniest Word", No. 7, February 16, 1987] when referring to agent-company relations in the life insurance business, I expected to get some healthy rejoinders, and I did.

Not surprisingly, most of the defense of the word came from home office sources. Field people, on the whole, could get along without ever hearing it again, particularly when it refers to their tactics of placing business.

One of the most interesting letters I received was from Sy Raboy, president of Connecticut Mutual. He chided me for missing one of his principal points when I quoted him in my previous column that a career agent need not engage in the practice of "shopping each situation." He put it this way:

"Clearly, professional agents will walk the line of balancing a commitment to a company, to a client, and to themselves in a fair and responsible manner. To shop each, and I underline each, situation is what we expect of a broker and not a career agent."

Then he hit me with the 16-pound hammer:

"On a broader front, Don, I'd be most interested in having you define for our public what should be expected of a 'career' or 'full-time' agent?"

I'll try. If an agent is theoretically full-time in a company whose rates are clearly in the ballpark, I don't believe he should shop around trying to show his client what a bright boy he is by saving nickels and dimes. It will probably even out in the end. But if there is a substantial difference in what his first-line company has offered and what he can get for his client somewhere else, he owes it to his client to show him what's on the market. And if his first-line company is consistently and substantially inferior, maybe he should consider switching to one that isn't.

Other Side Of Coin

But that's only one side of the coin. The other side turned up in two articles in the April *Probe* section of *Life Association News*—one by Dave Woods, president of NALU, the other by Bill Macfarlane, managing editor of the section. Between them, they alleged that two major companies had been engaged in practices that were apparently not in the best interest of their field force. Here they are:

- Until March 1, Mutual Benefit Life "openly allowed its products to be used to replace existing insurance." Further, "it was doing so through a series of savings banks in New York State." It ceased as of March 1.
- A wholly-owned subsidiary of the Equitable Society, located in Arizona, was "soliciting the purchase of single premium life insurance as an investment product through advertising in *The Wall Street Journal* while the parent company was expressing concern about "the 'abuses' of the tax privileges of life insurance."

President Woods inquired, "What must the field force. . .think about company loyalty?" There's that word again.

While I question the prudence of bringing these instances into the open until their extent had been determined and the companies had been given an opportunity to state their cases, it's obvious that NALU, through the voice of its president, is deeply concerned about the loyalty issue. If names are going to be named casually, I can think of a stack of companies I would list before the Mutual Benefit and the Equitable, which are two of NALU's stoutest supporters.

Today almost every life company is experimenting with untried distribution procedures in order to increase their share of market. If they should be discouraged from doing so in the name of loyalty to their field forces, everyone involved might be adversely affected in the long run.

The business must face the fact that it has lost its innocence—all of it. Noble words describing our relationships with one another are empty words.

I don't believe that NALU or any of its presidents is going to turn the clock back to a simpler day. Nor will any company be able to hold its agents captive.

Sy Raboy's definition of "commitment" seems to be the most workable word in 1987. It implies honesty and decency in business dealings, and not blind devotion. A great majority of us ought to be able to live with it.

"The Ladies Opt Out"

No. 35, August 31, 1987, Page 21

After 98 years of experience, the National Association of Life Underwriters has its organizational housekeeping in good shape. Its members know what they can expect of it and what they cannot. It runs smoothly and expertly.

Consequently, when the word came out this summer that the Women Life Underwriters Conference was to be disbanded and reduced to committee status, old association watchers were surprised. This surprise was compounded when the officers of the WLUC said, in effect, "Thanks, but no thanks," and announced that it would continue to operate as an independent "Women Life Underwriters Confederation" incorporated in the state of Connecticut. In effect, the ladies were telling NALU that they knew what they could do with their committee.

Why all this unseemly ruckus? A little historical detail is necessary.

NALU has had a women's committee on and off for most of its existence. Its job was usually to encourage women to become life underwriters and then members. In 1935, after the Million Dollar Round Table had been established, the ladies formed the Women's Quarter-Million Dollar Round Table, which by no means was as ridiculous a production goal as it seems today. The name was later changed to the Women Leaders Round Table and enjoyed good standing among NALU's subgroups.

But active women saw neither the committee nor the Round Table to be adequate representation, the committee being appointed by the NALU board and the Round Table being limited to superior producers: Women in field management did not have much of a voice.

So in 1978, with the acquiescence and full approval of the NALU board, women leaders created WLUC. Its officers and directors had the perks of all

NALU subgroups, and its annual meeting occupied two full days before the beginning of NALU conventions, a tradition carried on from its predecessor organizations.

Its principal drawback—which I doubt anyone had fully anticipated—might be expressed by saying, "They gave a conference and nobody came." NALU has some 16,000 women in its local associations. In recent years, less than 1,700 of them have been members of WLUC.

It seems clear by now that women life underwriters fall into two groups: those who feel that meetings among members of their own sex will increase their skills, and those who are quite content to mingle with agents of both sexes. Some are taking strong leadership roles in NALU and its local and state associations; others prefer to lead women. (Of course some women life underwriters have taken high positions in both groups.)

To the board of NALU, this undoubtedly has become a financial matter. A conference like WLUC costs considerable money especially in its formative years. When barely 10 percent of those eligible choose to join, management has to decide whether it's worth the candle. The board's answer was obvious.

Of course, the new confederation isn't starting from scratch. It has some 50 chapters, and doubtless will seek to organize more. Whether it can generate the money to do on its own what NALU couldn't do for it is moot. Certainly, it should be given a fighting chance.

It seems to me that NALU was premature in starting WLUC at all. It was doubtless swayed by a few enthusiasts. If, as we now see, nearly 90 percent aren't sufficiently interested in such an organization to belong, a simple survey should have told them so.

If women were being discriminated against in insurance, if their commissions were lower than men, if they were prevented from full participation in the various associations of their business, a strong women's group would be vital. Under current circumstances it seems to be an iffy proposition.

I wish the new confederation well. It will, obviously, have to fight for its existence. If a group of women—no matter what the numbers—can give sustenance to their colleagues, something good will be happening.

"What The Big Boys Eat—And How Much"

No. 50, December 14, 1987, Page 19

Exceptional life insurance producers are a very lucky people, for a whole host of reasons. Not only do their regular commissions earn them a respectable amount of money, but their companies insist on heaping upon them a lot of perquisites not obtainable by ordinary mortals.

A recent LIMRA survey entitled *Compensating Exceptional Producers* provided the lowdown on how a group of 71 companies treated their big hitters, and it seems their motto is, "The more you produce, the more special money you get."

First of all, what constitutes an exceptional producer? Among the larger companies, the median seems to be about $75,000 in first-year commissions. In smaller companies, the median is nearer $50,000. In each case, of course, the producer is almost a sure bet to make the Million Dollar Round Table.

The easiest thing the companies provide is their ego-builders: production clubs that give the top boys and girls trophies, several conventions and special privileges, additional advertising allowances, clerical allowances, or computer assistance plans. While LIMRA didn't say so, I'm betting that these also include corner offices, deep carpeting and the distinct possibility that they get to call the CEO by his first name.

Most of these perks have been on the agenda for a century. But there are some new ones that tend to inflate the agent's income substantially: sharing overrides, sharing expense allowances, overrides on subagent production, production bonuses, accelerated vesting schedules for renewal commissions, special services (which can include special underwriting treatment) and accelerated security benefits, including profit sharing and deferred compensation plans.

Of course, not all the companies responding to the LIMRA study offered all these benefits; companies have assuredly not lost sight of the profit motive. But a striking number of them have close to half of them on their menus. And, because the project is so new, LIMRA did not survey what companies are doing in the area of producer-owned reinsurance companies. These are still being tested and, as LIMRA says, "a PRC is a long-term commitment for agents—profits are not expected for 10 to 15 years after a producer joins." A wait-and-see attitude seems to be the prudent one here.

Why do I bring all this up? It's obvious that if you have a fleet thoroughbred you feed him whatever will make him run faster. You don't waste your oats on mules. Unless a company gives its big hitters top dollar, they will drift to other companies that will. And since only a handful of companies are recruiting, training and supervising a full-time field force today, they can't afford to lose their star performers. These companies may have a stake of about $250,000 in an agent before he or she begins to blossom into a super-producer.

Philosophically, however, it seems obvious that the company must drain money from two highly-important groups of agents in order to keep the exceptional producer from straying:

1. The recruit. Because of the peculiar nature of life insurance field compensation, the new agent has a hard time surviving. Half the recruits who fail do so because they're incompetent salespeople; the other half because they can't meet their budgetary requirements and quit to go to a business where the front money is better. If life insurance companies are going to develop the big hitters of the future, they mustn't let them get away while they are freshmen.

2. The happy agent. This is the old pro who is supporting his family comfortably, working no harder than he has to, and is a contented producer with no desire to have his picture in the magazine or to call the prez by his first name. Some people will say he is the backbone of the business. But he wants his compensation—all of it. If he feels his commission possibilities are being stripped in any way to feed the big boys' egos, he will raise hell. He mustn't be tampered with.

While I agree that the exceptional producer is a valuable person to have aboard, if the company spends so much time pampering him that it loses sight of the two categories I have cited, there's trouble brewing. I bow to no one in my admiration for the exceptional producers, but they must not be allowed to control a company's marketing process.

"Continue To Learn Or You're Going Downhill"

No. 8, February 22, 1988, Page 17

Any life insurance agent who acquired a CLU designation in 1970 and stopped the learning process right there would probably be booted out of the business today. The idea that life insurance is an immutable force has probably caused more failures than any other single factor. The agent who doesn't know what's going on today doesn't know anything at all.

So it's a little surprising to read that Bob Knowles, southern editor of the *National Underwriter*, characterizes 220,000 Texas agents as "panicky" at completing up to 30 hours of continuing education courses in a two-year period or else losing their licenses for up to 12 months. Bob has been around, and I assume he knows what panic is, but the very thought of 220,000 Texans shaking in their boots at an itty bit of continuing education boggles my mind.

Most people spend more than 15 hours a year shaving.

At least 22 states now have some sort of continuing education requirement for agents, although there's not much similarity in what they ask of the producer. With some, certified attendance at sales congresses and certain other state and national meetings counts as continuing education. Apparently, as Bob Knowles tells it, the Texas law will be a little stricter than that since it demands "class hours" of agents and not merely sitting in on someone's talk. It also asks for graded examinations.

Some elements of the Texas insurance community seem to be more worried about the administration of the continuing education plan than its content. But unless the state launches a vendetta against its agents in the form of impossible examinations, this shouldn't be a problem. I cannot conceive of a state wishing to put its agents out of business.

Like all states, Texas has its "Nowheresville"—a town called Muleshoe, which I happened to visit about 50 years ago. "How could someone from Muleshoe attend classes?" they ask. Well, if I could get out of Muleshoe a half-century ago, I assume that its current residents are able to.

The only sustenance I can see for the forces opposed to continuing education is the rather curious example set by the American College and the American Society of CLU/ChFC. Neither requires any further study for the retention of one of these designations by a student who has passed the courses. You would think that these estimable organizations would be setting a proud example for the business. It must make their advertisements boasting of the intelligence of the CLU/ChFC a mite hard to write.

Jim Ballew, who has been writing for life insurance people over many years, has recently published a book entitled *The New Generation of Life Insurance Products—In Plain English* (64 pp., $6.50—The Rough Notes Co., Inc., P.O. Box 564, Indianapolis, IN 46206). In it he cites 11 life insurance products that have come to the fore since 1970: adjustable life, universal life, variable premium life, interest-sensitive whole life, annual renewable term, variable life, variable universal life, single premium whole life, last survivor life, graded premium whole life, and deposit term. While not all these products are brand new, they have all come to flower in the past 20 years. What would happen to the agent who isn't abreast of all of them? And that doesn't even include the various tax laws that keep changing year by year.

Of course, companies that have agency forces realize all this, and feed their people current material until it comes out their ears. But with more and more agents unaffiliated with a specific company, weight of learning rests more than ever on the individual.

While I'm not happy with government playing Big Brother in the field of continuing education, if that's the only way to motivate a certain percentage of producers, I say go for it. Most agents are self-starters and don't need to be told that they had better know all the answers to the pertinent questions, but if some of them need a shove to keep them in the business, so be it.

Maybe even the CLU/ChFC people will mandate continuing education someday.

"Shall We Join The Ladies?"

No. 11, March 14, 1988, Page 19

There has been considerable tohu-bohn (as they say in Paris) lately about the organizational status of female life underwriters. The National Association of Life Underwriters started it by reducing its Women Life Underwriters Conference to the status of a standing committee. The ladies countered this move by establishing a Women Life Underwriters Confederation, independent of NALU.

The discussion then hit the trade press. Norman Levine, the Sage of San Francisco, came down heavily on the side of NALU in the *Probe* section of *Life Association News*. Several women defended the formation of the new Confederation. I kicked in with some words in this column that expressed sympathy with the women's position but doubt that enough of them were willing to support it.

For the moment the situation seems to lie fallow, but I don't think it will continue to be so for very long.

NALU apparently dismantled the Conference for two reasons: because it felt that it was economically unfeasible to support, and too many women expressed not only disinterest in but active hostility to the project. So be it.

The new Confederation, operating totally outside the structure of NALU, is not taking the rebuff lying down. For many years the Saturdays and Sundays prior to NALU conventions have been partially the preserve of women life underwriters who have conducted seminars, sales congresses and banquets at those times. NALU has turned its back on these events. But, according to Linda Turner, executive head of the fledgling Confederation, it will still be there in 1988. The NALU convention will be in Dallas, from September 25 through 28, with its official headquarters in the Anatole Hotel. The Confederation has obtained a block of rooms in the Dallas Market Center, near the Anatole, and it will conduct meetings on September 23 and 24, and until noon on the 25th. The Confederation will invite the women of NALU to attend.

It's unfortunate that the situation has turned into a Mexican standoff. For the first time in its history, as far as I know, NALU has rejected a group of its own members who felt they had good and sufficient reasons to convene periodically. (The Confederation requires currently that its members join NALU after two years, but some of the NALU hierarchy believe that this is too long a wait.) NALU's rationale—lack of financial support and interest—makes sense, but is it sufficient?

Many women entering the life insurance sales field today are—let's face it—up against considerable male chauvinism. I don't think this is a calculated position taken by men but, as I have written before, simply a lack of knowledge and training in how to handle the female salesperson and motivate her properly. Some women brush this off and march straight ahead with their male colleagues. Others, with a sensitivity that might in the end make them superior agents, are put off by it.

The members of the latter group tend to rely heavily on the advice and guidance of their successful female compatriots. This isn't a sign of weakness or instability. Many are members of two-income families who may also be rearing children, and there are many men who can't understand their regiments and how to cope with them. Other women can. Thus, the perceived need for a confederation.

As far as I can see, the insurance business is generally abysmal now in the teaching of how to train and supervise women. I'm not aware of a single course on the subject open to field management. The prevailing philosophy seems to be that the sex of the salesperson has nothing to do with selling skills, so let's forget the whole matter.

If some women can guide others into successful careers, I'm all for an organization that formalizes this procedure, no matter how small it may be. (The current Confederation has about 20 chapters and 500 members.) NALU should lend it benign support, but not necessarily financial assistance. It should be able to find its own financing. If it is simply a self-serving organization it will fall by the wayside.

But if it can show some success stories among a group of people who need guidance, it deserves a place in the business.

"More News On Continuing Education"

No. 15, April 11, 1988, Page 19

On rare occasions, sheer coincidence can make on ordinary person look like a swami, a genius, or a Very Deep Thinker. Very often he is none of the above.

In the February 22 issue of the *National Underwriter,* I wrote some words under the headline "Continue to Learn or You're Going Downhill." In the course of the article I was sharply critical of the American College and the American Society of CLU/ChFC for not having some kind of continuing education mechanism built into their designation-granting procedure. I concluded by saying, "Maybe even the CLU/ChFC people will mandate continuing education someday."

In the April issue of *Society Page*, the American Society's internal house magazine, just such a program is announced. It is imaginative, far-reaching, and just what the doctor ordered.

It would be lovely to believe that the Society, stung by my criticism, got together and assembled this program during the month of March. It would also be stupid.

The plan, called Professional Achievement in Continuing Education (with the appropriate acronym of PACE), is the end result of many months' work on the part of an Ad Hoc Committee on Continuing Education of the American College and the American Society. Like any good committee working on a tough project, its members kept mum about it until they had something concrete to talk about. I was writing on the basis of the best information I could collect, but my sources either weren't talking or not in the know.

PACE lies in the mainstream of all good continuing education programs, in that it stipulates continuing attendance at designated classes, institutes, national meetings, seminars and other formal educational programs. The news columns of this publication will give you the complete formula.

The major question is: Will those who have already earned the CLU or ChFC designation be "grandfathered" into immunity from PACE? The tentative answer seems to be that they will, since it would be difficult to strip a designation, which had no strings attached when it was earned, from those upon whom it was conferred.

However, the board of directors of the Society has publicly petitioned the board of trustees of the American College to consider denying the use of its designations to future graduates who do not meet the continuing education standards set by PACE. The same board has also resolved that if the trustees approve the denial of use of the designations, then the College and the Society should move to replace the Society's program with a jointly sponsored, mandatory program.

It's to be hoped that this will be done. A designation is not quite akin to a college degree, which is usually conferred in perpetuum and cannot ever be revoked except under extreme conditions. A designation can be revoked—the College has done so several times for cause, including failure to live up to its exacting code of ethics.

If this prospectus strikes fire, the whole complexion of continuing education in the life insurance business will never be the same again. Every organization that has pretensions toward educating the agent will be forced to go along in its own way—although "forced" is certainly not a word that need be applied to such forward-thinking entities as the Life Underwriter Training Council. The concept, once sternly applied, will permeate the business. And this will most assuredly be true even of those "grandfathered" CLUs and ChFCs who might be tempted to rest on their oars but will certainly want to associate themselves with the PACE program, if for no other reason than self-defense.

Sometimes I have felt that the American College has become so bogged down with the realities of the present that it has failed to dig into the possibilities of the future. The advanced masters' degrees that it confers are invaluable, but an affirmation of continuing education for those who have neither the desire nor the capacity to add more initials behind their names should be a blockbuster.

If posterity should try to tell you that my February 22 column started this surge, just show them this piece.

"Front-End Load Or Level Commissions"

No. 42, October 17, 1988, Page 13

Archives of the National Association of Life Underwriters show that the argument about how an agent's commissions should be allocated over time began in 1899. NALU, desperately trying to find a way to curb rebating, recommended to the companies that they reduce first-year commissions and increase renewals.

This was a major surprise to the companies; agents had traditionally wanted as much front money as they could get in order to take some profit out of a sale even if there were an early lapse (or rebate). Owing to the cutthroat nature of the business at the time, those few companies that went along with the NALU resolution found their agent ranks immediately raided by other companies that continued to offer a generous up-front dollar. The visionary idea slowly died, aided not a little by NALU general agent members, who saw their ability to give recruits a living wage seriously hampered.

Ninety years later, the discussion is just as hot—and for many of the same reasons, including the resurgence of rebating. There is a certain amount of level-commission selling around today, chiefly in the area of group, annual premium annuities, annual renewable term, and home service policies. But the vast majority of individual policies still reward the seller with 55 percent or more—sometimes a lot more—in first-year commissions, plus 7.5 percent or more for the next nine years, plus a service fee for the life of the policy.

I wrote here some months ago that no company wants to be the first to drop first-year commissions to, say, 25 percent and build subsequent compensation correspondingly. Indications are that such a statement may not be true any longer. Both the John Hancock and the Metropolitan have begun experiments in the area, and if the giants are doing so the rest of the business pays close attention.

All companies, given their druthers, would obviously embrace a levelized compensation plan, but only if all their colleagues went along with the idea.

The matter of persistency of business, now a cause for concern to almost all home offices, would effectively be turned over to the agent. The larger the renewal commission, the greater impulse there would be on the part of the selling agent to keep the policy on the books.

It is now the field force that is deeply divided on the matter. Agency managers have little interest in digging deeply into their own pockets to finance new agents, and would doubtless beseech home offices for enough funds to tide them over until salesmen were able to support themselves on half—or less—of the first-year commission money that they are now receiving. Without such company help, recruiting would be an almost impossible job.

The only kind of agent I can visualize as being thoroughly comfortable with some form of level commission scale is the substantial producer who is confident of his clients and his ability to generate consistent business. Such a plan would, after a few years, give the agent a financial stability undreamed of under current compensation plans.

But even the old pro is likely to have nightmares about early death claims or lapses. Persistency of business would be an absolute must under a level-commission scale, and we are all aware of what happens to the best laid plans of mice and men.

If there is to be any measurable experiment in levelized compensation, it is likely to be instituted by a cohesive group of high-powered agents working in close harmony with one or more high-powered companies. There will probably be stock options involved, and quite possibly elements of ownership. If it succeeds, it will probably be transferrable to other groups, but it is hard to imagine it pervading the business. The present compensation system is so ingrained that overhauling it completely would make the labors of Hercules look like child's play.

Still, it is a magic dream, and perhaps some latter-day Hercules can bring it to reality.

"Agent Education In The Fast Lane"

No. 2, January 9, 1989, Page 17

Some 6,000 members of the National Association of Life Underwriters have asked their association for greater access to educational programs. Alan Press, NALU president, made this somewhat surprising statement at the Tom Grant Breakfast at the annual meeting of the American Council of Life Insurance. (The breakfast has been sponsored by Business Men's Assurance for some 53 years to give the incoming NALU president an opportunity to meet and consult with company CEOs on both the association's and the industry's problems).

I say "somewhat surprising" because, at first blush, it would seem that with the Life Underwriter Training Council, the American College, the American Society of CLU/ChFC, and educational meetings of state and local associations as well as companies, the educational cup of the agent ought to be quite full.

But no. As Alan Press explained it to company officers, "Our members told us that there was a void in the menu of available industry educational programs. There was a lot of the educational equivalent of fine, full-fare family restaurants around. . .They were telling us that their need was for the educational equivalent of a bunch of different, high-quality, fast-food restaurants, all conveniently located near one another. They wanted quick, short, intensive and inexpensive education."

He listed some educational gaps they defined: traditional fixed equity and variable equity products; traditional fixed premium and flexible premium products; term rate wars; interest rate wars; traditional, levelized, and negotiated commissions; personal computers to enable agents to vary mortality and interest assumptions; tax laws; advanced underwriting techniques, etc., etc.

The first questions that come to mind are obvious: shouldn't the organizations that NALU created, such as LUTC, the American College and CLU/ChFC, be the proper repository of such "quickie courses?" Isn't NALU, which has been pushing education of the agent for 99 years, simply adding another layer to an educational system that has been rocking along with huge success over time?

The answer seems to be that the agents are looking elsewhere for a fast-food, highly selective program that will enable them to dip into issues that confuse them, and dip out again when they are satisfied they have the answers. This isn't formal education on a long-term basis; it's a taste-here-and-a-nibble-there process, which educational professionals look upon with something akin to horror. Most of them have the notion that you do not acquire an education as a chicken picks up corn.

However, it is unthinkable that NALU will not work closely with its fellow organizations in developing what Press calls "its new educational initiative." The heads of LUTC, the American College and the Society of CLU/ChFC are certainly standing by ready to play whatever parts that they are asked to.

Another question pops up: are the agents who answered the NALU questionnaire lazy? All the issues that President Press listed as "educational gaps" are certainly discussed in courses that are available today. But they all demand consistent study over at least a year, and often much longer. Is there such a thing as a "quick fix" in the spectrum of an agent's knowledge of what he is marketing? There may be, but not many insurance scholars I know would admit it without the application of a hammer-lock.

Because the "educational initiative" is still in its swaddling clothes, I have few worries about its being brought into line with the flow of the various associations rather quickly. Every one of the 17 members of the NALU board of trustees has at least one designation behind his name signifying considerable study of his business. Some have three: LUTCF, CLU and ChFC. We are not dealing here with a group of men who are know nothings.

My only concern is that NALU use the enormous facilities of its fellow organizations to reach significant ends. Let them consider the closed-circuit TV of the American Society of CLU/ChFC; let them enlist local chanters to "help the huddled masses yearning to breathe free." It will work.

"The Return Of The Native Agent"

No. 5, January 30, 1989, Page 11

Those admirable surveys that spew forth endlessly from the Farmington headquarters of the Life Insurance Marketing and Research Association are beginning to show one pleasant and interesting trend: the so-called agency companies, those who used to dedicate themselves to a full-time field force, have begun solemnly rededicating themselves to this concept.

For a time in the past decade some of them had seemed uncaring about where their first-line agents placed business. Either they didn't equip their field people with a full portfolio, or they were simply non-competitive in some areas where business was brisk. Now they are breaking their backs to be competitive in all major scenes of action, even though the effort is causing them to trim large morsels of fat from their tables of operation, both in home office and field.

Not that the phrase "captive agent" is returning to vogue. Such people have become as extinct as the heath hen and the passenger pigeon because all but a few companies have ceased to insist on utter fidelity. But companies that used to pride themselves on a full-time cadre of old pros appear to be regaining that pride in word and deed. In some instances they had opened up a series of niche products, which failed to excite the troops. In others, they talked about loyalty and expected it, but failed to give much in return. There were other failures too numerous to mention.

But my crystal ball tells me that in 1989 many companies, most of which had forgotten their agency forces while they dabbled in arcane ideas, will get back to basics. I'm not alone in this notion, of course. People like Jack Bobo of NALU, Ernie Cragg of LIMRA and Joe Melone of Prudential were talking about it during the fall of '88. But when the cloud of evidence gets so big that even I can see it, there must be considerable truth in it.

But nobody says it's going to be easy.

One of my favorite profound thinkers and occasional correspondents is Peter Roberts, vice-president of LIMRA. Peter's thought processes enable him to challenge almost any conventional wisdom, ingrained though it may be. In a recent letter to me, in which he was discussing the re-emergence of the agency system, he wrote:

"Soon we will hear about the challenges of controlling financial losses. This will be followed by the rediscovery that a quality agent was a quality candidate.

"How long before we find ourselves once again patiently explaining that the quality of the agent is determined by the quality of agency management? And that the quality of agency management is determined by the quality of regional management?

"Will some bushy-tailed MBA emerge from the lead mines and recommend forming an organization devoted to the study of the dynamics of the agency system?"

To me, Peter seems to be saying that the pieces—tested and approved—are all there but we have neglected to put them together. I agree. I'm fond of quoting George Santayana's familiar sentence, "Those who do not remember the past are condemned to repeat it." The only worse people are those who don't think the past is worth remembering.

I cannot help but believe that one of the reasons the agency system has fallen upon evil times is that companies have brought into their senior executive ranks outside people who don't have the vaguest idea of how it works. It's not easy to dissect this unique system and explain how it differs from other sales corps. Perhaps the new breed of CEOs, most of whom were hired as money managers, is learning that life insurance is fundamentally a people business.

Once that recognition comes—and it seems to be coming—the future of the full-time agency system appears infinitely brighter. No business can afford to ignore or misunderstand its faithful salespeople for too long.

"Keeping Abreast Of The Business"

No. 22, May 29, 1989, Page 15

When I first became acquainted with the life insurance business (just after I returned from the California gold rush, if you must know), it was assumed that life insurance companies educated and trained the agents they hired. (To "educate" was to tell them what life insurance was all about; to "train" was to teach them how to sell it.)

The CLU program was just getting off the ground; the idea of the Life Underwriter Training Council had to wait until the end of World War II before it could begin. A few universities, like Purdue and Southern Methodist, had started "institutes of life insurance marketing" to bring advanced training to agents.

Now let's roll the film fast-forward a few decades: Most companies are trying to get out of any form of agent education and training as fast as they can; The American College is offering CLU and ChFC designations and two master's degrees; LUTC is cranking near 35,000 students through 2,200 classes yearly, and presenting graduates with the LUTCF designation; NALU is offering short courses (most of which are prepared by LUTC) to its state and local associations; the General Agents and Managers Conference and the American Society of CLU/ChFC are involved in closed-circuit TV, and the Life Insurance Marketing and Research Association has devised a course for general agents and managers. Add to that the commercial publishers and you have a God's plenty of educators, each ready to succeed or fail on its own merits.

And each depends, to one degree or another, on the beneficence of the companies which, in theory, no longer have to train agents in-depth.

But then came an occurrence that may have broken the camel's back: LUTC, growing by leaps and bounds, finally became too big to be housed in the Washington headquarters of NALU. It had to move out. And, instead of hiring a suite of offices somewhere, it decided to buy or build its own building. It figures the price to be in the neighborhood of $5 million, and it is going to its graduates, designees and companies to raise the funds.

A certain number of companies—it's too early to guess exactly how many—have balked at being the major contributors. They haven't said no, but it is apparent that they are going to have to have the answers to some specific questions before they say yes. Until the say yes, all insurance educators may be stalled.

The companies look at the various educational outlets and they see duplication, entrenchment and empire-building. Does each of them need its own special staff of educators, course writers and specialists? Is the CLU instructor unable to teach or write at the LUTC level? As Ken Frye, executive vice-president of Massachusetts Mutual, wrote to me, "The educational principles are common to all and many of the basic courses are common to all. The organizational structures of each are much the same."

Ken's idea is to monitor all educational organizations for 10 years in order to develop a goal for the year 2000. "We should continue to fund the inefficiencies and inequities but control the growth of these organizations," he says, "and as people leave or retire at least we would have identified the organization of the future, its location, the career path, the designations, recognitions, the rewards, etc."

Calls have been made for a career path before; the best one I have seen is PACE (Professional Achievement in Continuing Education) developed by the American Society of CLU/ChFC and The American College. But the determination of the companies constitutes a 900-pound gorilla that is capable of knocking heads together. Companies are short funds everywhere; they can be impatient with what they see to be duplications of effort and empire-building. They, after all, are being called upon to provide the bulk of the funding for agent education.

To my mind, Ken Frye's proposal has merit; it calls not for an upheaval but for a 10 year task force study. Any educational organization that is unwilling to have its functions and activities examined minutely over a period of years by a competent group brings suspicion on itself.

I don't know how many allies Ken Frye has, but I think his plan deserves measured consideration all the way down the line.

"Loyalties—And The Senior Agent"

No. 34, August 21, 1989, Page 15

Recently five senior agents—all CLUs and past or present members of the Million Dollar Round Table—have talked with me about their dissatisfactions with the life insurance business as they begin to slow down prior to retirement. They represent five different companies and live hundreds of miles apart. I have a notion that many of their peers can tell the same story.

In the late 1970s and early '80s, when loyalties were taking a heavy beating in home office and field, and companies were coming up with strange and wonderful policies, agents like these became almost totally independent. Their reason was, they said, that they were trying to find the best buy for their clients. As the excitement of searching for the lowest net cost waned—because most major companies became increasingly competitive—they drifted back to their No. 1 companies like prodigal sons. But there was no fatted calf.

All five want to throttle down as they get closer to 65. They believe that they have paid their dues. Each has been highly active in institutional groups. They would like to lie back and smell the roses.

But, in the case of these five, their companies don't see it that way. Over the last 10 years their written business with those companies hasn't been up to the standards established for full-time agents. Their break in service has more significance to the companies than it does to them. Unless they punch up their production they are going to start suffering, first in the medical coverage and then in their pension benefits.

The sad story seems to be that they didn't read the fine print in their contracts. (Despite the fact that we all indignantly deny there is fine print any more, it has to be acknowledged that some type is larger than other type.) Many years ago they listened to those who recruited them, and assumed that the promises made were eternal. They weren't.

But here we're not talking about marginal agents; we're talking about old professionals who have brought pride to their companies, their institution and themselves. Even though they may have strayed from the fold momentarily, and even though their production may be dropping as their ages mount, do their companies owe them anything for a lifetime of service?

A principal problem, of course, is that there is precious little portability in pension and medical benefits in the life insurance business. If an agent for one company places a jumbo policy in another, he is happy with the commission and doesn't think about any possible pension rights—at least until he nears retirement age and starts to count up the might-have-beens. Then he starts to have second thoughts.

The companies, of course, see service commissions for the life of the policy as a form of pension. But if we look at LIMRA statistics about how long policies stay in force, we are stuck with the conclusion that the slippered pantaloon—as Shakespeare calls the retiree—isn't going to collect any important amount from service fees. Nor, being slippered, is he going to give much service.

It occurs to me that, in addition to the bright print and the small print in agents' contracts, companies should consider the possibility of constituting committees that would evaluate an agent's contributions as he or she nears retirement age. As I have said many times, the word "loyalty" has been bandied about so meaninglessly, as it affects both the agent and the home office, that it has become almost farcical to both sides. Such a committee could focus on the subject, and perhaps bring a measure of substance to it.

It is the nature of the salesperson to be suspicious of his bosses (and it might be said that the reverse is also true). If the word "loyalty" is to have any meaning, its presence must be felt up front—particularly among career agents. Any action taken to devise a "senior agent evaluation committee" would have a profound impact on company-field relations.

"Life Of A Salesman"

No. 34, October 2, 1989, Page 35

Mike Royko, the syndicated columnist from Chicago, frequently reminds me of some of the old boys who inhabited the newsroom when I was a cub reporter: the ever-present fedora, the cigarette dangling from the lips, the two-fingered typing, the blazing vocabulary, and the ever-present desire to get to Bleecks, a newspapermen's tavern across the street, as soon as deadlines had been met.

A few weeks ago Mike mused about the worst job he had ever had before he made his mark as a writer, and he had some beauties: pinsetter in a bowling alley, hole digger for a landscaper, machinist, bartender, lathe worker, and pool-hall manager.

The one he hated most was selling. He didn't sell insurance; he sold tombstones on commission. But his comments on the life of a salesman deserve to be carved on a granite monument somewhere, perhaps in the lobby of the headquarters of the National Association of Life Underwriters. Here they are:

"For me, persuading people that they had to have a product—my product—was the most agonizing job I've ever had . . . Don't misunderstand. I'm not demeaning sales work. Just the opposite. I think that selling on commission is the hardest, most nerve-wracking way to earn a living there is. To deal with the uncertainty—the deflating 'Sorry, but no thanks'—takes the hide of a rhino and the nerves of a pilot.

"It amazes me that every morning, hundreds of thousands of men and women get up and hit the streets or the phones to face that uncertainty. But it doesn't amaze me that at the end of the day, many of them head for the nearest place that pours something with an olive in it.

"That's probably why the play *Death of a Salesman* has become an American classic. And why plays and movies such as *Glengarry Glen Ross* and *Tin Man* are so successful. The audience is full of people who say, 'That's me,' while their stomachs churn.

"So next Labor Day weekend, we might keep in mind that lifting something heavy or getting dirty hands isn't the only tough form of labor.

"Given a choice between calluses or an ulcer, I'll take the calluses. As any salesman with his back to the wall will tell you, 'You can't wear work gloves on your stomach.'"

Most life insurance salespeople I know won't admit to this except over one of those things with an olive in it, but the element that Royko forgets to talk about is the other side of the coin: the giddy, almost insane, pleasure that comes when an agent cracks a big case. The memory of past sorry-but-no-thanks incidents is wiped out and we are on top of the world, ready to face a thousand gorillas.

I have always held the belief that home office executives who have no idea what the sales procedure is like should be assigned to work with an agent for a full week. In the old days, no one could become a senior officer of the Metropolitan Life without having walked a debit for a specific time. I understand that some companies are today sending executives into the field to learn at first hand agents' problems. To some executive suites this must seem insanely simplistic. However, if the gulf between the manufacturer and the salesman is to be bridged, this is one means that should be grasped.

One of the great problems of the business is the turnover rate in the sales force. Many people, who see what thundering successes some agents achieve, opt for the job, but they find the same pains in their stomachs as Mike Royko did, and they quit. Part of this problem is that the selection process for new agents has never been perfected despite the application of some of the best minds in the business. But a good deal lies in the fact that the home office regards its agents as a group of curios, operating on a wing and a prayer.

That attitude needs to be changed before the recruit feels the confidence to hang in there, and the mature agent stops being ulcer-ridden.

"The Squeeze Isn't All On The Agent"

No. 50, December 11, 1989, Page 13

Companies are continually trying to master the art (it's certainly no science) of marketing life insurance at a profit, competing successfully with their opposite numbers, and keeping their corporate families happy and eager to get the chores done.

It hasn't been easy on a lot of people. The marginal agent is effectively out of the business. The middle-of-the-road agent in a protracted slump also faces a "produce or else" ultimatum. Even the Million Dollar Round Table has become the "$40,000 in First-Year Commissions" Round Table. Selling a million is no longer a certified way of getting to use the CEO's first name.

The squeeze is on the agent, all right, as you will read in an upcoming symposium on agent compensation in the *National Underwriter.* But are the companies trying to solve all their woes solely by leaning heavily on the field force?

No, indeed. Home office people are getting the same treatment. But because they are somewhat more sequestered than agents, who are right out there in front of God and everybody, they tend not to receive the same kind of sympathy. Perhaps they should.

Carol Robinson of the Life Office Management Association puts it this way:

"Mergers, acquisitions and downsizing among insurers have flattened organizational structures. So, more employees are reporting to fewer managers. And that means there's less supervision." Her logical conclusion: "Today's insurance employees need to be self-starters."

To me, that is an almost excessively polite way of saying, "Stop thinking that you can continue to lean on your bosses. They may not be there next week—and if you don't shape up, maybe you won't be either."

LOMA is not an organization to issue a warning like this and not back it up with some constructive action. It has produced an Employee Development and Growth Enhancement Program (called "EDGE," naturally) that is designed to arm employees against "flattened organizational structures."

It involves five training sessions: "Taking the Initiative," which helps employees discover how to take control in their jobs; "Using Time Wisely," which speaks for itself; "Opening Up to Change," which undertakes to remove some negatives from the future; "Communicating for Results," which also speaks for itself, and "Recognizing Your Customers," which talks about everyone the employee deals with.

The program looks like a good idea. Home office employees lead more structured business lives than agents (although they may not seem to on certain occasions), because the matter of prospecting doesn't face them when they wake up in the morning. Of course, they do have certain other restraints that members of the field force happily know nothing about.

The life insurance business has practically no firm statistics on the fluctuation of its agency and home office employee population. As Lynn Merritt, president of LOMA, explains it, "An agent can be listed as under contract with many companies. That means any one of them could be counted several times. An employee may work for an entire group of companies, performing a certain function for each of them. They, too, may be counted more than once. Up to now, we haven't found it possible to produce accurate statistics on how many are employed in either segment of the business." That certainly sounds reasonable.

But I tend to agree with Ms. Robinson's notion that things have "flattened" in every element of employment or contract. Consequently, courses that help people sharpen their skills are desperately important. The field has its LUTC and CLU/ChFC designations. The home office now have EDGE. People who don't avail themselves of these opportunities are likely to be the first to be "flattened." It's a vivid word, but a necessary one.

"The 'Average Agent' Is A Dinosaur"

No. 18, April 30, 1990, Page 17

For years I have heard the big hitters of the life insurance business prate from the platform about the virtues of the 'average agent.'

"He will never make the Million Dollar Round Table," they would say, "but he will get the National Quality Award. He has a good home and family, with kids he is sending through college. He is the backbone of the life insurance business."

The key word here is "average." Average means mediocre. Mediocre will no longer do as the pace of life insurance grows faster, the demands on salespeople more stringent, and the bottom line looms larger and larger. Today if an agent is no more than average, he or she is in grave danger of termination. The average agent costs too much.

If they hadn't already known it before, the General Agents and Managers Conference heard it from two of my friends at their LAMP meeting in Dallas: Bill Fenniman, the leading manager for the Manufacturers Life, and Vin Bowhers, who occupies the same status as general agent for John Hancock, both in Boston agencies.

New compensation systems are coming in that seek out mediocrity and punish it. Vin Bowhers is applying the profit-center concept in individual producers. He charges for service first and rewards productivity as an offset. This involves a bonus system that reaches down as far as the clerical staff. Salaries are reduced or flat and the bonus ties everyone's income into the productivity of the agency.

Some critics (lazy ones, mostly) may contend that this resembles the Stakhanovite system that the Russians have been toying with since 1935, in that it emphasizes productivity at the expense of professionalism. This is nonsense. It simply is placing the carrot before the donkey's nose (sorry about that, fellow donkeys), which is a tested method of helping people work more efficiently.

This is only one of a series of strictures Vin Bowhers has introduced in his efforts at cost-containment, but it is the one that will doubtless get the most immediate attention of agents. The reason: the figures are right there on the board for every individual to see, and those who don't measure up will, just as in baseball, be trying on some minor league uniforms.

Like Bowhers, Bill Fenniman has also moved from fixed to variable costs, or total incentive compensation. He looks at office services as part of the grand plan, and charges stiffly for them. Even pre-contract training for the novice agents is beginning to cost them under his plan so they can cease to be liabilities from the day they sign. He also holds brainstorming sessions that are aimed at motivating producers to buy into profitability.

Are Bowhers and Fenniman cruel men, obsessed with the bottom line? Hell no. They are competent businessmen who realize full well that their necks will be the first under the guillotine if they surround themselves with mediocrities or incompetents.

Too many agents, some of them veterans with a good many merit badges, fail to recognize the changing face of life insurance today. They have always been good soldiers, they say; they have paid their dues and they have brought a modicum of honor to their companies. Indeed they have, but it is no longer enough. If they paid close attention to the fiscal binds their agencies and companies were in, they might see the handwriting on the wall. Yes, many of these binds were created by the agencies and companies themselves in the '80s, but that's crying over spilled milk. Everything flowed easily for a few years. That's all over, and everyone in life insurance should realize it.

One reason for it is that the companies have been reluctant to tell their field people what their problems are, precisely and squarely. That might be a better cure for non-productivity than any other device.

I believe that Bowhers and Fenniman are moving in the right direction, but there has to be lots more creative thinking before agent and company lock arms.

"The Impossible Takes A Little Longer"

No. 23, June 4, 1990, Page 37

For some years now I have been worrying in print about the various educational organizations in the life insurance business tripping over each others' feet. The rush to educate members of the field force, both in management and selling, is unassailable but, in the immortal words (or woids) of Jimmy Durante, "Everyone wants to get into the act."

Duplication is costly; it is costly to the participant; it is costly to the agency; it is costly to the supportive company; and it is costly to the associations, their administrators and their faculties.

As recently as March 26 in this column I said, "Neither agents nor their companies can afford more proliferation. What is called for is an all-industry committee to determine what's needed in institutional areas, and then enforce its dictums."

Well, as the back-country magician said when he actually made the elephant disappear, "I'll be goldanged." What I asked for is apparently on its way to happening. Not that I did it (I understand that the elephant really fell into a hole), but the coincidence pleases me mightily. The credit belongs to the top people in the Life Insurance Marketing and Research Association, the Life Office Management Association, the General Agents and Managers Conference, the American College and the Life Underwriter Training Council.

They have announced a "comprehensive joint effort. . .to define and clarify emerging field management development needs, with regard to the individual niches and specialities of each association."

This is a giant Step One. If these associations can make progress in this area, they will be admirably positioned to take over discussion of all elements of field education and training. Not that the companies themselves are out of the act—far from it. If a company doesn't brief its own field force on its principles, policies and practices, it is neglecting a prime duty. But, especially in the area of intermediate and advanced education, the institutional groups are increasingly demonstrating leadership.

To make the circle complete, the National Association of Life Underwriters, in addition to all its subsidiary conferences, will have to join the act. And I assume this would include the health insurance group that is just being born. Plus, I would urge, the American Society of CLU/ChFC.

True, the original statement of the five participating associations said, "Deliberations to date have focused on the opportunity to develop an identifiable career path for field managers through various professional development programs." But they surely understand that what is beneficial to agency managers can be logically extended to the people they manage. It would be a neat fit.

Yes, gentlemen and ladies, I know what I am doing here is known in poker as "bulling the bet"—taking a logical sequence of events and trying to extend it beyond what everyone is currently prepared for. But I'd be willing to bet my bippy that the leaders of the current project, plus many onlookers, have the same idea in mind. If the business is smart enough and brave enough to attack the duplication that now exist, it will save millions.

The American College has already announced a major step in this direction: it will, as its announcement says, "enable a number of the 21,500 holders of the LUTCF designations to receive credits toward CLU/ChFC." Simple, you say? Inspired, I call it. One of the most tortuous processes in education is to study for a course and then, a couple of years later, have to study for it again.

Perhaps not many people will regard the GAMC-LUTC-LIMRA-LOMA-American College projects as a vast step forward in field education and training. I do. Over the years there has been too much talk and too little action in this critical area. If it succeeds, they deserve the credit. If it bogs down, shame on them—and, incidentally, on all of us.

"Stump Merrill Syndrome"

No. 32, August 6, 1990, Page 29

Across the Androscoggin River from where I went to college is a village called Topsham. One of its leading citizens is a man named Carl Merrill, who is universally known as "Stump"—possibly because he wasn't as big as some of the boys as a kid. Stump is a teacher of athletes—in the fall he is on the staff of the Bowdoin college football team. The rest of the year he is a baseball manager. . .somewhere.

He has managed minor league teams ad infinitum. Class A, Class AA and even Class AAA (the cream of the minor leagues). He has been universally successful. If he is a journeyman, he is the best of journeymen.

A calamity happened to Stump Merrill a few weeks ago. He was named manager of the New York Yankees baseball team. The Yankees have the worst record in major league baseball. Their CEO is a strange man named George Steinbrenner. He took a winning team and, through various maneuvers, lost most of his star players. In the 18 years he has been owner, he has had 18 managers. His motto seems to be, "When losing, fire the manager." As a matter of fact, he is so obstinate he sometimes fires the manager even when the team is winning.

Steinbrenner may have sacked old Stump by the time this reaches print. No matter. There is a parable here for those of us in the life insurance business, both home office and field.

Is the executive suite of some life insurance companies really the "Steinbrenner suite?" Are its occupants so out of touch with the daily problems of the field that "Fire the manager" is their only viable recourse? That's not true, of course, in most companies, but it surely is in some.

When management goes out on a limb, it must explain what motivated it to do so, or suffer the consequences. During the '80s, when companies were trying all manner of experiments to stay abreast of what they called the competition, some alienated many of their best agents who started going shopping for the best deal they could cut for their clients.

The obvious answer: fire the agency manager. He couldn't keep his agents loyal to the company. Agency production went down, and production is mother's milk to a manager. Management even fired some pretty good agents who, even though they might be members of the Million Dollar Round Table, weren't placing sufficient business with their prime company.

Good agents survive; someone wants them. It's tougher on general agents and managers. The conventional press release has always read, "John X has asked to be relieved of his managerial duties in order to serve his own clients better." What—all 20 of them? The dedicated manager is up to his ears in managing, not selling. If he has any clients they are either relics of his agenthood or happenstance sales. (I'm, of course, not talking about personal producing GAs who are a breed apart and live by a special state of rules.)

Have the companies, like Steinbrenner, forgotten the support factor that makes a manager look good or bad? In an effort to cut costs, have they shifted the total burden of recruiting, training, supervision and continuing education to the field? If they have, it seems to me that they are the chief culprits, not the manager.

There is a growing lack of rapport between the home office and the field—in some companies, that is. (It is unwise to generalize.) The division permeates conventions, and astute observers of the insurance scene comment on it. They should if the field people and those in the executive suite become adversaries; no good can come of it.

You may say that I should have named the syndrome after George Steinbrenner, not Stump Merrill. But, like Lou Gehrig's disease, I believe the victim should be celebrated and not the perpetrator.

"Ethics, Due Diligence and Other Imponderables"

No. 1, January 7, 1991, Page 31

As I recall, when you and I were somewhat younger we clearly understood the matter of ethics. If we were engaged in a friendly person-to-person sport, without judges or other officials, we called 'em as we saw 'em, and if we were beaten we acknowledged the fact. Oh, there were a few arguments on marginal calls, but nothing hair-raising. We were not young John McEnroes, the win-at-any-price, I'm never-wrong fellow.

In business, we went by the book or we got fired. When we arrived at a position where we were able to do the firing, we became even more ethical.

Where has the philosophy of good ethical behavior gone? It has seemingly strayed so far that four major educational organizations in insurance—the American College, the American Institute for Property and Liability Underwriters, the American Society of CLU & ChFC, and the Society of CPCU—have found it necessary to sponsor an Ethics Awareness Week this December.

They are on exceedingly solid ground in one area, for sure: people need considerable help when they are on the horns of an ethical dilemma. Always have, always will. The ability to reason one's way out of thorny situations has to be taught. Their videotaped panel presentations has attacked this situation forthrightly.

The problem lies with people who consciously violate ethical dogma for their own profit, heedless of what their actions may do to their clients or colleagues. Here we might as well be advising a congress of thieves on how to avoid thievery. Will anyone be listening?

We are all uncomfortably aware of the ethical scandals on Wall Street and in the savings and loan industry, as well as the tax-dodging that is constantly going on and the various other peccadillos that we witness daily. Will anyone dare arise and tell us that these people don't know what they are doing? The sole motto is: don't get caught.

I applaud any serious discussion of ethical conduct, but at the same time I realize that much of it will fall on deaf ears. This doesn't mean we should be silent, or even lower our voices. Maybe we will catch a convert.

Next in line we find the relatively new phrase, "due diligence," which, in its simplest form, means that a salesperson must be alert not to describe a mess of pottage as a five-course dinner. Brokers have always known it; members of other professions live by it. As salespeople spread out their smorgasbord of possibilities before a prospect, they must be sure that they don't offer a rotten tomato in the fare. It's their responsibility.

When agents represented one company only, this wasn't a major concern. But now that getting the lowest price has become the major goal of the client, and agents scurry to find it, they must be certain that what they come up with has stability.

If not, the client may sue the agent if he finds he has been handed a lemon, and the agent may well lose. "Due diligence" has much more substance to it than my shorthand comments, of course, but the agent has many more sources at his or her fingertips to mull over the matter.

Errors and omissions insurance may bail out the agent in many instances. If life underwriters have done their level best to present a substantial product to their clients, a claim against them may have a hard time finding recourse, which is as it should be. While E&O insurance used to be a filigree which many agents scorned, it is now a part of business life.

Words like all of the above should remind us how complex life insurance salesmanship has become. It used to be a case of "sell or not sell." Sell enough and you were a success; don't and you're a failure. Today it has become a question of precisely how one sells. The client has become more sophisticated. Let it be.

"'How Much Do You Make On This?'"

No. 26, July 1, 1991, Page 27

Relations between a salesperson and his or her client have usually been cordial, especially when earnings on a transaction have been concerned. You don't usually ask a salesperson who has sold you a car, "How much do you make on this?" It's always been a no-no; the seller might just as well reply to the buyer, "I'd be glad to explain my commission scale to you if you'd care to tell me how much you were paid last month for what you do."

Lately, however, consumer advocates have been urging buyers to ask the question. The ostensible reason is that all sales should be open and above-board. A less obvious suggestion is that the buyer is thinking about the possibility of some kind of a rebate. The transaction has become adversarial.

This kind of dialogue should remind us all of the old wheeze:

A person's machine (you name the machine) lies down and refuses to work. He calls a mechanic. The mechanic looks at the vital elements of the machine, pulls out a screwdriver and tightens three screws. The machine starts to purr like a kitten. "How much?" asks the owner. "Fifty dollars," replies the mechanic. "Fifty dollars? What for? It didn't take you five minutes." Comes the reply, "Three dollars for tightening three screws. Forty-seven dollars for knowing which screws to tighten."

The moral to the story, of course, is that the client has utterly no understanding of the education, preparation and knowledge that went into the five minute operation. The client could sit around tightening screws for a month and the machine wouldn't respond.

Or, as Luke said in the New Testament, "The laborer is worthy of his hire."

It would be possible for any agent to say, "Now, you just listen to me for a minute. I studied to get my license to sell. I took training courses from my company on my own time. I took courses from LUTC, CLU and ChFC, at my own expense and on my own time. I go to many meetings a year, at my own expense and on my own time, to learn to give you advice that is completely up-to-date and in conformity with the laws that both you and I must obey. Now, will you kindly factor that into your question of how much I make on this transaction? Didn't you have to do something along the same lines to get to the point where you could even consider my proposal?"

Naturally, you wouldn't be that rude. Yet consumerists, sometimes, seem to be asking for it. They casually accept the fact that they have fought the good fight in order to arrive at a position where you and they could be discussing a big-ticket purchase, but they believe they are the only ones who have done the homework to make a transaction possible. You, they contend, are simply a cog in a mammoth machine that transmits a product or a service from the manufacturer to the customer, and they feel privileged to know how big a profit you are making on them.

This entire concept revolts me. I don't even want to know what Lee Iacocca makes, although newspapers insist on telling me. I assume that if he isn't earning his keep, his board of directors will take care of him. Every day I read about senior executives who have resigned "to seek other opportunities," and I understand full well that they haven't been able to justify their salaries. . .and bonuses. . .and perks.

I respect the rule of privacy, except in the case of a publicly held corporation (including all insurance companies) where management is totally responsible to stockholders and policyholders. This does not extend to commissioned salespeople, whose compensation is set by law and who cannot circumvent the regulators in their states. But privacy seems to have become a lost trait; half the books on the best-seller list seem to be stripping people naked.

You may say that I am taking the simple question, "How much do you make on this?" and extrapolating it too far. To me it's just a matter of degree. If you invade my income, you start to invade life, and I don't like it.

You mind your business, I'll mind mine, and we'll both be OK.

5

The Political Arena

"The Future Of Rebating"

No. 45, November 8, 1986, Page 17

"Greetings, friends! This is Cut-Rate Cal, Your Insurance Pal. Say, you **know** you need more life insurance, don't you? How'd you like to get exactly what you want at **one-third off** the first year's payment? And not with some little ol' company you've never heard of, either. Just pick any of the big ones—the Pru, the Met, the Equitable, the Hancock—you name it.

"Here's all you have to do: go see your regular insurance agent and decide what you need. Ask him what the first-year premium is. Then tell him you'd like to think it over—and come see us. We'll guarantee you one-third off that first premium.

"How can we do this? Volume, that's how. Because we sell so we don't need the first-year markup your agent puts in his pocket. For further information call. . ."—A possible radio or TV commercial in 1989.

A fantasy? Don't count on it. The first rebating domino fell when the Florida Supreme Court reaffirmed in September its earlier decision to strike down the state's anti-rebating laws. California, approaching the issue via the legislative route, has seen a bill reaffirming its age-old anti-rebating procedures vetoed by Gov. Dukmejian. Other states are considering legal or judicial actions to make rebating wholesome. Ralph Nader is rubbing his hands in glee. Consumer activists are surely gearing up to take action in your state.

Equally alarming, as I discovered at the annual CLU Forum in San Antonio in October, is that many companies and agents have already prepared fallback positions if rebating strikes the public fancy, which they surely wouldn't have done unless they saw rebating as a real possibility. Some of them echoed the words of Richard Maurer, agency vice-president of the Metropolitan, which appeared in the August issue of LIMRA's *MarketFacts*:

"We would be inclined to go to level commissions. In other words, get the commission down so low and effectively reduce the front-end so that it wouldn't be meaningful to negotiate." My translation of this is: If you don't pay the agent enough to rebate, he won't rebate. And at that point I begin to get stomach cramps.

Joe Melone, president of the Prudential, was 180 degrees away from Dick Maurer in a panel discussion at the CLU Forum. He said that he saw "no chance" for a level commission system in his company.

Everyone who spoke seemed to feel that his own constituency would be most badly hurt by rebating. Rod Geer, executive head of the Million Dollar Round Table, expressed the belief that his big-hitter members would be hurt "more quickly and more often." John Driskill, executive vice-president of the American Society of CLU & ChFC, thought that the advanced underwriter, dealing with the most sophisticated client, would feel the first impact. And Jack Bobo of NALU mused about the plight of the recruit, who needs front money. He brought forth the thought that it—the rebating problem—was "not necessarily Armageddon," but might be solved by legislative remedy in states where the courts overturned current regulations.

But the recurring mutter that "rebating needn't be harmful" reminded me of the passionate outcries of the American Tobacco Institute about the intrinsic wholesomeness of cigarettes. Many of those who seemed to be in that corner were old pros who had spent much time in property-casualty insurance, where rebating is more of a way of life than it is in life insurance. But P&C has what already amounts to a level premium system and isn't accustomed to the front-money and longterm financial practice of life compensation. As one multi-line agent, Tom Roebig of Jacksonville, FL, wrote me:

"Property/casualty agents do very well on level commissions and I feel as a class are more professional, service their clients better, and certainly remain in the field for longer than 90 percent of those entering the life sales force."

But if the anti-rebating front is to be shored up, the entire insurance business has to get into the act. Several institutional groups stated at the CLU Forum that they had supported the California effort financially. Others are prepared to act as amici curiae wherever consumer groups raise anti-rebating as a legal issue. White papers must be carefully prepared to show the dangers to the consumer of unlimited rebating—forget the shedding of tears about the plight of the agents and the companies.

While the preparation of fallback positions if the Naders take over the henhouse is certainly prudent, I fear for the future of the career agency system if rebating becomes the norm. What bright young kids will want to come into a business where the practice is to give away a substantial slice of one's earned income?

"The PAC vs. The Voter"

No. 46, November 15, 1986, Page 11

Political Action Committees throughout America have by this time decided which candidates for public office merit their financial support, and have handed it out. While they talk about distributing it "fairly"–and most of them do, I guess—the chances are strong that candidates who agree warmly with the philosophy of the individual PAC will haul in the bucks, while those testy people who are of contrary thought or who haven't made their positions known will end up in a dry gulch.

There is no doubt that our election system needs some control over who gets what campaign money. Any other system—or lack of it—means that the candidate with the best-heeled friends will bring in the dollars. And how important dollars for exposure to the voters have become! The days of the whistle-stop campaigning, handshaking and baby-kissing are over. TV time is what produces the votes. And you don't need to be told what that costs.

Happy With PACs

Organized business and organized labor are thoroughly happy with PACs because the system gives them candidates' attention—although not necessarily their votes. People with no strong affiliations—and you'd be surprised how many of them there are if you look under the right rocks—tend to feel that candidates are no longer interested in them, and that they have become ciphers in the minds of legislators.

Senators David Boren (D.—OK) and Barry Goldwater (R.—AZ) have designed an amendment that would, for the first time, place an overall limit on the amount any House or Senate candidate may receive from all PACs. However, members of Congress have never become noteworthy for turning off any kind of Golden Spigot, so its future is in doubt despite the fact that it has passed the Senate by a 69-30 vote.

Largest One

The insurance business is up to its ears in PACs—company PACs, organizational PACs, institutional PACs. Considerably the largest is NALUPAC, the creature of the National Association of Life Underwriters, which produces about $1 million for federal races and a like amount for state elections. To see with blinding clarity the success of NALUPAC, one has only to attend a Congressional reception hosted by the association. Everybody who is anybody is there, from Bob Dole on down, behaving as much like kids under a Christmas tree as members of Congress allow themselves to be.

I have some small misgivings about political action committees for three principal reasons:

- Incumbents, unless they are obvious misfits, are more likely to benefit from PAC largesse than candidates who are challenging. The PACs know the incumbent's track record, and have certainly explained with great care their stands on the issues of the moment. The new candidate faces what *The Wall Street Journal* calls "the incumbency barrier"—the unwillingness to settle money on an unknown quantity.

- Most PACs are avowedly special interest groups—a phrase that sounds more derogatory than it should. Insurance PACs are interested primarily in how a candidate stands on insurance issues. Conceivably, the candidates could be blithering idiots on some matters—roads, treatment of farmers, state and local revenues, to name a few—but if they will protect the sainted inside buildup, they may gather enough money to televise their way across their state with vast success.

Here to Stay

- I am in great sympathy with individual voters who see their state as a whole, not as an agglomeration of special interests. I would not like to see the PAC become the primary constituency of the candidate rather than the broad gauged voter, but the terrifying impact of TV money tends to make this possible.

Don't get me wrong—I am convinced that PACs are here to stay. They perform a valuable service in bringing the candidate face-to-face with the issues that he or she will have to confront during the two or six years before the next election. But under current circumstances there seems to be no end to their expansion, and the three reservations I have mentioned above would become ever more acute.

The unlikely combination of the young Yale, Rhodes scholar from Oklahoma—a Democrat—and the crusty old fighter from Arizona—a conservative Republican if there ever was one—may be the answer. As long as all PACs and all candidates are treated alike, as they are in the Boren-Goldwater amendment, only the PACs with very deep pockets and no place to unload them should wail.

The Senate has passed Boren-Goldwater, but the House will be tougher because the number of people who need campaign funds is larger and hungrier. If it becomes law, it may strengthen the balance between the voter and the PAC, and between the incumbents and those who are trying to unseat them. That seems useful.

"The Sorry State Of Florida"

No. 11, March 16, 1987, Page 17

When most of us think of Florida, we visualize sunshine, bikinis, Disney and *Miami Vice*. Some of us also visualize a progressive, growing state, full of new ideas and a touch of madness.

Madness, however, seems to have taken over lately as far as the control of insurance is concerned. Companies and agents are trying to fight their way out of a bind caused by changes in law, regulation and taxation. Any one of these moves might cause panic; put together they most closely resemble chaos.

Here are some of the actions, promulgated by various arms of government, that have insurance interests shaking as if with palsy:

Early last year the state Supreme Court struck down Florida's anti-rebating laws, which were similar to those in most states. The protagonist in this action was Walter Dartland, Miami's consumer advocate. Shortly after this he was fired (for reasons having nothing to do with his attitude toward insurance), but he ended by becoming consumer advocate for the entire state, so he now has even more clout.

The state insurance department has issued several regulations that have blocked unrestricted rebating, including one that forces an agent who uses the tactic to do so with all clients, not just a favored few. But the worm of rebating is in the apple of insurance.

In the final hours of its 1986 session, the Florida legislature passed a bill that included insurance reform, tort reform, property/casualty rate roll-backs, a tort and insurance law study committee and physician financial responsibility. Just about everyone in Florida found one or two things to like in the act and a half-dozen to despise. The result has been that the lawyers, the doctors, the insurance companies, the agents and consumer groups have been trying to dismantle one part of it or another ever since. And first there was much talk on the part of companies of "leaving Florida." That has simmered down, but the wounds haven't yet healed.

Miami's Insurance Exchange of the Americas, a sort of Lloyds of London for the Western Hemisphere, has run onto such hard times that Commissioner Bill Gunter has stated that he may ask the legislature to repeal the law that brought it into existence. The *Miami Herald* calls it "yet another South Florida financial institution constructed on a shaky foundation of big dreams and little money. It tried to grow too big, too fast. It took shortcuts, kept sloppy records, let in some bad apples, and paid a high price for its early mistakes."

The Exchange is a for-profit organization that has had as many as 21 syndicates operating under its aegis. If the state is forced to take it down, the entire insurance business will feel the repercussions, although the financial repercussions will be limited.

Finally—and this is the one that hits the most pocketbooks—Florida has decreed that insurance premiums will be subject to the 5 percent state sales tax beginning in July.

(Insurance isn't the only business affected—the edict includes all "professional services" from doctors to beauticians.)

This is a scary proposition. It began when the 1986 legislature voted to let most of the sales tax exemptions, except for food and prescription drugs, expire this July 1. Now lobbyists are faced with the job they hate most: getting remedial legislation enacted. That's a far tougher task than blocking ill-advised bills.

Why Florida? Why now? And why should other states worry?

Why Florida? Because it's a bellwether state; other states are influenced by its experiments. And no political party is really dominant.

Why now? Because the consumer movement looms large in the state, with its enormous contingent of oldsters trying to get their due and with time to spend lobbying.

Why should other states worry? Because what has succeeded (or, in the case of the Insurance Exchange, has had trouble succeeding) is immediately examined from every angle by interested parties in the other 49 states.

As a citizen of Florida, I love sunshine, bikinis and Disney. I'm ambivalent about *Miami Vice*. I devoutly hope that all you non-Floridians out there will not look upon these kinds of capers as something caused by too much sunshine. They could just as easily happen to you.

"Pontificating On Wall Street"

No. 47, November 23, 1987, Page 25

Now is the time for all good columnists to haul up their socks and pontificate on the effects of the stock market's gyrations on life insurance. Since each of us writers comes to different conclusions there's very little chance that you will read the same thing twice.

I can sum up my principal reaction in one sentence: the single word that was the favorite of the life insurance business for its first 125 years and then fell out of favor—the word GUARANTEE—will once again be a major force in every agent's vocabulary. Those wonderful computer illustrations that took the possibilities for profit right out of our galaxy will be replaced by sober-sided statements about what the payoff on a policy will be come what may.

Agents will hark back to the Great Depression and remind policyholders that while other financial institutions were impaired or collapsing, life insurance stood firm and "no policyholder ever lost a cent." Although that statement has a great ring to it, I suspect that it's a mite overdrawn. Still, it's part of the lore of life insurance, and no one is going to change it now.

Salespeople who have been reaping hefty rewards on the sale of various universal and variable products may once again realize the manifest virtues in the impregnability of ordinary life and will find to their surprise that it's still in their portfolios. Cosmic thinkers like Bob MacDonald who have talked as though ordinary were a relic to be found only in the pyramids of the pharaohs are likely to see it once again as a useful object and not a crumbling papyrus.

To paraphrase Jack Bobo, a great many wheeler-dealers may remember that "the most important thing about money for future delivery is 'Will it be there?' and the second most important thing is, 'how much?'"

In other words, a great many sales presentations are getting overhauled, and tons of illustrations are being toned down so they will reflect what might be called the "new reality."

Of course, one of the so-called features of variable life policies is that the owner can switch the investment element from stocks to bonds or money funds, depending on the state of the economy. But, as Jane Bryant Quinn recently pointed out in her syndicated column, "Money funds pay barely enough to keep your policy values level, and bonds don't do much better. If that's your investment choice, you might as well be in a straight non-variable policy."

Fortunately, the strictures many states have imposed on insurance company investment in the stock market have kept investment managers from going overboard. While I have seen concern among top management about the state of the economy, nowhere have I witnessed any tendency toward panic. Some agents have reported to me that customer enthusiasm for universal and variable policies appears to have waned, but the idea of tossing life insurance out of a life estate is still unthinkable.

The business still faces a formidable hurdle: Congress is gathering strength to pass legislation taxing the inside buildup of life insurance policies. If this should succeed it would lay a heavy hand on sales presentations. It would demolish those who have been making a living on single-premium policies, and would make all forms of life insurance more difficult to sell.

But I am not ready to throw in the towel on this one. The reasons for the favored tax status of life insurance are as valid as they have always been, and the might of the insurance lobby that believes resoundingly in the maintenance of this status has yet to be tested. Congress has never been anxious to tamper with an instrument that is of overwhelming importance to widows and orphans, and it's hard to visualize it doing so in these times.

No, the stock market plunge didn't wreak havoc on alert life insurance companies and agents. The fact that it caused considerable shifting of gears in sales philosophies is apparent, but this will simply separate those who are uniquely equipped to market life insurance under any circumstances from those who aren't.

"'Feared Sting Of The Insurance Lobby'"

No. 21, May 23, 1988, Page 19

Not long ago, "lobbyist" was a nasty word. It conjured up images of balding, pot-bellied men who smoked stogies, pressing money on members of Congress in return for their "voting right." Nobody ever called himself a lobbyist—he was in public relations or communications or some other calling that could mean almost anything.

No more. Today the lobbyist stands tall and proud. Part of this is probably due to the fact that political action committees have legitimized him; his entree to congressional suites is completely accepted. His physical and mental dimensions have also changed. Instead of looking like Lyn Nofziger, he is young, impeccably groomed, and totally oriented to the issues he talks about. And he's not always a he, either; many women are in the front rank of the nation's lobbyists.

So it's no wonder that the *New York Times* headlined a recent article, "Feared Sting of Insurance Lobby Haunts Capital."

Writer Nathaniel Nash concentrated his story on the Independent Insurance Agents of America and its top lobbyist, Paul Equale, but he might just as well have been talking about the National Association of Life Underwriters and Paul's opposite numbers there. Insurance field-people have long since learned the advantages of working together on issues that involve them all, which is one of the reasons why their power has grown so measurably.

Nash quotes Sen. William Proxmire, chairman of the Senate Banking Committee, on why insurance agents are feared in Washington:

"There are more insurance agents in the state of New Jersey alone than there are banks in the whole country."

Coming from a man who is leading the determination of how far banks may move into the insurance business, that says a mouthful.

The very sales mentality of the insurance agent tends to make him a formidable lobbyist. This from Kenneth A. Guenther, executive vice-president of the Independent Bankers Association:

"It's like the difference between offense and defense. If an agent is not a good salesman, he won't stay in the business long, while a banker tends to have a more passive personality and expects people to come to him."

These people have learned that when an insurance association lobbyist sees hard going ahead and calls out the troops, he has at hand some of the most skilled semi-pros he could find anywhere. Both NALU and IIAA have had hundreds of agents knocking on the doors of Senate and Congressional office buildings at critical points when bills were about to go on the floor.

Nor do they come to Washington unprepared. They are veterans of local and state legislative committees. They know the issues, and they know their senators and representatives. So when they go to the capital, in their state or Washington, they are received politely—although not always with open arms.

The full-time lobbyists, like Paul Equale and his staff, and his opposite numbers from NALU, Jim Douds, Mike Kerley and their associates, serve as mentors and shepherds for the semi-pros brought in from the states. Elaborate briefings are held, and when they are unleashed on the Hill it's no wonder the *Times* refers to their "feared sting."

Nobody pretends that IIAA and NALU have the only effective insurance lobbies in Washington. Company associations and other groups with narrower interests also have plenty of clout. But when it comes to delivering tons of persuasion to the Capitol, they have no equal.

The key to their success, of course, as the bankers ruefully admit, is that they are insurance salespeople selling concepts about insurance. They know their craft, and they are prepared down to the last jot and tittle.

The same skills that make them successful agents don't have to be put in a greatly different focus to make them successful lobbyists.

"Speaking With One Voice?"

No. 38, September 19, 1988, Page 13

It is the fond wish of most members of the life insurance community that the business be able to "speak with one voice" on the major issues it faces—chiefly taxation and other legislative matters, but also field compensation, replacement of currently owned policies and other nuisances that keep coming up.

As Eliza Doolittle would say, "Not bloody likely."

Today the business has more mavericks, crackpots, visionaries and fast-buck entrepreneurs among its top management than at any time I can remember. Some of them are sincere, dedicated people who are trying to improve a conservative, slow-moving business; others have heard the ancient and controversial dictum, "There's no way a person can lose money running a life insurance company."

Here are some of the areas where life insurance is highly unlikely to speak with once voice in the future:

- Federal taxation of companies. For reasons that are abundantly clear to every student of insurance, stock and mutual companies have historically experienced cycles of confrontation on this issue. Last year it reached the point where the American Council of Life Insurance hired an organization named Conflict Management, Inc. of Boston, to undertake to mediate the differences between two singularly different types of companies that traditionally operate under the same fiscal umbrella. The experiment had some success, but as long as Congress tries to extract the same amount of juice from apples and oranges there is going to be an industry collision on how it does so.

- Field compensation. At a recent institutional meeting a senior executive of Metropolitan Life suggested that his company was ready to embark on a level commission plan for agents. When asked for his thoughts on the possibility of such an experiment, an equally senior man from Prudential replied, "Not in my lifetime." What a company pays to the people who bring in the business is certainly one of its most important exercises, but there appears to be no common ground today about what the intrinsic worth of a producing agent should be. The agent usually thinks it is too low; the company replies, "More productivity will earn you more money." There are possibilities for a deep and dangerous split here.

- Deregulation. Most companies and agents have been lobbying to keep the banking industry out of their business. But some companies, notably the John Hancock, are willing to let banks into insurance so they themselves can get into all areas of financial services, particularly banking. Despite the tons of overblown talk on the matter, the critical point seems to be the belief that banks will begin to put subtle pressure on customers who want to borrow money—that if they want the loan, they will have to buy an insurance policy. The Hancock's simple reply is, "That is illegal. If you find a bank that is doing it, you go to the attorney general and get the bank prosecuted." There is flat-out disagreement here.

- McCarran-Ferguson. This Act gives the various states the primary right to regulate insurance. Companies operating in a vast majority of states give lip service to it, but have been known to mumble that it would be easier to transact their business under one federal authority. Smaller companies, licensed to do business in only a few states, are content to leave the business the way it is and go one-on-one with their commissioners. This will always be a thorny issue.

- Replacement. Despite state laws that are already in place, companies are of two minds about how to fend off the current wave of replacements, as exemplified by the A.L. Williams Co. Despite the fact that they have lost many millions of business, they have been reluctant as an industry to insist on the enforcement of statutes they helped put on the books. Some say it is a problem for the agent to solve; others believe it comes with the territory. There has been no concerted effort to do something about it.

"Speaking with one voice" is a slogan with a great ring to it, but perhaps the business is more healthy with occasional dissent. It keeps the establishment on its toes.

"Guess Who's PAC-Bashing"

No. 51, December 19, 1988, Page 17

"I'll tell you the kind of campaign reform I'm supporting, Senator Bentsen. I think it's time we get rid of PAC money. Support our legislation, where we totally eliminate contributions by special interests and political action committees, and let's have the individual contribute and the political parties contribute. That's the kind of tax reform that Republicans are for. They want to get rid of this special interest money and rely on the individuals, and also the political parties." —Vice-President-elect Dan Quayle, during the course of his "debate" with his political opponent, Senator Lloyd Bentsen.

When I heard this comment, delivered live from the bowels of my TV set, I had to dive deep into may vocabulary and come up with the only profound remark I could think of. "Golly-gee!" I said to myself. "What will Bob Dole say?"

I have heard politicians give away the store before in order to get elected, but I have never heard a truly conservative Republican line himself up on the side of Common Cause, the liberal lobby of John Gardner, Archibald Cox and

Fred Wertheimer, all gentlemen who seem to have no problem calling themselves liberals.

Because more important items were discussed on that semi-memorable occasion, no members of the press or TV to whom I listen brought the quote up for scrutiny. Perhaps they thought that Dan Quayle hadn't been sufficiently backgrounded—to use a newly-coined political verb—on the tortuous history of political contributions. Was he implying that individual citizens who contribute heavily to campaigns have no special interests? Or does he yearn for the good old days when backers with the deepest pockets could get their man elected?

For years I have been ambivalent about political action committees. When they are run with scrupulous fairness they provide valuable input, both financial and ideological, to government. But when they are used purely for political hand-kissing (on one side) or bashing (on the other), they leave much to be desired.

In the ten years during which PACs have been major factors in elections, it had become clear that most PACs are Hamlets. Almost uniformly, they would "rather bear those ills we have than fly to others that we know not of. . ." In other words, they tend to go with the incumbent whose quirks they understand rather than take a flier on an untested neophyte.

This makes the Congress—and most particularly the House of Representatives—almost monolithic in nature. In 1988, well over 90 percent of the incumbents who chose to run again won. They did so with the spirited help of PACs. One reelected candidate from Indiana expressed it this way:

"I think they found out when I got elected that they could deal with me. And I think they look at the situation and say, 'Well, he's going to be here for a while.'"

Insurance PACs like a legislator, federal or state, who will hew to the industry line and vote "right." They tend not to worry about a candidate's general ideology. He or she may be flawed in many ways but, "Buddy, if you're against increased taxation of life insurance, both on companies and policyholders, we're for you." Presumably, the members of a PAC wouldn't have it any other way.

If I were parceling out PAC money, I believe I'd try to look at the whole man or woman. I could stand a legislator voting against my industry's position now and then if his general philosophy matched my own. And I'd spend a lot of thoughtful time assessing challengers who had no track record. They might prove to be a lot better than the good ol' boys.

I doubt that Dan Quayle will have his wish—if it is indeed his wish—to destroy PACs. They may be somewhat more limited by law, but someone has to pay for the TV commercials, which are the mother's milk of a political campaign. If your memory is sound, you know this as well as I do.

I just wish PACs would look as carefully at the aspirants for a Congressional seat as they do at the incumbent.

"Three Curious Moves"

No. 14, April 3, 1989, Page 13

The *New York Times* can publish long and probing articles about it, and does so.

The *National Underwriter* can report about it fully to the life insurance community, and does so.

But no life insurance agent or company can mention it to a policyholder or prospect, under pain of at least censure and possibly penalties.

"It" is the New York State Life Insurance Guaranty Corp. which protects policyholders to a considerable degree against the perils of company impairment. It is not a government organization, but is run by companies admitted to do business in New York. It performs many of the same protective functions as the Federal Deposit Insurance Corp. does for depositors in the nation's banks. While banks boast openly—and quite properly—about membership in FDIC, life companies and agents must remain mute about the guaranty fund because "it is a non-profit organization with a limit on its liability."

So states the Life Insurance Council of New York, a 59-member domestic life insurance trade association. It voted 21 to 12 with 25 abstentions not to amend the disclosure statute, a move that had been sought by the Unity Mutual Life, one if its members.

Two groups would certainly be comforted by common knowledge of the existence of the Guaranty Corp.: the great body of policyholders, and the smaller companies doing business in New York, whose claims to financial soundness are not as well-known as those of the giants. The possibility that unscrupulous companies might use it as a sales tool seems remote because the New York Insurance Department is highly vigilant in regulating the companies that are under its control.

I think that further consideration ought to be given to full revelation of this protective blanket.

* * * *

In his monthly newsletter, the *Insurance Forum*, Joe Belth has been examining some aspects of the financial structure of Executive Life, an up-and-coming company with interesting notions in all areas of management. He has been the victim of dirty pool by some anonymous individuals who have started to publish something called *The Insurance Bore Em* which attacks him personally by innuendo and parody, and defends Executive Life in every area. The most recent copy I've seen features an eight-page interview of "Dr. J.M. Wealth" by "Reraldo Givera" and suggests that he find another company to attack.

The issues here are too serious for innuendo and parody. If Joe Belth is out of line, the company's officials ought to call him to task through proper channels. If Joe Belth is right, Executive Life officials should be busy amending their practices.

In all probability the responsible officials of Executive Life had nothing to do with this fatuous publication. They are probably saying, "I can defend myself from my enemies. Heaven defend me from my friends." It's a shabby business all the way.

* * * *

Everyone understands that, chiefly owing to furious intervention by the various old folk's lobbies, the Social Security system has been made as fiscally sound as it is ever likely to be. Now word comes from Washington that some departments of the government have begun to borrow on the stockpile of money being set aside for future payments. Generations that are now paying in heavily in order to have assurance of an ultimate payout to themselves and their families ought not to be happy about this turn of events.

The federal government is apparently incapable of setting up a financial system that promises to work and then leaving it alone to perform its function. The claim is immediately made that the system is "overfunded" and the little foxes start nibbling away at it.

The responsibilities of Social Security over the years to come are awesome. If the system is impaired by borrowing on it in order to support the promise of "no new taxes," the younger ones among us will ultimately suffer. Prudence needs to prevail.

"Politics Made Difficult"

No. 29, July 17, 1989, Page 21

Since there are no major political contests in 1989 (unless you are a New Yorker and must decide whether you want Mayor Ed Koch for another term) would it be OK if we talked politics in general for a few paragraphs?

I am concerned about what political action committees (known generally as PACs) are doing to our form of government, even though most of them are well-intentioned. They have become the prime source of political funding in an era where television costs make a senator collect $4 million to get elected, and many congressmen at least a quarter of that.

PACs—even the most liberal ones—tend to go along with incumbents if their voting records are "right" to the dispensers of the funds. Indeed, in 1988 PACs gave four times as much money to incumbent senators as they gave to challengers, and rewarded sitting congressmen over their opponents by an 8 to 1 margin.

That's why about 98 percent of the members of Congress who choose to run for reelection make it, and why any shift in the leadership of the houses of Congress seems to have become impossible. This should give the insurance business pause, since it has PACs galore, ranging from some of the largest, like NALUPAC, to much more modest ones.

Last year, 10 congressmen received more than $200,000 apiece from PACs even though no one was running against them. My favorite columnist, Dave Barry, hazards the guess that the money was used to buy bumper stickers that expressed the campaign theme: REP. BILL BLOOTER—"You Have No Choice."

These Congressmen have probably put away such a war chest that no one will **ever** run against them.

Until now, my chief concern about insurance PACs has been that the steering committees that parcel out the dough were chiefly interested in how Congressman Blooter would vote on insurance issues, and not on whether he was a good citizen and a thoughtful legislator. In other words, if he could be counted on to preserve the inside buildup it didn't matter how he stood on education, child care or gun control.

But my concerns have broadened now that I see the self-perpetuating (or PAC-perpetuating) Congress. It looks as though we were fated to see the same old faces forever until, like my old friend Claude Pepper, they simply fade away.

PAC dispensers will reward the same old cronies and try to reform the same old enemies. (My insistent use of the word "old" here is by design. Congress is getting to be a bunch of old folks. Fresh faces and fresh ideas are at a premium.)

Dave Barry points out that while the populace seems to dislike 98 percent of congressmen, they keep electing their own. "Which tell us," he says, "that people tend to view congressmen pretty much the way they view body odors. They can tolerate their own, but they can't stand anybody else's."

Calls for reform, although certainly not demolition, of the political action committees are coming from all corners. President Bush, who is certainly concerned with Republican inability to gain ground in either house of Congress, has said, "PACs weaken the parties, restrain competition and deaden the political debate." He plans to propose major changes in the way campaigns are financed. David Boren, a liberal Democratic senator from Oklahoma, proposes a voluntary ceiling on total campaign spending, "providing for strong inducements to comply with the limits." He is realistic enough to say, "There's no use trying to ban PACs."

Such measures would probably dismay the TV stations, but not many others—if all candidates were provided with a level financial playing field. Issues might be debated more evenly, and we might even get some commercials that make sense.

Everything I have said is debatable, and because so many insurance people are putting their money into PACs, I'd like to see it debated in these columns. If PAC leaders have points of view, send them to me at 611 Ocean Drive, Key Biscayne, FL 33149. Letting fresh air into a situation never hurts.

"Was Rebating Never Really A Problem?"

No. 30, July 24, 1989, Page 13

The National Association of Life Underwriters and its various state and local associations were founded many years ago with two or three major issues in mind—and one of them, front and center, was the problem of rebating. The fear that the system of agents' compensation could be completely destroyed by rebaters was very real to agents.

They did some mighty effective lobbying, which was a dirty word at the time, and managed to get some firm anti-rebate laws on the books in all 50 states. The first chink in that dike came when the Florida Supreme Court ruled, a couple of years ago, that rebating was legal on a regulated basis. Then California's Proposition 103, which spared nobody anywhere in the insurance business, overturned the state's anti-rebating law.

Did these actions presage the tumbling of the entire dike, with any client free to suggest that an agent return part of his commission, or that an agent could win a competitive case by slyly suggesting that he would be glad to perform that heinous act? Some people thought so, particularly when little Proposition 103s began to be introduced in a host of state legislatures.

Now a couple of professors at Arizona State University have concluded that rebating never is—and possibly never was—the bugaboo that agents thought it might be. "Rebating in the life insurance industry appears to be an idea whose time has come and passed," according to Drs. Lawrence Crosby and Kenneth Evans. They have concluded, according to their press release, that if life insurance agents were allowed to rebate their commissions, there would be "little, if any, positive effect on the selling process and outcomes for life insurance."

One of the major citations for their conclusion is the statement that the one Florida agent who received approval from the insurance department to rebate his commissions "stopped rebating earlier this year after he became convinced the practice was unprofessional."

While I have never been sure of the total omnipotence of researchers since the *Literary Digest* declared Alf Landon was going to be a big winner over Franklin D. Roosevelt, I grudgingly concede that they have come a long way since those days, and I have used them extensively myself (particularly when I thought they might support my point of view). In this instance, however, I don't believe Drs. Crosby and Evans have made rebating a dead issue. For two reasons:

- They have limited their research to "the effect of insurance rebating on consumer buying decisions." This isn't quite the same as agent sales decisions, which also belong in the mix.

- In their own words, they concede that "rebating is likely to produce considerable job dissatisfaction and turnover among agents who feel that they are less able to serve the customer correctly and are unfairly perceived as being manipulative and underhanded."

Aye, there's the rub. What the researchers seem to be saying is that the consumer isn't greatly interested (presumably since rebating in life insurance is likely to be a one-shot deal), and the agent who gets involved in rebating is more likely to quit. But, added up, these two reasons don't tell me that the days of rebating "have come and passed."

It is exceedingly tempting to take a current issue and research it out of existence. We then drop our guards and go on to other problems, of which we have many. But I can't help believing that if a certain number of smart agents, with the consent of the states in which they operate, embrace rebating as a way of life, it will continue to be a thorn in the sides of producers. Crosby and Evans reached their conclusion on the basis of 116 structured interviews. I need more evidence than that to convince me that rebating is part of our past.

But I must say I hope they are right.

"After McCarran-Ferguson. . .What?"

No. 47, November 20, 1989, Page 13

Conventional wisdom has been telling us for some time now that Congress—after it receives appropriate instructions from Ralph Nader—will take steps to dismantle the McCarran-Ferguson Act. As every schoolchild knows, the Act declares that insurance regulation by the states is in the public interest and the federal government should keep hands off.

Of course, the idea that the feds itch to get into the regulation of insurance is anything but a secret. Observers inside the Washington beltway say that a few government agencies, such as the Securities and Exchange Commission, are already exerting clout in defiance of McCarran-Ferguson, because (in the case of life insurance, at least) some of the activities the companies are involved in weren't even on the drawing board when the Act became law.

Publicly, insurance people are united in opposing repeal or even stripping down McCarran-Ferguson. They are content in dealing with each state individually because, as someone has indelicately put it, "They would rather fight 50 mice than one gorilla."

Privately, the situation is not so precise. Smaller companies, operating in a few states, are bitterly against change. They are comfortable with the insurance commissioners they report to, and they haven't the slightest desire to haul their wishes and problems across the Potomac. They will fight to the end against any downgrading of McCarran-Ferguson. Their stand seems perfectly logical to me.

The major companies, licensed to do business in virtually all states, are not so sure. Some of them would like to have a shot at making friends with the gorilla and getting rid of the mice. But to say so from a platform would be to court disaster. The split between stock and mutual companies, already traumatizing life companies in the field of taxation, would be exacerbated. It cannot be forgotten that most of the smaller companies are stock, while many of the larger ones are mutual. To add a contest about the form of regulation to the tax battle would cause wounds that might never heal.

The McCarran-Ferguson Act is the clear and present danger. Congressional leaders cannot tolerate the notion of a business with well over $1 trillion in assets being beyond their reach. A bill will appear on the floor sometime soon that will put the issue up for grabs.

The insurance business has done remarkably well in lobbying lately, except when it gets into internal fights, such as the stock-mutual tax issue, and then isn't able to come to Congressional committees with a united front. When it acts as a unit, its power has been awesome. Possibly its belief in this power has convinced it that it can't lose. Like a superior football team with a scarcely blemished record, it brims with confidence.

But even the best of teams has a two-minute drill, a super effort when the going gets tough. Is the insurance business practicing one?

Here are a few of the issues it may run up against:

- If McCarran-Ferguson is repealed, will the federal government instantly create its own Department of Insurance, adding another layer of regulation to those already in place? Who will staff it?

- What powers will be left to the 50 state insurance commissions? Will the feds assume most of them, or will they simply become presiding justices over the states?

- Will the states, and the companies operating in the various states, accept the roles assigned them, or will there be court battles?

I'm sure that committees of the various insurance associations, operating behind closed doors, are already considering these questions, plus a great many others. It would be interesting to see them debated in public, as a rehearsal, of the two-minute drill that may be upon the business at any time. At this writing we've not seen much discussion of the alternative to McCarran-Ferguson. I'd certainly like to listen to some of them.

"Can NAIC Acquire Real Clout?"

No. 17, April 23, 1990, Page 11

If the camel is an animal constructed by a committee, the National Association of Insurance Commissioners is an animal constructed by 50 committees, plus a huge flock of advisers, lobbyists and hangers-on. It has no corporate power—each state insurance commission has varying degrees of power within its own jurisdiction, but NAIC itself is simply a group of people who gather semi-annually to discuss mutual problems and possible state-by-state solutions.

The McCarran-Ferguson Act, which cedes most insurance supervision to the states, is NAIC's Holy Writ. Let McCarran be repealed or seriously diminished in power and the various commissioners would find their own powers fatally impaired or they might become mere functionaries—depending on how much supervisory leadership Congress might choose to take. It might decide to take it all.

NAIC has had a rocky history over the nearly 100 years that states have had insurance departments. In its early days its members served as tax collectors from companies domiciled within their confines, and not much else. The taxes, incidentally, were hardly ever used to supervise insurance, but became part of the general revenues.

But as insurance began to grow into a financial giant, insurance departments acquired more attention. Their staffs, which had sometimes been pathetically small, acquired more power, and regulation became more firm, although some states still looked on their departments as cash cows and not much more.

Now we arrive at 1990, with McCarran-Ferguson in grave danger and the fate of insurance departments in deep trouble. Happily, NAIC is taking some positive steps to assert itself even though, of course, each state must do its own asserting. In late March, it convened a special committee "to discuss the strengths and weaknesses of the financial condition examination process." Of insurance companies.

It's about time. Some states, like New York, have strong departments with the ability to perform adequate financial examinations. Others have few people at all to pore over companies' statements and must rely on the help of other states for what are called "convention examinations."

NAIC states that "since last December government solvency has received increased visibility in the public policy arena." Since last December? Members of the media have been darkly hinting for some years that the solvency of some insurance companies was in question, and that someone ought to take a searching look into the problem. Who but the state insurance departments, under the benign leadership or NAIC? If they can't do it, and do it right, goodbye, dear, old Senator McCarran.

For nearly half a century companies and agencies have supported the viability of McCarran. But unless they get behind their state insurance departments and shove, they are asking for federal supervision. Every time a company—and you can name the state—goes down the tube or has to be rescued by its colleagues, another nail is being driven into the coffin of the McCarran Act.

Like most bureaucracies, state insurance departments, tortured by the legislatures and their regulations and the constant patter of the tiny feet of lobbyists, are slow to move. Their national organization, with no conclusive power, is even slower. If NAIC's "Solvency Policing Agenda for 1990" drags its feet it may find that it has no feet left.

NAIC plods because its "model" regulations are, in effect, advisory only. Any state can consider, adopt, or ignore them. After a committee espouses what is usually a middle-of-the-road recommendation, usually after long debate, it is freighted to the states to do with it as they will. Then, further debate ensues in each state. There has got to be some speed-up in this process or the various commissioners will find themselves in the buggy-whip business.

Strong commissions usually move rapidly and decisively. Weak ones vacillate. And it's the weak ones that Congress has in its sights. NAIC must magnify its clout.

"Gov. Florio Explains It All To Us"

No. 38, September 17, 1990, Page 25

Gov. Jim Florio of New Jersey has never been a particularly great and good friend of the insurance business. As a congressman he was an active member of committees nibbling at the flanks of insurance—particularly auto insurance.

One of the first things he did after having been elected governor in November was to spearhead the passage of the Fair Auto Insurance law, which became effective in February. It enabled the state to set tight boundaries on premiums and gave the insurance commissioner, Sam Fortunato, considerably more power in regulating companies doing business in the state.

The ITT-Hartford Insurance Group didn't much like the strictures placed on its subsidiary, The Twin City Fire and Casualty Company, and announced its desire to cancel its auto policies in New Jersey.

Jim Florio's answer was terse and to the point:

"If they won't sell us car insurance, we won't let them sell us anything."

Auto insurance is no big deal for the Hartford in New Jersey. It controls, through its subsidiary, about 1 percent of the market. But it is very big in property, casualty, life and health insurance in the state. And it carries the group auto insurance program of the American Association of Retired Persons. If Florio throws the company out of the state completely, the repercussions would be serious.

And that's not all; 31 other companies have petitioned to stop selling auto insurance in New Jersey. Some of them may be pure auto insurers but others, undoubtedly, are multiple-line companies that would be seriously hurt by getting a total heave-ho. Aetna? Travelers? Allstate? State Farm? Just to name a few.

Gov. Florio may have bitten off more than he can chew in this instance. In a spiteful move to defend his position on auto insurance, he may have affected the income of thousands of sincere agents whose interest in the issue is minimal. As far as I know, he has no quarrel about how life agents, as an example, sell, and whether their rates are logical.

No company likes to withdraw from any jurisdiction. But if the actions of a legislature make staying in business feasible, it should be acceptable for the company to discontinue the sale of a specific product. Florio is throwing out the baby with the bath water.

As might be expected, ITT-Hartford has temporized on the matter. It will continue to sell auto insurance in the state but its president, Donald Frahm, has said the company would still pursue all available administrative and legal remedies because it does not believe Gov. Florio's position is correct. This seems to be a sane, if temporary, action. When a company run for profit is pressured into supporting a state run insurance pool to cover high risk drivers, something is amiss. No company is a charitable organization. If the New Jersey legislature passed an act to give high-risk drivers a break, why should low-risk drivers have to pay for it? The courts will, obviously, have something to say about the matter.

At the risk of twanging one string on my guitar too often, let me say this. Florio's action is simply the latest example of a public official's vendetta against one form of insurance affecting all forms of insurance. California's Proposition 103 had become the classic, and it is likely to be copied in many states. Beyond that, who knows, as Orson Welles used to say, what evil lurks in the hearts of men?

The inability to distinguish one kind of coverage from another, particularly in the case of legislators, has caused the insurance business mortal pain. Yet there seems to be neither the will nor the finances to make the issue clear.

If I had the same name as someone who had been accused of being a vile criminal, I would do my best to clear my name. But it seems apparent, as Gertrude Stein might have said, that insurance is insurance is insurance, at least to the leadership of the insurance business.

"I'm Sick. . .Get Me Some Insurance!"

No. 4, January 28, 1991, Page 23

"I'm sick, I'm Dying. . .Get Me Some Insurance!" Some people seem to think that the person who is dying of an incurable disease has every right to buy health and life insurance, presumably at standard rates. Commercial companies, they argue, are in business to provide insurance, not to deny it.

What a pity that the insurance companies don't agree! What an injustice! Does anyone around here give a single, solitary damn about the prudent man or woman who buys life or health insurance before any illness or injury befalls them, and who hopes against hope that such will never happen—but is ready and insured if it does occur? And does anyone realize that the premiums of the prudent person who insures himself and his family when he is alive and well will go to support the laggard who decides he needs insurance only after the doctor has told him the sad facts about himself?

It appears that New York State does. . .maybe. The Court of Appeals—New York's highest court—recently ruled that health insurers may test applicants for the AIDS virus and can reject those who are affected.

The deputy executive director of Gay Men's Health Crisis had an immediate reply: "The private insurance sector has been all too successful at avoiding its share of the cost of AIDS care," he said. "You're effectively screening out a whole group, making them totally uninsurable."

One of my closest friends has been diagnosed as having incurable cancer. Underwriters turn aside when he appears. But since he bought his insurance years before his illness was diagnosed, he is in good financial shape. He paraphrases Groucho Marx and says, "I wouldn't want to be insured with any company that would insure me today."

New York Gov. Mario Cuomo's aide has a different story: "Our overall objective is to make health insurance as available as possible to people who are HIV positive," she says.

To me, this is politics at its worst. If the Governor isn't looking for votes, why does this aide say, "Our overall objective is to make health insurance as available as possible to anyone who shows a tendency toward a serious illness"?

Somewhere along the line too many have forgotten that people buy insurance when they are unscathed to guard against the perils of disaster in one form or another. The insurance business couldn't possibly exist under any other concept. You and I doubtless spend thousands of dollars with insurance companies. We hope that we will never have the need to make a claim—at least, until we are ready to retire or have died. We understand that the money we have deposited has probably gone to pay the claims of people less fortunate than we have been. We don't begrudge our payments; we are happy that we are well and our property is intact.

On the one hand, legislatures are worried about the possibility of insolvency on the part of all sorts of insurance companies. On the other, they are urging those same companies to insure people who are admittedly under considerable risk of becoming claimants. Catch-22 is rambling unchecked among the legislators, the lobbyists and special interest groups.

Insurance people seem to believe that most consumers understand the basics of their craft. This can't be so if they say with a straight face that the business should be insuring the lame and the blind.

The American Council of Life Insurance and the Health Insurance Association of America are busy undertaking to educate legislators, state and national, on the fundamentals of life and health insurance. The Insurance Information Institute is doing the same job on the property/casualty side.

Might it not be appropriate for them both to send a plaque to all statesmen and legislators inscribed, "There is no such thing as a free lunch"?

"Who Makes The Best Lobbyist?"

No. 7, February 18, 1991, Page 15

Not too many years ago, if you called a person a lobbyist it was an almost automatic invitation to fisticuffs. But in recent years the profession has become so sacrosanct that legislators fawn upon it. Today, I don't hesitate to boast that some of my best friends are lobbyists.

The reason, of course, is that in addition to giving what they conceive to be sage advice to politicians, they also dispense huge wads of money through political action committees. Sound advice and sound money are treasured by politicians beyond jewels. The lobbyist with a checkbook in his attache case is an 800-pound gorilla.

Lawyers will tell you that only lawyers are qualified to be lobbyists. This is particularly true in insurance, a business that is fighting tax and legislative problems, including the possible repeal of their favorite staff and prop, the McCarran-Ferguson Act. Lawyers, they tell you, are like the little Dutch boy with his finger in the dike. If we are to be saved, they will save us.

I guess I believed this wholeheartedly until I read a letter in the *New Times* for January 18, 1991. It was written by Scott M. Cutlip, dean emeritus of the School of Journalism and Mass Communications at the University of Georgia. He quotes the public relations consultant, Ivy Lee, a revered name in the business, twice. I would like to repeat his quotes:

- "If you go to the people and get the people to agree with you, you can be sure that, ultimately, legislatures, commissions, and everybody else must give way in your favor." And:

- "I have seen more situations which the public ought to understand and which the public would sympathize with, spoiled by the intervention of a lawyer than in any other way. Whenever the lawyer starts to talk to the public, he shuts out the light."

In my opinion, he is partly right. When, on the other hand, a lawyer who is a lobbyist speaks directly to a lawyer who is a legislator, it is a matter of deep calling to deep. Two people who have the same vocabulary—abstruse though it may be—ultimately end up in mutual understanding, if not agreement.

But where Dean Cutlip and Ivy Lee (among others) seem to have the right notion is that politicians don't react as strongly to the lobbyists who call upon them as they do to their own constituents. And lawyers are just not very good at reasoning with laymen, except in rare and wonderful cases.

When dollars get tight and budgets have to be slashed, insurance companies and their associations tend to pit lobbyists directly against legislators, leaving the vast majority of voters without facts on which to base their opinions and their voices. The lobbyists are inevitably lawyers.

People who study law have been taught from their first class to know the facts about which they speak, and to act as though they knew those facts. The uncertain lawyer will shortly be cleaning windshields. Public relations people have no similar discipline. They have to improvise, and they do it well, but they don't have the force of the law behind them. That leaves them at a distinct disadvantage when they get into the lobbying game.

I have a generalized suggestion that might compromise the situation and give both Dean Cutlip and the legal profession some gratification: let the lawyers talk to the legislators, and let the public relations people talk to the legislators' constituents. I discussed this with Mr. Cutlip and he seemed to think that this was a fair division of the labor. The chief trouble with my plan is that politicians are easy and cheap to reach, but the public—sprawling and almost endless as it is—is expensive. It is difficult to get its attention. So those who are in charge of the lobbyists say, "Forget it. Let's hit the direct target."

I believe they are wrong. The public has a right to know, to understand, and to influence. The business that doesn't give it a chance to do these things is divided against itself. Ivy Lee and Dean Cutlip are right.

6

Challenges In The Industry

"Risk Classification: Dig It?"

No. 50, December 13, 1986, Page 25

For nearly 150 years, life and health insurance customers accepted the fact that if you were in poor health or in a risky business or in the twilight of life you were expected to pay more for your policies than those without such problems.

It made sense: if your paying period was likely to be short, the company had to collect its money more quickly in order to satisfy its obligations to you or your beneficiary.

Then someone—maybe a columnist or an activist of some persuasion—asked, "Why? Why shouldn't everyone pay roughly the same amount? It will all even out in the end."

When actuaries had recovered from the initial shock of the question, they patiently explained the theories of risk-bearing and risk-sharing. Their explanation was couched in an insurance vocabulary that had served them well for over a century. It was logical, it was understandable, and, by God, it was right!

Advertising Program

However, a great many people chose not to understand it. Instead, they kept repeating, "Why?" So this year the companies, through the American Council of Life Insurance, decided to launch a three-to-five year advertising program in major magazines and TV outlets. It will reach millions of people dozens of times.

But because of the vocabulary the business is stuck with, it has to be called "The Risk Classification Program." In this day of red-hot, sophisticated advertising in print and on the tube, doesn't that grab you? "Look, hon, want to hear why the insurance companies charge us the way they do?"

Don't blame ACLI for this. Don't blame its estimable agency, Gray Advertising. Rather, blame two factors that the business created generations ago and has never corrected:

- The vocabulary of the business has always been technically oriented. The technicians who dominated it seldom allowed it to be simplified because "it had stood the test of the courts."

- No one has consistently tried to devise a simple road map to lead the public through life insurance phraseology. A high percentage of the public believes that many of the industry's spokesmen are obfuscators. They aren't trusted because they use a language that isn't plain English. Granted, they sometimes try, but ACLI and LIMRA surveys show that most laymen aren't buying the notion that the companies are putting all their cards on the table.

So now insurance people are faced, believe it or not, with sincere questions like these:

"Why can't I get health insurance when I'm sick?" "Why can't I get life insurance when I have lung cancer?" "How dare you test me for possible exposure to a dread disease like AIDS?" "Why do I have to pay more for my life insurance than my son or my wife does?" "Can you defend what you charge me for anything?"

Research Backs Statements

People who are immersed in the business may privately conclude that I am out of my gourd when I make such statements, but all you have to do is go to industry research to prove them out.

The result: at this point in its noble history, life and health insurance industries have been forced to come up with an advertising program headlined "Risk Classification." And in case you don't believe that the institutional organizations are serious about it, listen to the ACLI speak:

"No issue faced by the life and health insurance business at this time may be more important to our survival than Risk Classification. . . Legislative and social pressures are fast eroding public support for the principle. . . Ever-increasing numbers of people find it to be 'unfair,' unfair to women, unfair to the elderly, and unfair to the infirm."

Santayana said, "Those who cannot remember the past are condemned to repeat it." The life insurance industry in its unceasing—largely successful—efforts to convince the Congress of the validity of its tax treatment, seems to have forgotten that its principal constituency consists of people who own its product or who are considering buying it.

So now ACLI is faced with the monumental project of telling people why their premiums are fair and just, and neither picked out of a hat nor determined casually by avaricious executives.

Was it so hard to see this coming? At the ACLI annual meeting in San Francisco in November, Bill Tremayne, senior vice-president of Prudential and chairman of the ACLI advertising committee, exhibited a series of charts that showed an ever-accelerating lack of public faith in the product. Research people of ACLI and LIMRA have been blowing the whistle. It is time for institutional leadership to respond, at an even more accelerated rate than announced.

Columnists and other writers—but columnists especially—are often accused of asking hard questions and never coming up with answers. Not here—at least not in this case. If we are faced with a public that seems to be becoming increasingly hostile or confused or just plain dumb about what we are offering its members, the situation had better be redressed by communications—and quickly.

Let us not be Santayana's people. It says here that we are too smart for that.

"The Tragedy of AIDS"

No. 4, February 2, 1987, Page 9

Certain dread diseases seem to be taken for granted by the public, terrifying though they may be. Cancer, for instance, or the various forms of cardio-vascular-renal ailments appear to be looked upon as part of our burden for having become human beings. We eternally seek for cures, as we have found at least a partial one for polio, but our optimism is always tempered by the reality of the present.

But every generation or so a disease appears that scares us beyond belief. In 1918 an influenza epidemic made millions of parents almost hysterical in their efforts to protect their children. That very epidemic hastened the cure so that today the flu is looked upon in most instances as a minor ailment.

Today we have Acquired Immune Deficiency Syndrome (AIDS). This horrible affliction has a sort of bizarre fascination for some people because of its sexual overtones and its tendency to strike down the famous.

Because of this and other unique qualities well-understood by anyone who can read, AIDS has become singularly politicized—probably more so than most social issues in modern history. When politics lays its heavy hand on the field of human health, the life and health insurance business inevitably suffers. The business may look upon itself as an innocent victim, but the results can be just as devastating as if it were the villain of the piece.

Here are some of the portents, none of them any good:

- AIDS is epidemic; despite optimistic newspaper stories, there is no current sign of a preventive vaccine or a cure. Responsible, and highly conservative, estimates are that the disease may kill about 60,000 persons in 1991, and that's only the beginning. If the virus invades all elements of the American community, it may call for a complete restructuring of the nation's health care system.

- Because sexual activity is admittedly the prime method of transmitting AIDS, gay rights activists and others consider that any questions or other screening of applicants on the subject is an invasion of personal rights. This inevitably means that companies are forced to accept into their body of policyholders people who may have a quickly fatal and highly expensive disease. Obviously, the cost of paying benefits to this group will have to be passed along to other policyholders or a company, in the long run, will go belly up.

- As reported in the news columns, new AIDS guidelines have been approved by the National Association of Insurance Commissioners and uneasily endorsed by the insurance industry and the gay community: any state that allows AIDS testing should allow insurers to ask applicants about prior testing results. Conversely, in those states that ban testing, no inquiries into past testing would be allowed. This is a dubious net at best, with holes for every state where testing is not allowed.

- The matter of "entitlement" to health care or health insurance has now moved center stage. People with dread diseases of any nature cannot be permitted simply to waste away and die in indigence. But does this entitlement permit them to be on the policyholder rolls of a corporation operating for profit and with an obvious responsibility to its current policyholders? Gay rights attorneys appear to think so. As I read it, their notion is that commercial companies should insure sick people against the hazards of sickness. That, as the fellow said, is a hell of a way to run a railroad.

This is undoubtedly one of the principal reasons why the American Council of Life Insurance has launched a major advertising campaign to educate the American people about the intricacies of risk classification. Private industry simply cannot exist in an atmosphere of total entitlement, and ACLI is undertaking to tell the public why. When it said, "Legislative and social pressures are fast eroding support for the principle (of risk classification)," AIDS had to be one of the considerations behind its words.

The upshot? Whenever the commercial life insurance business has come across a risk it felt it couldn't handle without endangering its current policyholders, it has asked the federal government to do so. Government insurance for servicemen in World Wars I and II are the prime examples. If the incidence of AIDS burgeons to the point where the companies just cannot handle it, the federal government will simply have to embrace the risk as part of its catastrophic health insurance package.

The private business will probably squirm at this "incursion," but it can't have its cake and eat it, too. Nothing quite so terrifying and politically charged has ever been visited on this country except the immediate presence of war, and the manner of insuring against its hazards will have to be the same as it has been against war.

"Talking About The Unspeakable"

No. 33, August 17, 1987, Page 25

You are doubtless as unhappy reading about AIDS as I am writing about it. If there were nothing new to be said on the subject, I would hold my silence. But the tide seems to be rising, and we cannot afford to look in the other direction.

AIDS affects the people in the insurance business in two ways: like everyone in the population, they are subject to the rising risks of the pestilence as it starts to take hold of "normal" people; beyond that, AIDS has in its ugly hands the power to destroy the insurance concept that has been built up over years, and the companies that sell it.

When I stop following the most recent discoveries about AIDS—which I sometimes do—I become complacent, and it takes some doing to regain my attention. The most recent person to grab me by the collar and jerk me back into reality was a most unlikely one: Donald K. Ross, chairman of New York Life.

Don Ross is not your lectern-banging high-decibel type of speaker. He is low-key in his approach, and mild in his delivery. But when he began to tell some 5,000 members of the Million Dollar Round Table meeting in Chicago in July some of his personal fears about AIDS, you could hear a pin drop.

He began with this perfectly bald statement:

"A year ago, based on reasonable assumptions, we determined that if we did not combat anti-selection by AIDS carriers and did not raise our premiums, New York Life would probably face insolvency within a decade."

Here we have the CEO of one of the big five life insurance companies speaking. Insolvency? If it could happen in one of the oldest, most stable companies, what would happen to the newer, more adventurous ones?

After reciting some of the more reliable statistics about the prevalence of AIDS—including, "By 1991, at least 180,000 deaths will almost certainly have occurred in the U.S. alone"—he arrived at this shocker:

"While the AIDS problem has appeared confined to drug abusers and gay men, our society and our government have been content to do too little. By the time it strikes close enough to home to truly galvanize the public, and hence, our leadership, it may be too late. We simply do not know the rate at which the disease is entering the mainstream of heterosexuals. But we have some indicators and they are scary."

As for the problem to the companies he said, "If we cannot underwrite for this risk, anti-selection will set a dangerous chain of events in motion: Those not at risk will be unwilling to shoulder the higher premiums and simply not buy our products. But we will see large numbers of companies giving up their medical expense, disability income, and life insurance lines completely in an effort to maintain enough reserves to fulfill their existing obligations."

There was much more. You get the idea—perhaps not anywhere near as well as if you had been there and listened to Don Ross pile fact on fact, but enough to realize that the situation is growing worse and action right now is necessary to keep it from becoming uncontrollable.

Americans have always held the fond belief that as soon as a terrifying national issue reached the brink, a concentration of the country's best minds would solve it. Influenza. . .cholera. . .polio. . .even World War II. But here we have a situation where the will to win and the dedication to work hard aren't enough. The only thing we can be sure of is that if we do nothing the problem of world overpopulation may be solved in a way that none of us wants.

More than any other business, insurance has a stake in this formidable mess. In its early days it was looked upon—misguidedly, it seems now—as a problem for the gay element in our society. No longer. Research, while it hasn't done much to get at the wellsprings of the disease, has proved beyond doubt that most of us are susceptible to it, even though we are total innocents.

As Don Ross concluded, "Agents, companies, and the industry must join to educate the public. . . Agents must do it at the point of sale and in every civic forum they have access to. Companies must do it through government and public relations. And the industry must do it through the media."

The alternative isn't pleasant to contemplate.

"Joe Belth And The IRIS Revelations"

No. 4, January 25, 1988, Page 15

You knew that when Joe Belth set out to expose the IRIS program of the National Association of Insurance Commissioners there was bound to be smoke and fire if not hell and brimstone. There indeed was, and is, and there is likely more to come.

For those of you who came in late, the cast of characters looks like this: Dr. Joseph M. Belth (to give him his academic moniker) is editor of the *Insurance Forum*, a muckraking publication devoted to "the unfettered exchange of ideas about insurance." He is one of the few consumer advocates who is part of the insurance establishment, although certain elements of the establishment wish they could disown him.

IRIS (the Insurance Regulatory Information System) was created by the National Association of Insurance Commissioners as a kind of distant early warning system to inform its members about "companies likely to experience financial difficulties." Its IRIS ratios don't accuse any individual company of any wrongdoing; it simply recommends to its constituency that certain companies receive "immediate regulatory attention" while others, presumably in better shape, should get "targeted regulatory attention."

NAIC started IRIS as a confidential system in the '70s, concluding that it was nobody's business except the regulators themselves, who would then keep a sharp eye on the particular companies that had been fingered.

Joe Belth disagreed. He saw IRIS as a valuable tool for consumers. He felt that if NAIC had enough doubts about a company to put it on any kind of a list, the public ought to know about it. The state insurance departments, he reasoned, are public commissions and accountable to the public.

He went through lawsuits in several states to get access to IRIS information, and finally succeeded in the District of Columbia. He then published in the December issue of his *Insurance Forum* the complete list of companies, life-health and property-casualty, "designated by NAIC for regulatory attention."

Hell has been for breakfast ever since. Insurance companies, which have a tendency to circle the wagons when a threat comes from the outside, have behaved predictably. Dick Minck, executive vice-president of the American Council of Life Insurance, wrote Joe Belth that "your publication did a disservice to many readers who are in no position to distinguish those companies on the list that are financially very sound from companies that are not, and who may be led to make unwise financial decisions."

Undoubtedly, a company can look bad for a year or two without being in any kind of a precarious position, but as I read the IRIS list it seems to me that NAIC is undertaking to be scrupulously fair. The number of companies that are undergoing financial changes in order to strengthen themselves constitute a small minority of the IRIS hit list.

We are here returning to the old platitude that the public must be protected against its own naivete. I have never bought this. The public has seldom been so naive as to fail to ask questions of its agents, and most agents will give people answers based on the best facts they can assemble. The person who reads a statement and then runs around crying, "The sky is falling," is bringing his fate on himself.

Yes, writers like Jane Bryant Quinn have praised Joe's publication of the IRIS list without surrounding their comments with the caveats that Joe carefully inserts into all his writings. But I suppose that's all a columnist untrained in insurance can do.

As you can see, I tend here to ally myself with Joe Belth. This is a personal belief, and not a statement by the *National Underwriter.* I cannot help but believe that a company not straining to get off any and all IRIS lists is foolhardy. Publication of those lists makes the strain just a little more visceral.

And when we hear that Georgia State University is now at work refining the IRIS tests, Joe's revelations seem even more important. These are no days for us to rest on our oars.

"When AIDS Hits Nearby"

No. 17, April 25, 1988, Page 29

Most of us resemble the intelligent mule: we are wise enough, all right, but you have to hit us over the head with a two-by-four to get our attention.

This is particularly true with the miserable AIDS. As long as it stays completely out of our business or neighborhood turf, many of us tend to turn away from it—even though we would realize, if we sat down and thought it through, that the more we ignore it the more chance there is it will enter our territory.

Furthermore, public pronouncements about the disease tend to confuse us. The eminent sexologists, Masters and Johnson, declare that it may be contracted through casual sexual contact. Dr. Everett Koop, surgeon-general of the U.S., calls this nonsense. He says that only certain specific acts transmit the disease, and then only under certain specific conditions.

In a previous article about AIDS I called us all "innocents" about the malady, and received a blistering anonymous letter from Indianapolis saying, in effect, "No one is innocent." My use of "innocent" meant merely "unable or unwilling to grasp the facts," and the Masters-Johnson-Koop controversy underlines why it is so difficult.

One of the positive elements beginning to emerge is that life insurance companies, in common with their opposite numbers in business and industry, have begun to put in place affirmative policies about steps to take if AIDS invades their workplaces. The most complete one I have seen thus far is that of the Metropolitan Life, although there may be others just as good.

But the most inspiring occasion I've come up against so far was a talk before the annual meeting of the Association for Advanced Life Underwriting called "When Your Employee Gets AIDS." It was presented by Howard M. Koff, chairman of Integrated Financial of Encino, CA, a company with 280 employees.

He described in totally compassionate terms how his organization tackled the knowledge that "John," an employee in his central support department (we used to call it the mailroom, but it does lots more these days) had been diagnoscd as having AIDS. Likc many organizations of a similar sizc, Ilowic and his colleagues had never had occasion to think the matter through. They were alarmed when the rumor mill (which was apparently in full cry at Integrated Financial just as it is everywhere else) created something closely resembling panic throughout the company. Since John had constant contact with almost every worker, the questions were quick to pour in: "What will happen if I use the same urinal or drinking fountain?" "What if John gets a paper cut when delivering the mail, bleeds on an envelope and I touch the envelope?", etc.

Howie Koff had to get information fast, and then act on it. He was faced with some irrational people and others who were, to some degree, informed and concerned about preserving John's dignity and being as supportive as possible.

He quickly found that, compassion aside, federal and California state laws prevented discrimination against John. Letting John go or isolating him was not an option.

Howie went to the AIDS Foundation. They responded immediately with speakers, videotapes and literature that spelled out the true nature of the disease. As he says, "Education has a tremendous and immediate effect on defusing fear. As our people became more knowledgeable, the discussion gradually shifted from the danger and focused on compassion for John. . .The supportive and caring part of our company's culture started to take over and the divisive factions within the company came together."

When John could no longer work, the employees helped sustain him both emotionally and financially. The result of a little education was full support until the death of a sick lad.

If you want the story of how a group of people turned a situation of panic into one of support, I suggest you write Howard M. Koff, Integrated Financial, 16530 Ventura Blvd., Suite 500, Encino, CA 91436. You may just be the next participant.

This article wouldn't be complete without a bow to AALU, which had the guts to spotlight the AIDS issue on its main program through Howie Koff.

"The Smokeless Century"

No. 20, May 16, 1988, Page 29

When I was a tad we called them "coffin nails" and laughed as we sneaked a smoke where no one in authority could see us. During World War II billions of cigarettes were shipped free to members of the armed forces. In the decade after the war, smokers were riding high; non-smokers retreated to their own little rabbit warrens of fresh air.

But sometime in the late 1950s the tide began to turn. The life insurance companies, as far as my research shows, took the first widely hailed step with specially-priced policies for non-smokers. Then the Surgeon General came down hard on the issue by forcing the cigarette companies to put dire warnings on packages.

Then came the flood. Supported by a solid front of the medical profession, the non-smoker hauled up his socks, told the smoker to get lost, and sent him over into the corner. Municipalities, states, and even the federal government have issued restrictions on smoking that come close to an outright ban. Airlines have acquiesced to a federal order prohibiting smoking on short flights, and one, Northwest Orient, has outlawed it completely on domestic flights.

The smoker now cowers in his bathroom with the exhaust fan on, hoping that his neighbor won't sense the aroma and turn him in.

Which is exactly the way it should be.

Enough evidence has been piled up about the dismal effects of smoking (even among the old boys who relished an occasional cigar or pipeful) so that every decent social pressure should be exerted on those who puff in places where others can be affected by it.

Many experts are predicting that the 21st century will be smokeless, at least in the United States. That's a worthy goal, and it will doubtless come about.

Yet, it is an apparent fact that nearly 30 percent of the population still smokes. Probably half of these are "social" smokers who light up because their friends do or because they think it is cute. They can probably quit just as soon as they are sufficiently motivated.

The other 15 percent are addicts—in the worst sense of the word. For them, hospital treatment, hypnosis or various popular nostrums have no effect. I happen to be one of them. They have become the pariahs of society, fearful of their shadows, and full of the knowledge that they are offensive to their fellow creatures. I have never met a single addicted smoker who wouldn't quit today if he or she could. What do we do about them?

To begin with, most of them have developed a tolerance for a non-smoking stance of two or three hours. They can go through a party, a flight or a theatrical performance without visibly quaking. They have become acutely sensitive to the wishes of non-smokers, and they will go to almost any lengths to avoid offending these non-smokers. (I have no patience at all with the surly smoker who challenges the world to make him put out his butt.)

It is estimated that there are about 5 million such people—a rather large nuisance. But I believe that with their own patience combined with the understanding of non-smokers, society can reach an accommodation with them. They tend to cringe when shouted at, so don't shout at them. They are pathetically willing to obey the rules of the house. They should never be invited into long-term occasions, like a weekend at the lake, where they might embarrass themselves or their hosts. If smoking is out of order, tell them so.

They are not happy creatures. They have an overwhelming desire to please, within the limits of their own endurance. They should be pitied, not scorned.

Meanwhile, the country should take all feasible steps to make the 21st century smokeless. Most important are the kids, who have to realize that smoke can kill them. Then the social smokers, who are beginning to learn that it's more acceptable to abstain than not. Finally, do what you can for the addicts. They will appreciate it.

"Health Insurance In 1989"

No. 26, June 27, 1988, Page 25

Regardless of whether Michael Dukakis or George Bush wins the presidential race, mandatory health insurance coverage is likely to be pretty high on the nation's agenda in 1989. If the attention of the new man is distracted by issues like foreign policy, Senator Teddy Kennedy and Congressman Claude Pepper will be right there, cracking him over the knuckles with a ruler and telling him to pay heed.

At this writing, Vice-President Bush hasn't devoted much speaking time to health insurance. It's probably premature; he has to go through the formality of being nominated in New Orleans before he starts enunciating his programs if he is elected.

But Governor Dukakis is well on the record with the brand-new Massachusetts mandatory health insurance plan. Insurance people are looking at it carefully, and some find it more digestible than might have been imagined from a liberal Democrat. The law has great attractions for employers to fill in the gap between individual private coverage on one end, and Medicare and Medicaid on the other. Significantly, they can do it through the private sector, which has a two-pronged advantage: governments in all areas will be trying to reduce expenses in the years to come, and private industry will not only get a piece of the action, but almost all of it.

Are private insurers buying this approach, which they had some part in forging? I talked with David Isgur, editor of the *Insurance Times*, a publication that takes the pulse of the New England insurance community weekly. He says:

"This approach is so new and so innovative that many top executives are reluctant to take a stand on it until they see it unfold. It's a highly complicated statute, and you don't want to endorse it until you get some sense of how it's going to be administered."

This might be called the traditional insurance reaction—"Don't shoot until you see the whites of their eyes." In this instance it seems wise. A "Department of Medical Security" will oversee the act. Sometimes such departments behave like Stephen Leacock's knight who "flung himself on his horse and road madly off in all directions." Until we know precisely where such a department is going, it's well that the whole process not be commended too much.

On the face of it, the mandated benefit approach seems good for insurance companies because it will expand their share of market measurably. Business in general should like it: it provides a level playing field for health insurance benefits. And organized labor ought to find, as the *New York Times* declares, that it reduces the cost edge enjoyed by nonunion employers.

Of course, any mandated health insurance plan is going to cost money, and that money will have to be provided by employers, either through the kindness of their own hearts or by shifting the burden to employees. But, like so much insurance, employees will never discover how much they need it until it goes into action for them.

Massachusetts is certainly not the ideal testing ground for such a plan; its economy is booming, unemployment is low, and almost every worker is above the $3.65 state minimum wage. Disruption would be felt more sternly in states that are still undergoing hard times. But the very prosperity in the Land of the Bean and the Cod means that if there are unforeseen problems they can be mastered more easily.

If the Massachusetts plan seems to work, it may well be the forerunner of a federal health insurance plan, no matter who is elected and which party controls Congress. Activists like Kennedy and Pepper are not going to let up, nor is the gradual recognition on the part of older citizens of the unholy financial costs of long-term disability. This recognition is being passed along to their children, who are not interested in paying the health costs of mom and pop through their declining years. There will be action.

Private insurance sees here a plan in which it is intimately involved. It can hardly afford to turn its back.

"Guaranty Funds: A Second Look"

No. 29, July 18, 1988, Page 15

Last August in this column I wrote a glowing piece about state life and health guaranty funds and their umbrella organization, the National Organization of Life and Health Insurance Guaranty Associations (NOLHGA) ["NOLHGA A Happy Acronym", No. 34, August 24, 1987]. After discussion with several people who are intimately involved with guaranty funds, I'm afraid I painted too rosy a picture of their current status.

While no one I talked with disagreed with the fact that guaranty funds have had a beneficial effect on bailing out policyholders of failed companies, some of the funds prescribed by various state laws have, to the insurance community, certain failings. Here are a few examples:

- The companies, in return for participating in the funds, quite naturally want tax offsets. Most state laws permit partial or total offsets, but at least eight states give none at all. Uniformity with the model bill of the National Association of Insurance Commissioners is just not there.

- The NAIC's original model bill contemplated that an insurance insolvency would trigger only the guaranty fund of the state of domicile, which would provide protection for all policyholders regardless of where they reside. Under the NAIC's revision, a guaranty fund of a particular state will protect only residents of that state. Thus, if an insurer doing business in 30 states becomes insolvent, the funds of all 30 states will be triggered. Each will then have the responsibility of not only paying outstanding claims but also keeping life and health policies in force as long as premiums are paid.

- Some people look upon the funds as an endless source of rescue for policyholders of insolvent companies. This certainly is not the case, because in the unlikely instance that a major company foundered, demands on others in the fund would be insupportable. All such funds have a terminal point somewhere.

- There are those in life insurance companies who believe that the industry should handle insolvencies through a voluntary plan similar to the successful enhancement plan carried out in the Baldwin-United instance. However, a majority appear to view the various state guaranty funds, created by legislation, to be a fait accompli, and to try to replace them with an all-industry voluntary plan in 1988 would cause chaos.

Another stumbling block for the funds is the provision that prohibits life insurers from mentioning their existence in conjunction with the sales or solicitation of life insurance. This is the precise opposite of commercial banks and savings and loan associations—everyone is aware of the phrases "member FDIC" or "member FSLIC." Agents are forced to leave the question of the stability of the industry and consumer protection unanswered.

Smaller and newer companies, whose names may not be household words, are particularly aggravated by this restriction. In a brief addressed to the Life Insurance Council of New York (the association of New York-domiciled companies) Unity Mutual Life of Syracuse has challenged the constitutionality of the provision. It calls the restriction "paternalistic" and says it is "unconscionable and should not stand." At this writing the Council is still considering it.

In Utah, it has been felt appropriate that the insurer be required (through its agents or otherwise) to inform prospective policyholders of the limits of guaranty association coverage. This seems to be working.

The question, of course, revolves around the ever-popular issue of the '80s called "consumer disclosure." Do the people have the right to know they are protected, or not? Or will certain insurers take advantage of the guaranty associations to go out on a limb at the expense of the more stable companies?

I raise all these questions simply to point out the fact that the guaranty associations and NOLHGA don't have their act totally perfected yet. But they seem to be getting closer every year.

In putting these paragraphs together I have been considerably aided by George A. Hardy, legislative counsel for the Northwestern Mutual, Deborah Roffman, second vice-president of Unity Mutual Life, and Arthur O. Dummer, CEO of the Donner Co. in Salt Lake City. I am grateful to them.

"Simplifying The Verbiage In Life Policies"

No. 15, April 10, 1989, Page 15

I doubt that any candidate has ever run for insurance commissioner anywhere without having as one of the planks in his platform the statement, "We will fight to see that the language in insurance policies is made more understandable to the policyholder."

This is a notion that sounds as American as chocolate malted milk, and I know of no one who objects to it except one group, of which more later. Some 30 years ago I worked on a volunteer basis with three companies that were deeply interested in simplifying their policies, and I came away with some beliefs that stand me in good stead today. Here are a few of them:

- Policies are not as complicated as they are long. They speak in relatively understandable language, but they can't understand what's going on.

- Policies are designed to protect both their holders and the companies that issue them from all sorts of occurrences, from outright fraud to petty errors. Most of these possibilities have to be listed so that both parties will know what they are getting themselves in for.

- There is a common thought that life insurance policies are simpler than property and casualty policies because of the old saw that says, "We feel you. If you are cold we pay off. If you are warm we don't." Maybe that was the way it was when the Corporation for Relief of Poor and Distressed Presbyterian Ministers and of the Poor and Distressed Widows and Children of Presbyterian Ministers was formed in 1759, but with our sadistically successful efforts to complicate everything we have come a long way from the old simplicities. (Incidentally, the company that I referred to above ultimately decided to change its name to the Presbyterian Ministers' Fund, to the relief of all.)

- By the same token, the policies themselves have become more complicated. The modes of settlement and the beneficiary set-up, to name two of the more obvious ones, can go on for many paragraphs at the insistence of the client. Some policies are built like accordions to satisfy the whims of the buyer.

But the group that will wear you down if you decide to simplify your policy forms consists of members of the legal profession. It is their insistence that every word in every policy form has been tested by the courts, and any changes may be made only at your peril—which may consist in your having to fight every word in your "simplified" form through the same courts that have approved the old one.

This isn't a whim; lawyers on both sides of any insurance litigation and the judges who preside over it will concede the intent of any phraseology that has stood the test of time. Overturning it will make the plaintiff look like Sisyphus, the legendary Greek who kept rolling the boulder up the hill but was never allowed by the gods to reach the top.

By now there is merit in this, I suppose, if there is merit in any of the strangleholds that the legal profession has imposed on us in the sacred name of precedence. Few lawyers lose cases by citing decisions that have been made again and again by courts over the years. Only a Clarence Darrow or a Charles Evans Hughes is capable of turning around a rule of law, and they seldom get involved in nit-picking expeditions.

So let it be clearly understood that anyone—new commissioner, consumer advocate, or fighter for special interests—will not change the language of insurance policies lightly. He or she will run up against the courts and the lawyers, and both are content with the level playing field they have smoothed out over many years. Changing the dimensions of this playing field may not be impossible, yet it will be a test of anyone's intelligence, guts, and ability to put their money where their idealism is.

"Ups And Downs Of Interest-Sensitive Products"

No. 20, May 15, 1989, Page 23

These are the days when financial analysts know everything. If a newspaper reporter hears rumors, good or bad, about a company, he doesn't go to the company for an interview because he suspects he won't get the truth. Instead, he calls up a financial analyst from Salomon Brothers or Drexel Burnham or Moody's or any one of a hundred other firms that employ specialists in the insurance market and asks, "What's the scoop?"

This is particularly true when we get into the heavy stuff like universal life or variable life, where the answers aren't so easy to figure out. Unhappily, like economists, financial analysts are anything but unanimous in their opinions, so today we are getting a lot of random quotes on the future of interest-sensitive life insurance policies. One group sees them as having topped out, and sliding down to oblivion like the 20-year endowment. Another says they will be revitalized when interest rates rise. A third says they have become a part of the fabric of the life insurance business and will be with us to one degree or another for the foreseeable future.

All three have reasons for their predictions. LIMRA, the research organization in life insurance, tells us that universal life slid from 38 percent of market share in 1985 to 27 percent in 1987. Disillusionment came when companies offered illustrations of future values that simply didn't come true, causing policyholders to dump their variable policies and go back to guaranteed ones. But there is a segment of the buying public that enjoys the minor gambles of universal life, knowing that the basic guarantees will keep them from going under.

Ah, but isn't the question of the future going to be not what the public is buying but what the agents are selling? I think so.

Let's face it: both the companies and agents have taken a beating on interest-sensitive products. Companies have cut premiums to the bone and come up with highly imaginative illustrations for the future that they haven't been able to deliver. Agents are getting smaller commissions on smaller premiums, a fact that speaks for itself.

Interplay between companies and agents has been a considerable mess over the last ten years. Companies, deserting their faithful flock, have invited stockbrokers, realtors and mutual fund salesmen to sell universal and variable life. Such people, unaccustomed to selling the permanent values of permanent life insurance, have taken to churning their clients' holdings, looking for a best buy (and perhaps a new first-year commission) every year. Career agents have countered by taking their clients to the lowest net-cost companies. "Loyalty" became a term inviting derision on both sides.

But now the pendulum seems to be swinging back. Companies are tiring of having virtually untrained people sell their products, particularly volatile ones like universal life. Agents are convincing their first-line companies that persistency has measurable virtues, and that they are the ones who have been trained to sell with persistency in mind. Buyers—at least the smart ones—seem to be embracing the belief that buying any kind of life insurance is a long-term proposition and nothing like ducking into and out of the stock market.

There seems to be no doubt that universal life, variable life and universal-variable are with us to stay. They, along with uncounted new products that are now being invented, are certain to be in most agents' portfolios from now on. Interest-sensitivity is never likely to leave the life business. But now that the companies have had their fling with alternate distribution systems and speculative illustrations, normality seems to be oozing back into the life insurance marketing operation.

As in the case of many conservative businesses (men and women, for that matter) life insurance overreacted when it got a taste of the high life, casting aside old friends and habits, and embracing the unknown. Today it seems to be coming back to home and family, which will be blessed relief to its loved ones. And not a minute too soon either.

"When Compassion And Judgment Clash"

No. 26, June 26, 1989, Page 13

A new idea is afoot that is attracting considerable attention in the life insurance business: if you are certifiably terminally ill, an organization will pay you an agreed-upon percentage of the face value of your life insurance policies, and take over your policies, becoming the beneficiary itself. It will ask for a waiver from all current beneficiaries. Upon your death it will receive the face value of the policies.

The notion started either in the fertile brain of Ron Barbaro, president of Prudential's Canadian operations and former president of the Million Dollar Round Table, or in the presumably equally lively minds of an Albuquerque father and son team, Rob Worley Sr. and Jr., under a plan called "Living Benefits." No matter. While the details of the plans differ, the thrust is the same—to give a dying person a little chance for financial independence in his or her last days.

The horrible phenomenon of AIDS was what caused the germination of the idea, of course. No cure has been found, and the victim slides into an irreversible depression. While money surely can't buy happiness—particularly in this instance—it can give the sufferer a last fling. The same is probably true of other terminal diseases, such as amyotrophic lateral sclerosis ("Lou Gehrig's disease") and others that any physician can reel off for you.

It is a tempting proposal, and I have no doubt that other insurance companies—plus organizations not primarily involved in selling life insurance—will offer it to people who are, as the medical records say, "terminal." All are taking the risk that a quick fix won't be found for these killers.

Nevertheless, I find that I regard the whole plan with something approaching loathing. Here are some of my reasons:

Most people buy life insurance to protect their families. If the policyholder takes it upon himself to collect a fraction of the policy, a beneficiary will probably agree with the idea, out of a sense of compassion. The purpose of the insurance has thus been thwarted, and the holder trades a few weeks of dubious happiness for what may be a lifetime of debt on the part of the beneficiary.

If the policies have cash value, owners are free to take a loan on them, leaving some of the principal for the beneficiary. This action continues at least a portion of the reasons why the policies were bought in the first place.

After an illness has been judged to be terminal, and the victim understands or suspects the fact, tender loving care becomes more important than cash. I know something about this; a person very close to me died of Lou Gehrig's disease not long ago, and what she wanted most was close friendships, not the ability to spend money on personal gratification.

No organization is likely to buy a policy from a terminally ill person before the contestable period of two years has run out. At that point, we must assume that the policyholder, unless he or she is alone in the world, is past the "last fling" stage.

Finally, if a terminally ill person suddenly acquires a reasonable amount of money, the facilities that have been treating him or her may demand at least a part of it. This defeats the plan of some relatively happy last days.

I was surprised that *Newsweek* spotlighted the Worley's "Living Benefits" plan in its May 8 issue, although it tried to reach a balanced conclusion—almost balanced, anyhow. It said, "Living Benefits is clearly helping some people that insurance industry giants have failed," then it concluded—"but not without generating troubling questions as well as profits." Which side is the magazine on?

It surprises me that AIDS, in the minds of most journalists, seems to be the only terminal ailment today. While I am happy that people are rallying to help AIDS victims, there are many other diseases that are just as painful, debilitating and terminal. My heart goes out to the people I know who suffer from cancer, but there doesn't appear to be the universal compassion for them. What did they do wrong?

"The Prudential's 'Living Payouts'"

No. 8, February 19, 1990, Page 15

When the Prudential announced its "living payouts" plan in late January, it received remarkable press coverage (even though the self-styled "paper of record," the *New York Times*, state that the company "has three million policyholders nationally," hardly a drop in the Pru's bucket).

Prudential simply refined a plan originally devised by the president of its Canadian operations, Ron Barbaro, that surfaced about a year ago, and has been mentioned more than once in these columns. The idea is simplicity itself:

a policyholder who is certified by his physician as having six months or less to live, or is permanently confined to a nursing home, can receive in advance almost all death benefits on current policies of $25,000 or more, or on new ones of at least $50,000. All that would be deducted is the interest the company would have earned over that six months.

Almost every insurance person I know has a strong point of view about the plan, and most are based on a single question: How will the payouts under the "Living Needs Benefit program" be used?

One group contends that if the money will be used simply as "last-fling insurance" it perverts the reason for which the insurance was originally bought—usually to give the beneficiary at least a start on building a new life after the policyholder has died.

Another contends that the last-fling notion is ridiculous, and that the money will simply be a source of financial comfort to both the policyholder and his or her beneficiaries.

Both raise questions about how the taxing authorities will regard such income. Today, the plan has been approved by regulators in 10 states—Alabama, Alaska, Arizona, Colorado, Florida, Idaho, Kentucky, Montana, New Jersey and West Virginia. Prudential has filed for approval in most other states.

This is simply the latest in a long series of moves that elements of the life insurance business have taken in an effort to keep up with the times. Incurable diseases have always been with us, but they have never been so clearly in the forefront of peoples' minds as AIDS has caused them to be, along with Alzheimer's disease and ALS ("Lou Gehrig's disease"). There have never been any miraculous cures of these ailments; there has been no "fighting back," as sometimes happens in the case of supposedly incurable cancer. Apparently accepting this fact—at least until cures are discovered—will ultimately make life insurance more valuable to an uncounted number of people, other companies are sure to offer their own versions of living payouts, although they may add their own codicils to them.

Janet Patterson of the American Council of Life Insurance said to the *Times*, "A lot of companies have started thinking about living benefits because of the high cost of long-term care, the aging of the population and the pressure from gay groups about handling AIDS. But the Prudential is the first to be offering it in this form."

She is perfectly right, although many more people than "gay groups" are concerned about the AIDS situation, including the insurance companies that have contributed millions to AIDS research. Of course, the gay groups are the best organized and most vocal.

Whether the Pru plan will turn out to be a significant part of the company's future or simply a magnificent gesture remains to be seen. The *Times* reported that the pioneer Canadian plan of Ron Barbaro had attracted only 14 policyholders. Still, the time is early and the possibilities are endless.

It's probably true that life insurance companies took too many tricky chances in the '80s, with new types of policies and glowing illustrations for them. But Prudential appears to be taking another kind of chance in its living payout plan, provided its underwriting alertness doesn't allow too many people already terminally ill to slip into it—and I can't imagine that.

What we have here is a sense of compassion coupled with judgment, and no industry can have too much of that.

"Health Insurance Bites The Bullet: I"

No. 10, March 5, 1990, Page 49

In the vast family that constitutes the entire insurance business, health insurance has always been something of an orphan. Most insurance companies, with a few notable exceptions, don't consider health insurance as their primary product. But the incredible army of policyholders, seeking insurance of all kinds to cover their risks, isn't interested in company theories or beliefs. It wants insurance, period—and health insurance is one of the types it wants most—for short-term health care, nursing home care and a variety of ancillary coverages.

So health insurance has come in out of the cold. It is now a full-fledged member of the insurance family, and not to be considered an ancillary part of some greater insurance scheme.

The person on top of the heap as far as the destiny of commercial—or private—health insurance is concerned is Carl Schramm, president of the Health Insurance Association of America. To me, he is an ideal man for the job. He is a Ph.D from the University of Wisconsin and a J.D. from Georgetown. He has been director of the Center for Hospital Financial Management at Johns Hopkins, a member of the Maryland Health Service Cost Review Commission, and an advisor for the U.S. Department of Labor. At the age of 44, he is in the unenviable position (at least to me) of helping to determine what part of health care can be made available by the private sector, and what must be a function of government, which has the taxing power.

The federal government's current mood is to load everything it can on private business, but in the case of health care there is a fearful mixup among doctors, hospitals, pharmacists, nursing homes, and a myriad of other organizations whose avowed intention it is to keep people healthy and, if not healthy, at least alive. Since each seeks a profit, the consumer has a good chance of ending up either broke or dead, or—God help us—both.

So here sits Carl Schramm. I decided it would be fruitful to have a considerable conversation with him, and we did so, although he was in an auto going from somewhere to somewhere, and I was on a pool deck (as is my wont) with my cordless 'phone.

One of the first things Carl did upon assuming the presidency of HIAA was to separate it physically from the American Council of Life Insurance, which had always been its Big Brother and mentor. This was more than just a symbolic gesture; it underscored the fundamental differences between health insurance and the other forms of insurance coverage. "Ours is an industry that conceives of itself as special," Carl told his constituents, and he moved its headquarters to Connecticut Avenue in Washington, away from the looming presence of ACLI on Pennsylvania Avenue.

Part of the reason for this, of course, is that health insurance is an industry that works chiefly with groups, while life insurance deals with millions of individual policyholders. Carl estimates that some four thousand influential policymakers hold the future of health care in America in their hands, while life insurance has such a broad constituency that its set of goals must be considerably different. You can't put the future of both of the industries under just one umbrella.

The Senate Finance Subcommittee on Medicare and Long-term Care and the Pepper Commission (named for the late Florida congressman who cradled the elderly in his arms as though they were his children) will take up the matter of health care in March. HIAA, which represents 90 percent of the private health insurance in force, will be there with its proposals, developed by industry consensus. Will HIAA undertake to prove that the private sector can take care of the 37 million Americans who are currently uninsured or underinsured?

No, according to Carl Schramm. It will advocate a public-private approach that will give each segment the opportunity to do what it knows best: the private companies working with companies that can afford cost-sharing, and the public sector to develop a plan where cost-sharing is prohibitive or insufficient.

Does HIAA have the support to swing it? Where is the opposition coming from? Next week this column will get into those issues and into many more affecting health care.

"Health Insurance Bites The Bullet: II"

No. 11, March 12, 1990, Page 17

Last week I discussed (and I hope you read my remarks) the emergence of the Health Insurance Association of America, under the presidency of Carl Schramm, as a major player in the health care future of Americans. But it goes beyond that: in my discussion with Carl, it became abundantly clear that he feels consumers have no understanding, even the foggiest, of the various kinds of insurance and how they work. And so, he says, all elements must strive together.

He was one of those who devised the "Help Line" which undertakes to answer all kinds of insurance questions. (The number, which I didn't have in hand when I first mentioned it, is 1-800-942-4242.) My understanding is that it is already in full swing, and has nowhere to go but up.

Will the Senate Subcommittee on Medicare and Long-term Care, together with the Pepper Commission, come up with some kind of all-encompassing health care legislation during the 1990 session of Congress? Carl's guess is no, and it's easy to see why. This is one act that everyone is getting into, and the insurance business itself is only one of the factors. All manner of social reformers have on their agenda notions of how health care can become affordable. There will have to be an incubation period.

This was, of course, to be expected. Some people have no patience with business, which must either make a profit or die. They would rather see big government, whose only sources of revenue are taxes and interest accrued from tax money, put a blanket around all of us who are ill or hurt. Lee Iacocca, whose professed business is making automobiles, has a representative in Washington who espouses his ideas for health care. And so it goes.

This incubation period, Carl believes, will be a time in which the various forces involved will either thresh out their differences or find that elements of Congress will do it for them. It seems certain that Congressional leaders will understand that firms organized for profit cannot handle charity cases without jeopardizing the investments their dues-paying members have made. Even Congress has limits on its largesse (which might be freely translated as "giving away other peoples' money").

The nation's press isn't quite so well informed. The *New York Times* recently published a front page story, widely reprinted, under the headline "Health Insurers, to Reduce Losses, Blacklist Dozens of Occupations." Who's kidding whom? Ever since health insurance was devised, hazardous occupations have had to be recognized. Is the daredevil steelworker, whose job is swinging gird ers of high-rise buildings into place, supposed to be charged the same premium as the computer technician whose greatest risk is falling out of his chair? If skydivers pay the same premiums as newspaper reporters, who's going to get rooked? Yet the press reports these "inequities" with ill-concealed indignation.

Nor can the insurance business itself coalesce, despite the urgings of its leaders. The National Association of Life Underwriters has announced the formation of a "conference on health insurance and employee benefits." This appears to signal a breakdown of many years of negotiations with the National Association of Health Underwriters, a much smaller group. NALU has at least 100,000 people in its fold who sell health insurance, nearly ten times as many as NAHU. This would seem to be a time to close ranks. If not, it is to be hoped that the two organizations retain a speaking acquaintance. Their motives should certainly be similar.

The Book of Mark says, "If a house be divided against itself, that house cannot stand." In the field of health care, and even more so in the field of federal taxation, insurance is in grave danger of being such a structure. Leadership, provided by men like Carl Schramm, Dick Schweiker of the American Council of Life Insurance, and a half-dozen more of their institutional cohorts, stoutly supported by their constituent chief executives, must prevail. Failing this, government will step in and you can forget all about the McCarran-Ferguson Act and the legislation that has forestalled the itchy fingers of government getting into the insurance pie.

If greed outweighs statesmanship, it will be the greedy who will suffer. That's the history of American business and industry.

"It's That Time Of Year, Isn't It?"

No. 14, April 2, 1990, Page 33

KEY BISCAYNE, FLA., APRIL 1, 1990–The General American Life of St. Louis, always known for boldly moving into areas where no man has gone before, has now topped itself. It is announcing "the introduction of a new plan of insurance designed to cover the risk of premature male pattern baldness."

Its press release states, "This is a new form of disability coverage available to males 7 through 60, and will help by providing financial compensation to those who suffer the biochemical change that stops hair growth prematurely."

According to Charles L. Larance, corporate relations vice-president, research has shown that individual hair follicles that stop growing hair are loaded with a protein form that impairs hair growth. In its single-strand form, he says, the protein is able to carry testosterone, a hormone, into the cell nucleus and to short-circuit hair growth.

General American says it is the first insurance company to offer this inventive new form of disability coverage, although it does not expect to be the last. Its disability income staff has been working with the Dermatology Institute of South Florida for more than a year to establish underwriting criteria. The Institute has issued a white paper covering its research, which is available through Mr. Larance.

Among its multifarious findings, the Institute determined that men who have hair loss from more than 50 percent of the crown surface were found to be 90 percent more virile than men with full hair growth. It also revealed the same group had 98 percent fewer opportunities to prove their virility. Mr. Larance also stated that the policy will not be available to females, not because of discrimination, but rather because hair loss is a far less severe problem among women, with only partial losses in an insignificant percent of the female population. "There is no need for insurance where the risk does not exist," he added.

A second major breakthrough in the technology of insurance coverage became known on the same day, although its originator, a major eastern company, was not able to confirm its existence because of ongoing negotiations with several state insurance departments. Reputable sources, however, state that it is in the process of forming a corporation known as the Hypochondriacs' Health Insurance Co., which will probably be known under the acronym H-HIC.

One executive of the parent company, who declined to be quoted directly, owing to the sensitive nature of the negotiations, said it was his belief that hypochondriacs—people who aren't really ill but who are convinced they are—are poorly treated by health insurance organizations. "People who think they are unwell are usually in as much discomfort and pain as those who are truly unwell," he said. "It seems to us that the insurance industry owes them the same tender loving care that it is accustomed to lavishing on the sick and injured. We cannot afford to turn our backs on a major segment of the American public."

It is reported that policyholders of H-HIC will have a sliding scale of premiums. If they are thrown out of a physician's office because they are in fact as strong as oxen, the cost will be nominal. If the doctor must perform tests on them to prove that they are perfectly healthy, the cost will increase. If it turns out that the patient is actually faking hypochondria and has a true ailment, a stiff additional premium will be charged. "This," the executive of H-HIC indicated, "will separate the wheat from the chaff."

It is notable that two such significant advances in health underwriting should be announced on the same day, April 1, 1990. It is devoutly to be hoped that we don't have to wait a year until some new miracles are revealed.

"A Fool For A Client"

No. 41, October 8, 1990, Page 15

There is an old saw among lawyers that says, "An attorney who chooses to defend himself before the bar has a fool for a client."

Recently, some respectable columnists have brought forth the notion that companies might be well-advised to design and insure their own health benefits. The *New York Times* hazards the guess that more than 50 percent of the nation's employees with health insurance provided by their employers now work for companies that do just that.

"Self-insurance lets companies buy just the services they want," according to one blurb. Of course, this whole idea stemmed from the Employee Retirement Income Security Act (ERISA), which exempted self-insured plans from mandated benefits and state insurance premium taxes. To protect themselves, some self-insuring companies buy catastrophic "stop-loss insurance" from a carrier. But they are taking part of the risk themselves.

The prevailing notion is, of course, that commercial health insurance companies load the employer down with benefits he doesn't need. Many health insurers indignantly deny that, stating that they can cut the cloth of a program to fit a company's desires. And I know many that do.

The machinery that makes any form of insurance is precise, indeed. If companies could simplify it, they would. They need the actuaries, the investment people, the underwriters, a medical staff, the legal section—and you can name many more. Self-insurers cannot get away without any of these experts. They must put them on staff, or retain them as outside contractors. Self-insuring is, in fact, starting your own little insurance company.

And you assume the risks inherent in the plan. If something catastrophic happened in your group, some very deep pockets might be needed for the bail out. With the cost of doctors, hospitals and drugs constantly on the rise, the tab for a cancer or AIDS case in your organization could easily exceed $100,000.

One of the principal reasons why all types of insurance companies exist is they spread the risk among many individuals, many businesses, and many cities. A non-insurance company, unless it is massive, has a hard time doing this. Just a few serious cases and the entire economy of the self-insurer might be badly skewed. In fact, there would probably be no insurance companies at all if it weren't for that "spreading the risk" factor. Every company would be running its own insurance operation, with the hazards involved.

* * * *

While I was trying to figure out a balanced approach on self-insurance for group health benefits, I discovered that Woody Woodson had written a perceptive article on individuals self-insuring their life insurance, in his "Back Page" column for *LAN*. He approached the issue in an entirely different manner than I had (the prosperous person vs. the agent), but his conclusion was so close to mine that I think it bears repeating here (his friends, who are legion, know that Woody has a delicate way of laying facts on the line). Here it is:

"Of all the risks with which we daily live, in our complex economy and our complex lives in this complex world, few risks are as great as the risk that self-insurance for any large amount will at best be insufficient, and at worst will be ruinous.

"Life is hard in this modern world in which we live and struggle, but real insurance, having arisen out of necessity simply because self-insurance could not meet the large-scale risks of modern life, has made the difficult facts of life just a little more difficult for those who use it."

To me, self-insurance is like mixing your own prescription drugs or building your own airplane. These can be done, I suppose, but what are the experts there for?

"The Miracles And Failures Of Medicine"

No. 16, April 22, 1991, Page 25

Here are two platitudes for you to grind your teeth over:

- Modern medicine has refined its techniques to the point where the number of people in their 70s, 80s, and 90s is increasing almost exponentially every decade. Very soon Willard Scott, the NBC weatherman who introduces centenarians on his program every day ("Isn't she lovely!") will either have to up the ante by a decade or be swamped with lovelies.

- But in many, many cases the body of an elder will not obey the dictates of the mind, or the mind atrophies in a healthy body. Either way, the result is slow tragedy, demanding almost total outside support.

As my wife, who suffered from ALS ("Lou Gehrig's disease"), said shortly before she died, "If they could only graft my head onto a healthy body with Alzheimer's disease, we'd show 'em a thing or two." Her mind was totally lucid; her body was incapable of responding.

We pray that medicine will soon achieve two breakthroughs: keeping the mind clear, and the body responsive. When these two miracles happen—and happen they will—the older person can say with confidence, in the words of Robert Browning, "The best is yet to be—the last of life for which the first was made."

At the same time the world's doctors are working away at such problems as cancer and cardio-vascular diseases. But the ultimate wearing out of the human frame is inevitable. The most anyone—may I be allowed to speak for "anyone"?—can ask is a little dignity and self-sufficiency in later years, marked by a modicum of enjoyment.

Meanwhile, we know where we stand. It is unbelievably expensive to care for a mind whose body withers, or a body whose mind has retreated into blankness. Experts have said that it takes at least four healthy people (including one who is skilled in medicine) to do so for every 24-hour period. Family can help, but family must have a life of its own, if only to earn its keep and help support the aging ones.

So we inevitably arrive at the absolute necessity for some form of long-term care insurance. Can the private sector provide it? Not if the patient cannot afford it. Private companies have to pay their employees, their agents and, in some cases, their stockholders—and make a profit while doing it. They are simply not geared to take care of the indigent, or even those with a restricted amount of funds. And disease knows nothing about income.

Can the public sector provide it? Of course, if the citizenry is willing to submit to the taxation that will inevitably accompany it. And, as the public sector always does, it will create a topheavy bureaucracy to oversee it.

Is there some way that the public and private sectors can work together? Of course, if each is willing to give a little. Private companies could examine and define the risk, and underwrite it to the point where the individual could afford it. Public money would then have to be used to make sure the patient wouldn't be thrown out on the street.

This solution appeals to me because insurance companies already have the machinery in place to determine who is in real need and who is just malingering. Big government would be spared the necessity of setting up its own army of investigators and examiners and, perhaps, building offices somewhere on the Potomac that would dwarf the Pentagon. Here is an area where public and private people might come together and demonstrate their ability to work in harness.

Both the rumblings in Washington and the headlines in newspapers indicate that something will be done about the long-term health care issue in this session of Congress. If the insurance companies and Congress choose to go separate routes, many extra billions will be expended, to no useful purpose.

I don't for an instant underestimate the complexities of what I suggest. The two sectors have been suspicious adversaries for as long as I can remember. They will probably continue to be. But if they fail to get together on this most pressing of problems, they both will suffer.

So will the progress of medicine, and so will the public.

"Who Rates Life Cos. And How Good Are They?"

No. 29, July 22, 1991, Page 11

For nearly a century, only one commercial organization—the A.M. Best Company of Oldwick, NJ—had the temerity to "rate" life insurance companies on what it considered to be their relative solvency. Most consumers were content to rely on the state supervisory authorities to keep companies in line, and to administer sound spankings if they strayed from the straight and narrow.

In the booming economy of the 1970s and 80s, however, life companies felt that the strictures laid upon them by the states put them at an unfair disadvantage, especially in their ability to take somewhat more liberal investment risks, and pleaded with the states to extend the leash. The states, caught up in the euphoria of good times, did so—sometimes reluctantly.

You know what happened thereafter. Some companies took advantage of the relaxed regulations and got into trouble. Three companies that had rated various other kinks of investment firms—Standard and Poor's, Moody's, and Duff and Phelps—entered the business of rating insurance companies. A total newcomer, Weiss Research, also has gotten into the act, without any particular credentials I could discover.

In all instances, if a company wants to be rated at all it has to pay a hefty price for the privilege. The rating company then turns its research microscope on you, and comes up with a series of ratings. If you disagree with its conclusions, you can drop the whole thing and go unrated. Few companies do so; the turndown is perceived by some to be a sign of weakness.

All ratings are, of course, put together by people—skilled people to be sure, but those with strong points of view about what constitutes wise investment management and what doesn't. The human factor can never be ignored. In most instances, the four seasoned rating services come up with nearly the same results, except among marginal companies where there may be some differences of opinion. (I'm not including Weiss Research in my comments because it is in the process of undergoing significant public criticism from the American Council of Life Insurance, which doubts the validity of its research.)

The problem I find with all the rating services, even A.M. Best, which has been involved in the process for the longest time, is that their judgments are almost impossible for the layman to understand. When we went to school, we were graded in all subjects with the letters A, B, C, D, or E, with occasional pluses or minuses if we were on the cusp between one grade and another.

Not Best's, Standard and Poor's, Moody's, or Duff and Phelps. The worst you can get is a B, which means terrible. You can be awarded an A+, a AAA, an Aaa, an Aa2, all the way down to a Bl. If you and I had gone through school with nothing worse than a B, we would probably have graduated with honors and be flaunting a Phi Beta Kappa key from our tie clips.

Not with our sainted services. Each of them operates on a two-letter alphabet. Is that fair to the lay person who remembers his school grades and is trying to find a safe haven for his life insurance money? I think not. All that results is confusion.

Recently, I showed to a group of my academic friends, who have been giving out grades for years, a listing of the major companies and what the four services had thought of them. It had been compiled by my friend, Joe Belth, for his *Insurance Forum*. Their results were unanimous: total incredulity. They laughed until they cried. "Is everyone in your business nearly perfect?", one asked. Another ventured, "If you're marking on a curve, have they invented a new alphabet?" We will draw a curtain over their other comments.

Since we are all not as smart as we would like to be, rating services have a place in our economy. But, like Caesar's wife, they must be above suspicion. If investigation shows that they are in hock (moral, legal, or ethical) to anyone, they deserve to be exposed. The four of whom on which I have some knowledge have no blight on their reputations.

It would please me if they spoke in English, but that doesn't seem to be the way of things.

Index

All articles appeared in the *National Underwriter* Life & Health/Financial Services edition unless otherwise noted and are listed in order of publication.